On Hobos and Homelessness

THE HERITAGE OF SOCIOLOGY

A SERIES EDITED BY DONALD N. LEVINE

MORRIS JANOWITZ, FOUNDING EDITOR

Nels Anderson

On Hobos and Homelessness

Edited and with an

Introduction by Raffaele Rauty

The University of Chicago Press

Chicago and London

NELS ANDERSON (1889–1986) was a pioneer of participant observation and the collection of life histories in sociological research during the early 1920s.
RAFFAELE RAUTY is professor of the history of sociology at the University of Salerno.

The University of Chicago Press, Chicago 60637
The University of Chicago Press, Ltd., London
© 1998 by The University of Chicago
All rights reserved. Published 1998
07 06 05 04 03 02 01 00 99 98   1 2 3 4 5

ISBN (cloth): 0-226-01966-7
ISBN (paper): 0-226-01967-5

Library of Congress Cataloging-in-Publication Data

Anderson, Nels, 1889–
    On hobos and homelessness / Nels Anderson ; edited and with an introduction
by Raffaele Rauty.
        p.   cm. — (Heritage of sociology)
    Includes bibliographical references and index.
    ISBN 0-226-01966-7. — ISBN 0-226-01967-5 (pbk.)
    1. Tramps—United States.   I. Rauty, Raffaele, 1947–   .
II. Title.   III. Series.
HV4505.A62   1998
305.5'68—dc21
                                                                    98-19274
                                                                    CIP

Contents

Introduction Nels Anderson 1889–1986

The Hobo, for Life

Nels Anderson was a paradoxical figure in the history of Chicago sociology. His book *The Hobo* ([1923] 1961) inaugurated the University of Chicago Press's Sociological Series, those nearly two dozen books published in less than two decades by which a larger public came to know the Chicago approach. By natural inclination he was thoroughly steeped in the social problems orientation that was central to Chicago sociology. He was, seemingly, a natural for sociological work. And yet, while other Chicago students' careers flourished in the decades following the 1920s, Anderson was unable to secure employment in academic sociology until the age of seventy-four due to prejudice on the part of other sociologists against his work with hobos and his work in the more applied areas of sociology. Unlike his fellow students, most of whom were the sons and daughters of clergymen or related professionals, Anderson was the son of an immigrant who could not understand the value of an education beyond the fourth grade—much less a doctorate. But, in the end, Anderson was able to synthesize his desire to know, his desire to help, and his unique personal history into a remarkable career that would span six decades. He is an underrated figure in the history of sociology.

Anderson was born 31 July 1889 in a tenement in Chicago. Like many American families of that era, the Andersons moved around in search of a better life, and his early years were spent in covered wagons in the West, in tenements in Chicago, and on farms in Michigan. In his midteens, Anderson resisted his father's desire to have him take over the family farm; he left home, and took up a series of migrant laborer-type jobs, "beating" his way across the country on freight trains. He was a dirt mover in Galesburg, Illinois, a horse driver in Montana, a farmhand in Kansas, a panhandler in Denver. Along the way, he was tossed off trains by railroad "dicks," jailed, and run out of town several times (Anderson 1980–81, pp. 10–16). These experiences would eventually sharpen his insights into the plight of laborers in general and hobos in particular.

It was also not uncommon for Anderson to beg at the back doors of houses when he traveled and, through one of a series of fortunate encounters in his life, he one day begged at the door of a Mormon family named Woods in Utah who took him in and essentially adopted him. He lived and worked with them for several years. Aside from the stability of this environment, the other great advantage to Anderson of his Utah stay was the Mormon view of education—"the more the better"—a view that contrasted sharply with that of his own family (Anderson 1980–81, p. 19). So, working summers and vacations on railroad maintenance and as a timberman in the Utah metal mines, Anderson was able to put himself first through high school and then college at Brigham Young University, with a sixteen-month interruption while he was a soldier in Europe during World War I.

Anderson arrived in Chicago on a freight train at the age of twenty-six. One of his professors in Utah, John Swenson, had dissuaded him from following his plan to enter law and told him instead to study sociology at Chicago since, as he put it, "they work with new ideas" (Anderson 1983, p. 396; 1980–81, p. 6). By his own admission, Anderson knew little sociology, and Albion Small, then department chair, admitted him essentially without credentials (1983, p. 399). The departmental faculty at that time included Small, Robert Park, Ernest Burgess, and Ellsworth Faris, who had been brought in to replace W. I. Thomas.

Anderson was never particularly close to other graduate students at the university in the 1920s; these included Roderick McKenzie (ecology) for whom Anderson taught at the University of Washington for a semester, Floyd House (industrial morale), Ernest Mowrer (family disorganization), Walter Reckless (vice), Ruth Shonle Cavan (suicide), Frederic Thrasher (gangs), Louis Wirth (the ghetto), and later the well-known figures of Herbert Blumer, Everett Hughes, Harvey Zorbaugh, and the anthropologists Leslie White and Robert Redfield, among others (see Faris 1967; Carey 1975; Matthews 1977; Bulmer 1984). Anderson reports that his fellow graduate students were "politely amused" at the idea of studying hobos. None would visit the Madison Street area that was the site of his research (Anderson 1980–81, pp. 5–6).

After some time in the program, Anderson learned one day that Ben L. Reitman, M.D., would give a lecture on the homeless men of Chicago. Perhaps because of his own background hopping freights, he was interested in hearing it. As Anderson reports: "Reitman proved to be one of those speakers who likes to attract harsh attacks in public debate. For him to give a lecture was to put on a show. He would lump [all the types of homeless into three categories]. . . . 'The hobos who work and wander, the tramps who dream and wander, the bums who drink and wander'" (Anderson 1980–81, p. 4). Anderson found himself objecting to the neat typology and, after a lively discussion, Reitman and Anderson continued their talk at a local restaurant. It was over coffee and pie that Reitman invited Anderson to do a study of the homeless in Chicago and pledged that he would be able to secure support and funds. The study that would become *The Hobo* was sponsored by the United Charities of Chicago and was funded by a private donor, William A. Evans, M.D., who wrote a syndicated column for the *Chicago Tribune* called "How to Keep Well." Anderson was supervised by a three-man committee consisting of Reitman, Joel Hunter, the director of United Charities, and Ernest Burgess as the committee's science advisor and chair (Anderson 1983, pp. 400–404; 1980–81, pp. 4–8). For Anderson, Burgess was the perfect mentor, for his interests appeared to be closer to the reality of "social problems" (Hughes 1979). Though he had no research experience and reported knowing "no sociological jargon," he says that he "never worked harder on a job, or with greater care" (Anderson 1980–81, p. 6). Anderson moved into a "workingman's hotel" in Hobohemia during his research, and the fruit of this project, after a year of interviews and observations, was *The Hobo*. After Burgess read it, he passed it on to Park who surprised Anderson with the news that he had made some small changes and that the University of Chicago Press was ready to publish it as soon as they could get it ready (Anderson 1980–81, p. 8). Departing from the usual order of degrees and publications, Anderson turned the book in as his M.A. thesis (Faris 1967, p. 65).

Within the context of a thematically eclectic scientific production, Anderson's name and interests remained linked to the hobos he studied early in his career and to his 1923 book *The Hobo*, which, he once remarked, "I have not been permitted to forget" (Anderson 1940, p. 1). Throughout his description, Anderson stressed that the era of the hobo ("a man who works and wanders") had come to a close in those same years, and he further succeeded in showing a set of relations between the phenomenon of the hobo and the social dynamics of the United States in the second half of the nineteenth century. He especially emphasized the historical link between the development of the United States, the process of Americanization, and the presence of the nomadic and casual laborer throughout the nation's social fabric. This approach countered the idea prevalent at the time that "their homelessness was . . . pathological in a society which assumes as axiomatic that every individual must belong somewhere, must have family, must have economic roots" (Anderson 1975, p. 168).

Because of his social background, his life experience, and his cultural orientation, Nels Anderson is undoubtedly the most atypical of the young students who gravitated toward the University of Chicago's Sociology Department of the 1920s. He was among the first, and perhaps the best, of those researchers to inaugurate a method for knowing the features of society based on direct participation and observation. He describes the world he sees with no mediation. He presents vividly the harshness of the vagrant's life and the contradictions inherent in the hobo's identity that form yet another variation on the theme of the breakdown of the American dream. Such a vivid narrative may be surpassed only by the more literary descriptions of Jack London or by some passages of Tom Kromer ([1935] 1986).

A Researcher in the Department

Anderson's early career was an expression of the processes of institutionalization and professionalization of a sociological discipline on its way to becoming "scientific." This was a discipline that was leaving the world of abstraction and coming to terms with real life. *The Hobo* is testimony to this process and, in all likelihood, is one of the most significant and powerful examples of research and narrative appearing in the Sociological Series. The book was highly reputed and positively reviewed, and Anderson's ability to draw on an intimate and autobiographical knowledge of American hobos endowed them, in his account, with a culture and a personality that they had lacked in earlier representations.

Not long before the publication of *The Hobo,* Beardsley Ruml, director of the Laura Spelman Rockefeller Memorial, had stressed "the absence of a scientific groundwork in the social field" due to the situation in the social sciences. These "were themselves very young. . . . The subject matter of the social sciences was extraordinarily difficult to deal with. . . . The universities have not been able to organize their programs so as to afford opportunities for social research." Above all, "as a result, production from universities is largely deductive and speculative, on the basis of second-hand observations, documentary evidence and anecdotal material. It is small wonder that the social engineer finds this social science abstract and remote, of little help to him in the solution of his problems" (University of Chicago Library, Special Collections, Reserved Papers, Laura Spelman Rockefeller Memorial Series, box 2, folder 31).

The theory of science that would guide the projects that fulfilled Ruml's criteria for a relevant, empirical social science at Chicago was derived from the pragmatist insight, dating from about the turn of the century, that it is attention to contextual, empirical phenomena that makes inquiry scientific. As Park put it in 1921:

> It has been the dream of philosophers that theoretical and abstract science could and some day perhaps would succeed in putting into formulae and into general terms all that was significant in the concrete facts of life. It has been the tragic mistake of the so-called intellectuals, who have gained their knowledge from textbooks rather than from observation and research, to assume that science had already achieved its dream. But there is no indication that science has begun to exhaust the sources or significance of concrete experience. The infinite variety of external nature and the inexhaustible wealth of personal experience have thus far defied, and no doubt will continue to defy, the industry of scientific classification, while, on the other hand, the discoveries of science are constantly making accessible to us new and larger areas of experience. (Park and Burgess 1921, p. 15)

Following the spirit of such a view, Anderson helped to pioneer the method that came to be known as "participant observation" as well as the collection of personal documents and life histories. In many ways, this approach was an articulation of the famous invitation that Park had addressed to his students: "Go and sit in the lounges of the luxury hotels and on the doorsteps of the flophouses; sit on the Gold Coast settees and on the slum shakedown; sit in the Orchestra Hall and in the Star & Garter Burlesk. In short, gentlemen, go get the seat of your pants dirty in real research" (quoted in McKinney 1966, p. 71). Park's scientific inclination was accompanied by a keen attention to research in which he synthesized his many years' background in journalism. This background led him to remark that the problem does not lie in the use of one method of analysis rather than another, but in the fulfillment of the requirements of knowledge, for which reason "it is important that we employ the best methods as they are" (quoted in Matthews 1977, p. 179).

Anderson did, and indeed *The Hobo* has been described as "an ice-breaking piece of direct reporting" (Faris 1967, p. 66). Anderson's attitude oscillates between an awareness of his intimate knowledge of the world of the hobos and a lack of confidence in his ability to render it well enough. However, he perceives that it is only by employing direct methods of description that one could get at the world of the hobos. His method was tied to his everyday relations, to the characters with whom he came into contact, and was a reinterpretation of Park's journalistic advice: "Write down only what you see, hear, and know, like a newspaper reporter." This process is based on the capacity to read the reality in which those characters live, to perceive their condition, to reproduce their stories, to recognize their emotions and ethics. Anderson accumulates countless, even too many, such stories given the boundaries of an inquiry that should have had, according to its author, a merely local character. Although the qualitative methodology Anderson introduced for handling his data counts as a milestone in the history of sociology, his vast project of collecting documents on hobos and poverty amounts to an archival milestone in its own right. The Chicago researchers have sometimes been criticized because their sources were not always or only firsthand data (Platt 1994, 1996)—a process of quantification affected those inquiries as well (Bulmer 1981). Even though he employs data from the existing literature on hobos, Anderson is definitely involved in the overall process of recording the hobo's experience despite the scarcity of means at his disposal, and he has received recognition for the intrinsic merits of his work from people whose approach was different from his own (Lofland 1973; Hannerz 1980).

Anderson worked at the tail end of the phase from 1916 to 1923, called a "period without funds," a "work conducted largely by the students" (Burgess and Bogue 1964, pp. 5–6), aimed above all at drawing maps of the city. Anderson's text belongs to (while distinguishing itself from) the phase called "Discovering the Physical Pattern of the City," during which the Sociology Department opened its doors to the city's various agencies, associations, and institutions. The Chicago that provides these social scientists with the site for their analyses is a diverse metropolis of immigrant ethnic groups. It is a commercial, industrial, and cultural center, a hub of roadways, railways, and waterways, where the individual's imaginary and real worlds are summed together in the anxiety and factuality of existence. "Social disorganization" develops "objectively" in the city. What takes place there, as in other great cities, is the process of modern transformation, which, together with the modification of the traditional conditions of order and social control, leads to the definitive and irreversible "corruption" of an American spirit that remained tied for many of those sociologists (Park in particular) to the rural realities and values of the primary groups.

These urban studies were heavily influenced by the concepts of ecological theory (see Gaziano 1996), including the notion of social disorganization and the zone-by-zone approach to the spatial patterns and the cultural life of the city's "natural" areas. Like other human ecological works in the Sociological Series, Anderson's book was committed to describing phenomena that had really never before been so treated—hence the need for participant observation and the collection of life histories. These were not neat little treatises of sterile theory. They were open ended. Thrasher, for example, emphasized that his book "has probably raised more questions than it has answered" and that "the study is primarily an exploratory survey designed to present a general picture of life in an area little understood by the average citizen" (1927, p. xi). Anderson remarked once that *The Hobo* "contained not a single sociological concept" (1983, p. 404). Like H. W. Zorbaugh's *Gold Coast and the Slum* (1929), Anderson's book was more description than theory and, whether he knew it or not, followed the example of the pragmatist emphasis on rendering the actual experience of people (e.g., James [1902] 1929) that Park admired so much.

In turn, Anderson also helped secure contacts with the Committee of Homeless Men and with the Chicago Council of Social Agencies while carrying out his research on hobos. Through these contacts, the university's Sociology Department made explicit its intention of following a path that would realize "an experience in social research" in Chicago (Smith and White 1929). This would become reality through the Local Community Research Committee, which established a close contact between the university and the community. This interaction increasingly turned the city into a laboratory for the social sciences, while at the same time providing the community with specific information based on more objective points of view.

Who Was the Hobo?

The hobo underworld constituted a variation on the world of poverty intrinsic and essential to the development of capitalism and to the structure of the American labor force. "The irregularity of his employment is reflected in the irregularity of all phases of his existence. To deal with him as an individual, society must deal also with the economic forces which have formed his behavior, with the seasonal and cyclical fluctuations in industry" (Anderson 1961, p. 121).

The object of Anderson's interest and analysis is the hobos, men who, in the condition in which Anderson found them at the end of an era, congregated in an area later dubbed "Hobohemia" where they could more easily sell their labor. They expressed the history and memory of a reality that saw them as protagonists of labor. The hobo Anderson described criss-crossed urban reality, although his existence was linked in an essential way to rural work: Hobohemia was in many ways "the main 'slave market' for Middle West agriculture" (1980–81, p. 11). The hobo was the protagonist of the "second frontier," no longer characterized by the westward movement of isolated men or single families, but rather by the mass migration of individuals who were completing a process of expansion and civilization.

The hobo is a generally unskilled, casual laborer who, on and off, carries the card of the International Workers of the World in contrast to members of the skilled, regular working class who support the American Federation of Labor. That laborer, whose skills have already been defined, acquires several names, depending on the type of classification one prefers. As Anderson recollects, "A hobo is a migratory worker in the strict sense of the word. He works at whatever is convenient." "Tramp" is a term used to indicate a narrower group, especially "an able-bodied individual who has the romantic passion to see the country and to gain new experience without work. He is a specialist at getting by" (Anderson 1961, p. 94). Davis has emphasized that, leaving aside the subdistinctions internal to the category of the hobo, "the category of 'nomad proletariat' avoids various confusions inherent in the term 'hobo' . . . and is also preferable because it includes the tens of thousands of transient outdoor laborers employed east of the Mississippi on railroad gangs and other major construction" (1984, p. 161). Hobos were generally in their prime adult years. The inquiry done by Anderson in Chicago in the summer of 1921 (Anderson 1923) showed that 36% were below the age of twenty-five. When in cities, they populated areas with names such as the "Main Stem," "Skid Row," and "the Bowery."

Anderson was interested in the problem of those isolated men. He believed that his study would provide him with the data indispensable for finding a solution to it. "The tramp problem cannot be dismissed with the assertion that it is all caused by unemployment: Nor can it be said that employment will cure all the evils connected with it." Later, in the same text, he stressed that the positive intervention of the middle and high-middle classes, rather than the lower ones, would be decisive for attaining a transformation of the problem. For this is a question which "weakens the strength of the nation," and regarding which "I would rather impress upon the minds of Congressmen and capitalists that it does not pay to have a large body of men tramping the country, living as the hobo lives" (letter to James Eads How, 3 May 1922, University of Chicago Library, Special Collections, Burgess Papers, box 127, folder 2, document 126).

Numerous since the mid–nineteenth century, hobos and tramps multiplied especially after 1873–74, when economic crisis created an unemployed mass of three million people. Tramps soon became identified with the jobless mass, and often with a "dangerous" class. Tramps and hobos are thus the product or by-product of foreign immigration and internal mobility, of poverty, of unemployment, and of the social dynamic of the frontier. In broader terms, they can be seen as the consequence of social incoherence and of internal fragmentation of a working class in the phase of industrialization (Berthoff 1971, p. 331;

Ringenbach 1973). They were thus a stable presence in American society and culture and form an important theme in the history of labor and industrial development. Tramps and hobos are one of the characteristic factors of westward expansion, shaped by the building of the railroad. They are themselves an expression of the force and the logic of expansion: "The frontier needed that labor force of mobile men who were versatile, who would move when not needed" (Anderson 1975, p. 72).

In this labor market, occupational precariousness and mobility were tightly linked to the consolidated industrial structure. The mobility of the masses of laborers ensured precisely what the factory required, that is, a reserve labor force capable of adapting itself to the fluctuations of an expanding market (Rodgers 1977, p. 667) and willing to replace those people who, by turns, were placed on the "blacklists" that barred workers from work and paved the way toward the selection process practiced within the industrial reserve army. In fact, those laborers increased and decreased in number as the national economy went through its cycles of boom and bust. The setting in which Anderson observes the hobo—that is, in an urban setting—is outside his characteristic experience treading American roads on foot, following the construction of the railroads, moving from farm to farm, hopping onto trains—all the features that characterize the temporary laborer.

The hobo is thus part and parcel of the mobility specific to a certain historical phase in which the governing principles are communication and mobility. "A rolling stone gathers no moss," a hobo reminds us, as if only in that mobility there could be an existential space for those people who recognize the irreversible formalization of relations as well as the contraction of space and time brought on by the development of capitalism. But they paid for their desire for autonomy with an almost constant exposure to the realities of the weather and with a high rate of mortality in accidents.

A specific feature of this working class, or proletariat, is the incessant turnover within its ranks due to the arrival of new immigrants or peasants, farmers, skilled artisans, and apprentices—all those who bring into industrial society a style of work and mores in conflict with the economic and ethical imperatives of industry (Gutman 1966, p. 40). Alongside the transformation and organization of labor, within and without the development of scientific management, a process of Americanization is taking shape, which for a long time maintains contradictory aspects. According to Thomas, Americanization demanded of every immigrant "a suppression and repudiation of all the signs that distinguish him from us" (1971, p. 283). These aspects are apparent primarily in those individuals who, finding it difficult to adjust to that very same process, preserve the "dangerous" traits that make them different from that organization—characteristics bordering on self-segregation. Those who, because of subjective or objective limits, are incapable of adapting to the new reality, threaten the new American industrial order—that modern America whose doors are open—while at the same time they inexplicably denied themselves the fruits of American capitalism (Katzman and Tuttle 1982). Though affected by the forces of immigration, the hobos themselves were generally not immigrants. Leiserson reports U. S. census data indicating that this kind of worker came mostly from the United States and that immigrants represented only a minority in the economic sectors in which the hobos' presence was especially strong: this is true for the key railway sector (26.7%), in the transportation sector (25%), in agriculture (9.6%), and in the forestry and lumber business (24.4%) (Leiserson 1924; see also Baran and Sweezy 1966). Anderson's own research showed that only 15.1% of the hobos congregating on Madison Street were foreign born (Anderson 1921).

For many, their lives as hobos or tramps ended after a certain period. The "home guard" represents an anticipation of that change: an individual who has experienced mobility in the past, but now has a sedentary life, a preliminary step toward attempting definitive integration into the urban structure.

The theme of seasonal, vagrant workers, mostly poor, stretches over time to become linked to the lives of the contemporary homeless. These homeless are the product of rich societies in which powerful processes of "detachment" are at work. Above all, the contemporary phenomenon of the homeless brings up again the question of mobility, of a nomadism seemingly inscribed in the genetic makeup of some individuals, of an internalized compulsion to wander. Work is desired, but subordinated to a rhythm in which the individual stubbornly wants to remain an autonomous subject, social control turned into individual will, inconsistency, detachment, distance from the social environment where one resides.

Hobo Culture

Anderson argued that the hobos "were a class of men quite apart from other worker groups. . . . [They form] a society with a culture" (Anderson 1940, p. 2). They had their own language (see Stiff [1930] and esp. Irwin [1931]) and autonomous patterns of organization. At the same time, however, they are individuals "without community" (Anderson 1975, p. 72), whose mode of life resisted integration into a group despite their shared cultural traits. Park thought that with his vagrant life the hobo represents "not only a 'homeless man' but a man without a country." He is an individual who resisted the efforts of organizations such as James How's Hobo College, or that of the Industrial Workers of the World, which tried to organize them. Park was inclined to believe that, given these circumstances, "the hobo finds in casual and seasonal labor a kind of occupation congenial to his temperament" (Park 1925*b*, pp. 159–60) through a process that seemingly turns reality upside down. The figure of the vagrant laborer finds coherence in detachment, emerges from it, and is reinforced and solidified by it.

The culture that Anderson claims for the hobos expresses itself in various directions: from the social life in the "jungles," or streamside hobo camps, where the oral transmission of patterns of behavior to the young occurred; to the organizing of Hobo College on Congress Street, mostly through the support of Ben Reitman (Beck 1956); to the *Hobo News*—the hobo's newspaper, since, as Anderson remarks, the hobo has a constant relationship with newspapers; to the social and cultural organization that comes to life among the hobos. That culture is also expressed in places such as the Proletariat bookstore, a public space where informal relations were established and mail could be held for those with no permanent residence, and above all in places where specific structures and ways of life emerged. An example of the latter is the saloon, a shelter from the hardship and insecurity of existence, a place where an autonomous morality prevails and where various and unexpected forms of social solidarity come into existence (Alt 1976).

There emerges the picture of a young population coming together around the fires of the jungle, eager to learn "the right way" in the hobo community. Interaction in such a setting hardly permits intimacy, which becomes replaced by a reserve about one's personal life; instead, interaction is characterized by the emergence of an autonomous code of relations and by reciprocal support shaped by immediate needs. The life of the hobo expresses a subjectivity at odds with descriptions of the hobo as a "vagrant," a "loafer," or, even worse, as someone cast into a "human junk heap" or, in Park's words, as individuals who "have fallen out of the line in the march of industrial progress" (1925*b*, p. 109). Anderson appears to understand this reality deeply, even though he finds it difficult to comprehend some features of that identity: the climate of homosexuality that takes shape within it and the prostitution of those women on the move who rely on heterosexual relations for making their wandering and their relationships less insecure. On these points Anderson shows hesitation or evaluations that are reductively moral, like the ones already existing in society (Weiner 1984). However, that prostitution—which appears to him and others (Flynt 1899; Laubach 1916) as the only form that the female presence assumes among the hobos—is neither, as Bertha Thompson remarks, an expression of vice nor the application of a "perverse" morality, but rather a way in which those "sisters of the road" express a female cultural identity. Though this female identity was certainly shaped by masculine structures and behavior, in certain aspects it distanced itself from them. This was a culture that made it possible for relations to survive and to remain on an even keel, which expressed the use of one's body as capital so as to ensure a less dangerous journey on the road. For a woman, life became much easier if she was not overly particular and if she treated her body as labor capital (Thompson 1937, p. 39).

All these modes of existence were expressions of a process that showed order in a life of marginalization and that came under attack with the various Tramps Acts, the first of which was passed in New Jersey in 1874, and with the campaigns of repression against tramps (Harring 1977). These attacks became generalized in the Volstead Act, which, opening the era of Prohibition in 1919, aimed at the destruction of the saloon and signaled an attack directed specifically against the hobo's reality and identity, his expressions and his relations within the urban structure. (Compared with the almost unanimous silence with which Chicago sociologists reacted to Prohibition, Anderson's account shows a countertendency; see Rouse 1991). The hobo, it seems, could have citizenship in American labor, but he was forced to remain outside the boundaries of the modern, middle-class order.

In time, people would return to the narrative on the hobos collected in the epoch-defining 1920s (the hobo "went off the scene as the second frontier was closing"), so as to show that the character of emigration and nomadism had been transformed by the end of the 1930s. "The automobile and the Great Depression brought a new type of migrant family, reported so well by John Steinbeck in *The Grapes of Wrath*" (Anderson 1975, p. ix). This variety of poverty and vagrancy is destined to reproduce itself in American society in forms and with characteristics specific to the ever-new historical conditions. Anderson's work has the most relevance for the study of homelessness today because it captures what is in retrospect a sea change of those conditions: a change from the diffused and itinerant labor pool of a developing frontier to the more familiarly consolidated and urbanized landscape of poverty-stricken homelessness today. Anderson, like Steinbeck after him, was able to express the memory of those who do not seem entitled to have memory, whose life was expressed in temporary labor. The hobos could provide the labor force that was demanded of them, but moving from place to place, which identified their laboring activity, made it impossible for them to belong to any one.

And in the End . . .

Anderson did not receive his doctorate from the University of Chicago. In an effort to escape the stigmatism of his research on hobos, he left for New York where he completed his degree at New York University with his 1930 dissertation, "The Social Antecedents of the Slum: A Developmental Study of the East Harlem Area of Manhattan Island, New York City." This move got Anderson into something of a double bind, since Chicago's urban research orientation, with which Anderson was identified, was regarded with disdain for some time in the older universities for its traffic with morally disreputable subjects (Anderson 1980–81, p. 11), whereas later the quasi-journalistic productions of the Chicago school were often derived as allegedly atheoretical and compared unfavorably with the more heavily theorized work of influential figures like Talcott Parsons and Robert Merton. Nor did he have any better experience with the smaller colleges: "It seemed that it was to be expected that, knowing about hobos, I would be acquainted with other doubtful characters. Parents . . . might be greatly concerned to learn that one of their family was taking a course from a professor who knows hobos and who sometimes talks about employment and poverty" (Anderson 1980–81, pp. 14–15). Worse, Anderson's friend Read Bain warned him that this experience working with agencies such as the relief administration would insure that he would not be hired by any university (Anderson 1980–81, p. 15). Indeed, more than thirty years would pass before he obtained his first teaching position at the Memorial University of Newfoundland in the fall of 1963 when he was seventy-four years old. In 1965 he became a full professor at the University of New Brunswick, where he was also awarded an honorary degree: "The goal of my dreams forty years earlier was not reached until ten years after entering active retirement" (Anderson 1975, p. 183).

In the meanwhile, Anderson acquired extensive experience in applied sociology in the United States and abroad: from his activity with the Chicago Juvenile Protective Association (JPA) and his inquiry into the city's nightclubs, to his study of the homeless in the New York area. Anderson was in Washington between 1934 and 1941 as the director of the labor division of the federal project that would become known as Work Projects Administration (WPA). From Washington he went to the Philippines, the Persian Gulf, and Russia, working in the social service for seamen from 1943 to 1945. From 1945 to 1953 he worked as a labor affairs officer with the military branch later known as the High Commission for Germany, helping trade unions to get reestablished after the Second World War. In 1953 he retired and began to work at the UNESCO Institute of Social Sciences in Cologne as the director of research for a year and as the de facto director general for seven years until the institute was absorbed by the University of Cologne in 1962. There he organized an annual research seminar, one on the family, one on work and leisure time. For thirty years Anderson thus worked outside academia until his appointment, already noted, at the Memorial University of Newfoundland. Since, in his mid-seventies, he could no longer be appointed professor, he was granted the title of visiting professor. In 1965 he became full professor at the University of New Brunswick. He retired voluntarily at eighty-five as professor emeritus.

The hobo is intrinsic to Nels Anderson's story and to his place in the sociological tradition. Although his work encompassed other related topics (the urban condition, the family), from the publication of his study in 1923 until his last days he returns to the hobo theme repeatedly as a topic of research and as a way of life. He appears unable and unwilling to divorce himself from the theme that was an integral part of his origins, his experience at the University of Chicago, and, in a more middle-class way, his experiences thereafter. In his writing, he returns to the theme in 1930 under the pseudonym of Dean Stiff, dispensing advice to hobos and criticizing intellectualistic attitudes toward them. He returns to the theme in 1934, while collaborating with the municipal authorities of New York. He digs more deeply into it and revisits it in 1940, aware of the changes that, in the course of time, have been affecting that kind of worker and the processes of immigration in their relationship to him. He would continue to add to the hobo theme with further contributions, communications, and recollections. His reflections on a social problem merged with the evolution of his and the hobo's life-long experience—indeed, his autobiography is entitled *The American Hobo*. In the end, Anderson's contribution consists of the rediscovery in daily life (Gouldner 1975) of the essence of a social figure that proves to be far removed from its stereotypical image. What we have emphasized here of Anderson's accumulated understanding of the hobo and of other laborers and urbanites is more than enough to assign him an eminent position in the Chicago sociological tradition as well as in the wider history of sociology.

References

Alt, John. 1976. "Beyond Class: The Decline of Industrial Labor and Leisure." *Telos* 28:55–80.

Anderson, Nels. 1921. "Summary of a Study of Four Hundred Tramps." Burgess Papers, box 127, folder 2, document 115. Regenstein Library, Department of Special Collections, University of Chicago.

———. 1923. "The Juvenile and the Tramp." *Journal of Criminal Law, Criminology and Police Science* 14:289–312.

———. (1923) 1961. *The Hobo: The Sociology of the Homeless Man.* Chicago: University of Chicago Press.

———. 1940. *Men on the Move.* Chicago: University of Chicago Press.

———. 1975. *The American Hobo: An Autobiography.* Leiden: E. J. Brill.

———. 1980–81. "Sociology Has Many Faces." *Journal of the History of Sociology* 3(1):1–26, (2):1–19.

———. 1983. "A Stranger at the Gate: Reflections on the Chicago School of Sociology." *Urban Life* 11:396–406.

Baran, Paul A., and Paul M. Sweezy. 1966. *Monopoly Capital: An Essay on the American Economic and Social Order.* New York: Monthly Review Press.

Beck, Franck O. 1956. *Hobohemia.* Ringe, N.H.: Richard R. Smith.

Berthoff, Rowland. 1971. *An Unsettled People: Social Order and Disorder in American History.* New York: Harper & Row.

Bulmer, Martin. 1981. "Quantification and Chicago Social Science in the 1920s: A Neglected Tradition." *Journal of the History of the Social Sciences* 17:312–31.

———. 1984. *The Chicago School of Sociology: Institutionalization, Diversity, and the Rise of Sociological Research.* Chicago: University of Chicago Press.

Burgess, Ernest W., and Donald J. Bogue, eds. 1964. *Contributions to Urban Sociology.* Chicago: University of Chicago Press.

Carey, James T. 1975. *Sociology and Public Affairs: The Chicago School.* Beverly Hills, Calif.: Sage.

Davis, Michael. 1984. "Forced to Tramp: The Perspective of the Labor Press, 1870–1900." In *Walking to Work: Tramps in America, 1790–1935,* edited by Eric H. Monkkonen. Lincoln: University of Nebraska Press.

Faris, Robert E. L. 1967. *Chicago Sociology, 1920–1932.* Chicago: University of Chicago Press.

Flynt, Josiah. 1899. *Tramping with Tramps.* New York: Century. Reprint, Montclair, N.J.: Patterson Smith, 1972.

Gaziano, Emanuel. 1996. "Ecological Metaphors as Scientific Boundary Work: Innovation and Authority in Interwar Sociology and Biology." *American Journal of Sociology* 101:874–907.

Gouldner, Alvin. 1975. "Sociology and the Everyday Life." Pp. 417–32 in *The Idea of Social Structure: Papers in Honor of Robert K. Merton,* edited by Lewis A. Coser. New York: Harcourt Brace Jovanovich.

Gutman, Herbert G. 1966. *Work, Culture and Society in Industrializing America.* New York: Knopf.

Hannerz, Ulf. 1980. *Exploring the City: Inquiries towards an Urban Anthropology.* New York: Columbia University Press.

Harring, Sidney L. 1977. "Class Conflict and the Suppression of Tramps in Buffalo, 1892–1894." *Law and Society Review* 11:874–911.

Hughes, Everett C. 1979. Epilogue to *Robert E. Park: Biography of a Sociologist,* by Winifred Raushenbush. Durham, N.C.: Duke University Press.

Irwin, Godfrey, ed. 1931. *American Tramp and Underworld Slang (with a Number of Tramp Songs).* London: Eric Partridge.

James, William. (1902) 1929. *The Varieties of Religious Experience: A Study in Human Nature.* New York: Modern Library.

Katzman, David M., and William M. Tuttle, Jr., eds. 1982. *Plain Folk: The Life Stories of Undistinguished Americans.* Urbana: University of Illinois Press.

Kromer, Tom. (1935) 1986. *Waiting for Nothing.* Athens: University of Georgia Press.

Laubach, Frank C. 1916. *Why They Are Vagrants: A Study Based upon an Examination of One Hundred Men.* New York: Columbia University Press.

Leiserson, William M. 1924. *Adjusting Immigration and Industry.* Montclair, N.J.: Patterson Smith.

Lofland, Lyn H. 1973. *A World of Strangers: Order and Action in Urban Public Space.* New York: Basic.

Matthews, Fred H. 1977. *Quest for an American Sociology: Robert E. Park and the Chicago School.* Montreal: McGill-Queens University Press.

McKinney, John C. 1966. *Constructive Typology and Social Theory.* New York: Appleton-Century-Crofts.

Park, Robert E. 1925a. "Community Organization and Juvenile Delinquency." In *The City,* edited by Robert E. Park, Ernest W. Burgess, and Roderick D. McKenzie, pp. 99–112. Chicago: University of Chicago Press.

Park, Robert E. 1925b. "The Mind of the Hobo." In *The City,* edited by Robert E. Park, Ernest W. Burgess, and Roderick D. McKenzie, pp. 156–60. Chicago: University of Chicago Press.

Park, Robert E., and Ernest W. Burgess. 1921. *Introduction to the Science of Sociology.* Chicago: University of Chicago Press.

Platt, Jennifer. 1994. "The Chicago School and First-Hand Data." *History of the Human Sciences* 7:57–80.

———. 1996. *A History of Sociological Research Methods in America, 1920–1960.* Cambridge: Cambridge University Press.

Ringenbach, Paul T. 1973. *Tramps and Reformers: The Discovery of Unemployment in New York, 1873–1916.* Westport, Conn.: Greenwood Press.

Rodgers, Daniel T. 1977. "Tradition, Modernity and the American Industrial Worker: Reflections and Critique." *Journal of Interdisciplinary History* 7: 655–81.

Rouse, Timothy P. 1991. "Sociologists and American Prohibition: A Study of Early Works in the *American Journal of Sociology,* 1895–1935." *American Sociologist* 22:232–43.

Smith, Thomas V., and Leonard D. White, eds. 1929. *Chicago: An Experiment in Social Science Research.* Chicago: University of Chicago Press.

Stiff, Dean [Nels Anderson]. 1930. *The Milk and Honey Route: A Handbook for Hobos, with a Comprehensive and Unexpurgated Glossary.* New York: Vanguard Press.

Thomas, William I. 1971. *Old World Traits Transplanted.* Montclair, N.J.: Patterson Smith [1921 publication attributed to Robert E. Park and Herbert E. Miller].

Thompson, Bertha. 1937. *Sister of the Road: The Autobiography of Box-Car Bertha as Told to Dr. Ben L. Reitman.* New York: Macauley Co.

Thrasher, Frederic M. 1927. *The Gang: A Study of 1,313 Gangs in Chicago*. Chicago: University of Chicago Press.

Weiner, Lynn Y. 1984. "Sisters of the Road: Women Transients and Tramps." Pp. 171–88 in *Walking to Work: Tramps in America, 1790–1935*, edited by Eric H. Monkkonen. Lincoln: University of Nebraska Press.

Zorbaugh, Harvey Warren. 1929. *The Gold Coast and the Slum: A Sociological Study of Chicago's Near North Side*. Chicago: University of Chicago Press.

The Hobos

1

The Hobo: Introduction to the Phoenix Edition

It is now thirty-nine years since *The Hobo* was published and forty years since I began assembling the materials out of which the book grew.

Not long ago I was lecturing at the University of Copenhagen, and I was asked to devote one lecture to the hobo. I was particularly asked to tell about the author, how the book came to be written, how the research was done.

In 1882 my father migrated to the United States after a boyhood in Sweden and some twelve years in Germany. Some labor contractor picked him up on arrival, and he was sent to a railroad construction project. For the next year, until he learned enough English to get along, he went from job to job trying to find German- or Swedish-speaking companions. The effort to get settled enabled him to acquire a facility for getting about. As he gained confidence in this respect, he lost for the time his wish to settle. My father found himself moving about through the Middle West, a real hobo worker: farmhand, miner, lumberjack, building worker, and for a while coachman in Chicago. Once he ventured west as far as Deadwood in the Black Hills during a gold rush. For my father, getting Americanized by this process of moving from job to job was a continuing adventure. He remembered later with pride how he learned to beat his way on freight trains.

Five years later in St. Louis he met my mother, who had been employed as a housemaid and as a factory worker. After the marriage they went to Chicago, where I came on the scene. While I was still an infant, my father heard about a great fire in Spokane. This opportunity he could not miss. Spokane would need bricklayers, and in 1889 we moved west.

Spokane was *the West;* here was plenty of land and much work. My father filed on a timber claim not far from Spokane. My mother, with two small children, and a third born soon after, lived in a shack on the

From *The Hobo: The Sociology of the Homeless Man* (Chicago: University of Chicago Press, 1961), v–xxi. © 1961 by The University of Chicago.

claim, looking after the garden and chickens. My father worked in town, coming home on horseback for weekends. This arrangement was not satisfactory, so the claim was sold and my family, in a covered wagon, trekked to Lewiston, Idaho. Here my father had an opportunity to farm Indian land on shares in the Nez Percé Reservation. The Indian reservation was not satisfactory either, so the family moved into Lewiston. My father built a good house, our first. He had steady work at good wages. But he wanted land where his family could take root; so after wandering in a covered wagon and sleeping in tents at night, we arrived at the Teton Basin in Idaho. The Teton Basin had rich land but no schools.

Everything was sold, and the family returned to Chicago less than ten years after departing that city. Chicago was disappointing. My father found work, but his wages were not enough. We lived in the worst kind of housing on the edge of Hobohemia. I turned to selling newspapers in the very streets and alleys, saloons and other places I was to study later. There was continuous sickness in the family. One baby born in Chicago died after a few months. My father could think only of finding a farm.

Less than three years after leaving the Teton Basin we were living on a rented farm in Michigan. Two years later, in 1903, we had our own farm nearby. It was my mother who called the halt. In the sixteen years since her marriage she had packed and moved ten times, and, in the course of this wandering, twelve babies had been born to her. Nine were still living when we settled on the Michigan farm. My father agreed he would not move again and put the farm in my mother's name.

When visitors came, if it was not my father telling his stories, it was Mother telling hers. My father usually tried to point out how in America even a "greenhorn" could get around. In his own way he saw the road as adventure. He never heard of Walt Whitman, but his thinking about the open road was no different.

Now that he had finished moving, his attention was on the dream that came with him from the "Old Country," to take root in the land. He would settle each child on a farm, and each Anderson would stick together against the world. In the end only two of his children became farmers, each of them only after he had done some wandering. Four of the boys became migratory workers before settling in other careers. My three sisters also left home and did some moving about before settling.

But none of my family became a drunkard, gambler, or loafer. All became self-supporting in some occupation above common labor. In that solid sense my parents did not fail.

I left high school and became a mule driver in Central Illinois. I was getting a man's pay, and I felt I had an occupation; besides entering the honorable ranks of the mule skinners, I had entered a select company of hobo workers. We had to widen the grade for doubletracking the Santa Fe railroad from Chicago to Kansas City. Every few miles along the entire stretch were grading camps. We lived in tents, and so did twenty span of mules. We moved the dirt with an elevating grader and dump wagons. Work was ten hours a day, six days a week.

In this crew of good names, the respected old-timer was Shorty Carroll. He symbolized much that "hobo" came to mean to me. He had driven string teams in the West. He had been on all the big railroad construction and canal-digging jobs, and he knew about levee building along the Mississippi. He had been a prospector, a stagecoach driver, and had marched with "Coxey's Army." A good worker and a better storyteller, Shorty had a weakness for strong drink. Four years later when I met him in Montana his health was breaking. He had finished working as a blaster in a railroad tunnel, his money was gone, and he was recovering from drinking his earnings. He said he was going "over the hump," over the mountains to the Pacific Coast. He was really going over the hump in another sense, but he was still a hero to me, and I felt it an honor to lend him money and to see that he boarded a train. There were other good names in that group: Rickety Bill, who talked little but about whom many stories were told, Kansas City Dick, Yellow Kid, Memphis Joe, and other "monickers," each having a character of his own.

Like the student who learns the "theory" of his occupation in school, I learned how the hobo behaved, or should not behave, in town, how he went about from place to place on freight trains, how he evaded train crews and railroad police, and how he found his work. But I had no experience of my own, and after six months in the outfit I began to feel self-conscious about holding on so long. I had become what the hobos called a "home guard."

Under this compulsion I went to Chicago, to remain only a few days. I met a man who had worked for the Santa Fe outfit, whose money was gone, and who was ready to ship out on the Chicago, Milwaukee and St. Paul Railroad, then in the process of extending its line across South Dakota, Montana, Idaho, and Washington to the Pacific. This was the last big American railroad building project and, as I realized later, the "last roundup" for the hobos, who had formerly performed such work. For a month I worked for this road in South Dakota.

I decided to move on into Montana, where I found work again as a skinner. My next job after that was on a rock contract, driving a railroad tunnel. Before another year had passed I had also worked in a lumber camp and a metal mine, and another four years were spent in pursuit of experience. I learned to ride freight trains and even passenger trains. I tried my hand at different kinds of work. While I was never given to spending money on drink, I did find myself penniless a number of times. I used these occasions for getting another kind of hobo experience, begging from passersby on streets ("panhandling") or begging at back doors for food.

Something like five years after leaving home I decided to go to Los Angeles, but I found the going difficult. Twice in the course of the night I was put off the train, but each time managed to get back on. The third time was at a lonely station near the Utah-Nevada line. The stationmaster gave me a drink of water and told me to move on. The next water tank was seven miles ahead. When I reached the water-tank station, the stationmaster warned me to move on. Another five miles nearer Los Angeles I came to a small valley with four ranch houses.

I saw a man mowing hay in a meadow near the track. When I asked him for a job, his answer was negative, but he did take me to his home for supper. The next day I helped him get in the hay, not asking about money, and learned there was a job some twenty miles away in Utah. The rancher from Utah happened to be present, and I was hired by him.

On that ranch I liked the variety of the work. I was taken in as one of the family. I found myself being persuaded to return to school. For the next several years, whether I was away at school or working, the ranch was my home. My high school work was taken partly in the academy branch of the Brigham Young University, partly in a school not far from the ranch. I earned money as a timberman in mines, as a maintenance worker on railroads, or as construction worker. Other students earned their money herding sheep, working on ranches, working in stores. I could earn much more through my migratory work.

From 1912 to 1920 I concentrated on getting through four years of high school and four of college at Brigham Young. Although learning was an absorbing interest, I had no goal except the vague one that I might later study law. John C. Swenson, chairman of the economics and sociology department, suggested that I would not be happy in the law, that I should go to a graduate school to study sociology, and that the most dynamic center for sociology then was the University of Chicago. Going to Chicago was my final effort at riding freight trains.

In Chicago a new way of earning a living had to be found. I knew how to get in and out of cities, but I had never worked in one. Finding jobs was easier than adapting to an upper-level academic life, for which there was so little time.

Then came an unexpected demand on my time. In each class I had to prepare a term paper, which meant field research and reading. I knew the hobo, his work, and his urban habitat, and I was permitted in two classes to do papers about that world so little known to most professors.

Because these initial papers were well received, other possibilities opened to me. I chanced to meet people who were interested in the problem of the homeless in Chicago. I had never thought of the hobo in this way, but in Hobohemia, his Chicago habitat, he was indeed among the homeless. I began reading articles, reports, and books about the homeless and the vagrancy problem. None touched the hobo as I knew him. I came to know Ben L. Reitman, physician to the homeless, friendless, and wicked, who enlisted the interest of Dr. William A. Evans, author of a syndicated medical column, who gave a small sum to start a study. This enabled me for several months to devote my time to research.

From this beginning other support came from the Chicago Council of Social Agencies and the Laura Spelman Rockefeller Fund. I found myself engaged in research without the preparation a researcher is supposed to have. I couldn't answer if asked about my "methods." In my research efforts, however, I did have two resources that could be put to good use—a capacity for interviewing and a capacity for reporting what I had seen and heard. Still, even after the publication of *The Hobo,* when I was permitted to take the oral examination for my master's degree, I was not able to answer most of the questions put to me. Apparently some of my answers must have amused the professors. When I was called back into the room for the verdict, Professor Albion W. Small pointed to the street, "You know your sociology out there better than we do, but you don't know it in here. We have decided to take a chance and approve you for your master's degree."

To return to the story of *The Hobo,* I took a room on Halsted Street near Madison, the heart of Hobohemia, and continued my research. Of the guidance I received at the University of Chicago from Professors Robert E. Park and Ernest W. Burgess most was indirect. The only instruction I recall from Park was, "Write down only what you see, hear, and know, like a newspaper reporter."

At last I had to write a report for the Chicago agencies which had displayed interest in the study. I had many "documents" but no idea how they might be put into a report. The task was one of arranging my materials into some sort of pattern. When I delivered it to Park and Burgess for their review, I had an unsure feeling because it seemed ordinary, a little naked, and lacking in literary style. But Park, usually slow to praise, put aside other work to read it, and without my knowledge, even without my thinking of such a possibility, interested the university in publishing the report.

Years later Pauline V. Young, writing about noncontrolled participant observation as a field research method, described the author of this book as "an intimate participant observer of the life of the hobo on the road, in the 'jungle,' in lodging houses, at Hobohemia, at work and at Hobo College in Chicago. He identified himself with the life of the hobo for an extended period and gained insight into the inner life which would have been almost impossible had he not been able to eliminate social and mental distances through intimate participation."[1]

Although I appreciate the compliment, I must respond. Both Dr. Young and her husband were graduate colleagues at the University of Chicago when *The Hobo* was written. I think at that time that neither she nor I had ever heard the term "participant observation," yet at Chicago that type of research was gaining a vogue. While this method was faithfully followed in my work, it was not in the usual sense of the term. I did not descend into the pit, assume a role there, and later ascend to brush off the dust. I was in the process of moving out of the hobo world. To use a hobo expression, preparing the book was a way of "getting by," earning a living while the exit was under way. The role was familiar before the research began. In the realm of sociology and university life I was moving into a new role.

Perhaps we understand the hobo better today than in 1923, when this book was first published. For example, we have a better understanding of the frontier, and the role of the hobo on the frontier is more clearly seen today. We need no longer think of the hobo as a problem, for he has just about disappeared. There are still the homeless, but the hobo has moved into frontier history. His counterpart may still be found in other new countries such as Australia, but the American hobo was unique.

Let me now use "hobo" in a collective sense and speak of the "typical hobo." The first observation is that he was American. The foreign-born who moved into that way of life were primarily Scandinavians, Germans, or from the British Isles. While most who entered hobodom moved out within a decade, the foreign-born turned even sooner to a settled existence.

The hobo was American in the same sense that the cowboy was. The cowboy emerged in frontier history for the same reason that the hobo

1. Pauline V. Young, *Scientific Social Surveys and Research* (New York: Prentice-Hall, 1951), p. 203.

did: there was a labor market need for him. The cowboy was a hobo type.

Again, the hobo was seldom an illiterate person. Even when illiteracy was high among urban and rural workers, the hobo was a newspaper reader and an ardent follower of the sport page. He had a higher degree of mental curiosity and cosmopolitan interest than most workers.

Apparently the hobo way of life was severely selective. Continuation in it called for a capacity to move from one type of work to another and from one place to another. Adapting to the strange and new in tools, work, machines, and scenes was for him a normal consequence of moving. Such resourcefulness was expected of all who went out into the wide areas.

Not uncommonly, the hobo would resolve that, on the next job, if not on the present one, he would begin saving money. Each time he quit a job and took his money to a town, he was determined to spend carefully. He would buy clothes, eat well, sleep in a clean room, and take it easy. He would do some reading, see a few shows, and go to ball games. Only a few were able to realize such good intentions, especially if the first stop was made at a "barrelhouse." Usually all savings were gone by the second day. Then came a few days of begging, then a search for the next job. Few hobos ever learned how to use leisure time.

The Industrial Workers of the World, with headquarters in Chicago's Hobohemia, was long identified as a hobo organizational activity. This is only partly true. Many hobos carried "red cards"; most hobos did not. This does not mean the hobo was antilabor; he was too much of an individual to feel comfortable in an organization whose control was distant. Groups of IWW "organizers" would ride freight trains during harvest time and throw off anyone who did not have a red card. Many would pay the dollar for a red card as insurance, but throw it away later. Perhaps they did the same the next year. Perhaps the only mass expression of hobo labor consciousness was the march of Coxey's Army following the depression of 1893. In economic depressions during the frontier period the hobo employed on development projects was usually the first to be dismissed. Significantly, the unemployed "armies" that started for Washington came from the Middle West and the Far West.

Chicago's Hobohemia was only one of several well-known "main stems." Its counterpart was found in St. Louis, Kansas City, Minneapolis, and other western cities. Chicago, being the greatest railroad center, had the largest Hobohemia. In New York its counterpart was the Bowery, but the Bowery was not primarily a hobo street, although an occasional hobo did get that far east. Just as the private employment agencies, selling distant jobs, were more numerous in Hobohemia, so the rescue missions were more numerous on the Bowery. Hobohemia was the great labor market where the hobo spent or lost his earnings and started again on the road. There he was met by the horde waiting for a "live one": moochers and hangers-on who borrowed or begged, gamblers and tricksters, procurers who had prostitutes "working" for them, and a variety of "jack rollers," who lived by robbing. The narcotic handler could also be found, since an occasional hobo was a "snowbird." The same leeching horde could be found on the Bowery, but much more money circulated in Hobohemia.

Of Hobohemia's places where the hobo ate or slept or found religion nothing needs to be added here. Such institutions continue, whether the hobo is there or not. It must be kept in mind, however, that the descriptions in this book are for 1921 and 1922. At that time Hobohemia was brighter and livelier. Workingmen who were not hobos would go there to spend an evening. They found in Hobohemia a type of "downtown" atmosphere with all the friendly anonymity one might wish as well as any contact one might desire.

For twenty years I have carried a card announcing that I am a "Knight of the Road," a member in good standing of "Hobos of America, Inc." I was so honored by Supreme Knight Jeff Davis, "King and Emperor," in tribute to the author of *The Hobo*. But perhaps the only man to acquire anything like a leader role among American hobos was Jacob S. Coxey. When he was leading the unemployed to Washington, he was "General," and he was never called a king. It was evident in his old age when I knew him that he liked to be called "General." It was reminiscent of a colorful episode in his life.

Finally, a word about "wanderlust," a term that stems from the writings of a German authority on vagrancy. I cannot now find the source, but I think it was a French authority who invented the term "dromomania." Either term seems to assume a type of pathology in chronic wandering. Each term assumes an inborn urge to be mobile, an inability to resist the pull of the road. As Robert W. Service wrote of hobos, "Theirs is the curse of the gypsy blood, and they don't know how to rest." From science to poetry, this explanation of wandering is heard again and again. But if we use wanderlust to explain the hobo's mobility, it would be difficult not to explain other types of mobility in the same way. On the American scene mobility was imperative, else the frontier would still be wilderness. It was a real asset for the hobo.

Americans are beginning to recognize that the frontier was much more than the movement of land settlement from the east toward the west, a rush to appropriate the natural resources. There was a second frontier which also moved westward, two decades or so behind the first, and it followed in the wake of railroad building. Its main characteristics were the founding of towns and cities and the establishment of the major industries needed to exploit the natural resources taken from the land, the forests, and the mines. This second frontier brought in waves of population, filling the spaces between widely dispersed settlements. It also brought streams of immigrants who did not settle on the land but found industrial jobs in the towns and cities. They were content, for a time, to work for low wages, and the hours were long. They filled the poverty-level slums. The first frontier reached the Pacific about 1850, the second about thirty years later. The first began to die about 1890, while the spread of the second was being completed in 1920.

The first of these frontiers was one of amazing discovery, romantic adventure, and challenge to initiative. Timber and ranch lands were gobbled up and extensive mineral claims staked out. Men of imagination founded settlements which often became towns bearing their names. These westward waves usually found excitement and adventure but seldom wealth. The great majority worked for others. They worked and wandered, carrying their beds on their backs. They were the first hobos. Their number multiplied when railroad building began and when other types of firm structuring were needed. They worked in places where no labor supply existed.

The true hobo was the in-between worker, willing to go anywhere to take a job and equally willing to move on later. His in-between role related to the two frontiers. He came on the scene after the trailblazer, and he went off the scene as the second frontier was closing. We can hardly overestimate the importance of his interim role. His kind of labor was going out of demand at the time *The Hobo* was written. Migratory workers were still needed, and still are in agriculture, but they have been drawn from other sources of supply. They no longer belong to Hobohemia.

With the moving of more people to the land, the big ranches began to disappear. The wide empire of the migrating cowboy was broken into thousands of fragments. Mining camps depending on a mobile labor force have since become mining towns with a permanent labor supply within walking distance. The same applies to the old-style lumber camps. Certain kinds of seasonal work, like ice harvesting, have been eliminated by technological change. The harvesting combine in the grain fields reduced the old rush each summer to the harvest. Extra workers are still needed to move the crops, but the demands are much less compelling than before.

While the hobo reflected the mobility tradition, his occupation made mobility a virtue. Distant jobs were always calling to him, and if no job beckoned, he went looking for it. Going from place to place, he followed the railroads. Highway travel was too pedestrian. If he had to walk, it was along the railroad track, and only to the next water tank where he waited for a freight train. His kind of mobility belonged to an era which was his own. When the automobile came in, he began to disappear. With the coming of the automobile, mobility did not diminish, but it took another form, making it possible for more people to become more mobile. The migrating family is now as evident as the migratory man once was; only the pattern of mobility has become more complex.[2]

Americans are clearly the most mobile of Western peoples. They are the most mobile residentially, as they move from one house to another. They are the most mobile in moving from place to place, between city and country, between city and suburb, between city and city, and between region and region. They are the most mobile professionally, changing from one job to another or from one kind of work to another. They are the most mobile socially, in their movement upward or downward from one social class to another. The hobo moved also in keeping with this tradition of mobility and may have contributed to it.

Once I attempted to list the reasons why the inhabitants of Hobohemia were in that almost womanless section. I asked questions about several individuals: Who they were, what they did or had done, the circumstances leading them to that area? I tried to determine if there was logic in their arrival and presence there. I tried to trace the road, the chain of events that brought them there. I found that each had arrived in Hobohemia by a different route.

In each of these cases arrival in Hobohemia had been preceded by a different series of events (defeats and disappointments). For some it was an interim station, for others the point of a new beginning, but for many the end of the road. In the competitive, complex way of modern life, Hobohemia served a different purpose for each of its habitants. Some have proposed abolishing Hobohemia as a slum, but the many roads that lead to such a place as Hobohemia would still have to terminate at a common point.

Hobohemia, as I tried to describe it, belonged to a great variety of types. After a fashion they could be classified, and I attempted to do that, but my attention was mainly on the hobo. He was still the important figure on the scene in 1921–22. Hobohemia then belonged more to him than to certain other types. He shared the area in a bigger way

2. See Nels Anderson, *Men on the Move* (University of Chicago Press, 1938). This is a study of the new migrancy, but it is not fully representative because its chief concern is the migration caused by the Great Depression.

than they could. He did not make Hobohemia, but he brought to it a unique type of cosmopolitanism. While utilizing the area, he also brought color and life to it.

It is clear now, although it was not recognized fully at the time, that the hobo was on his way out. That was fully understood by Jacob S. Coxey, but what he said—"The old timers will not be here much longer"—as we once walked through Madison Street did not have as much meaning then. He had in mind the types who had made up his "army" three decades earlier.

Since the hobo has moved on, this Introduction is my tribute to him. Whatever his weaknesses, and I knew them full well, I present him as one of the heroic figures of the frontier. With his work and help the railroads were built, out-of-the-way mines were developed, and outpost towns were established.

2

Hobohemia Defined

> All that Broadway is to the actors of America, West Madison is to its habitués—and more. Every institution of the Rialto is paralleled by one in West Madison. West Madison Street is the Rialto of the hobo.
>
> The hobos, themselves, do not think of Madison Street as the Rialto; they call it "the Main Stem," a term borrowed from tramp jargon, and meaning the main street of the town. "The Main Stem" is a more fitting term, perhaps, than the Rialto, but still inadequate. West Madison Street is more than a mere Rialto, more than the principal hobo thoroughfare of Chicago. It is the Pennsylvania Avenue, the Wilhelmstrasse of the anarchy of Hobohemia. (From an unpublished paper on the hobo by Harry M. Beardsley of the *Chicago Daily News*, 20 March 1917)

A survey of the lodging house and hotel population, supplemented by the census reports of the areas in which they live, indicates that the number of homeless men in Chicago ranges from 30,000 in good times to 75,000 in hard times.

We may say that approximately one-third of these are permanent residents of the city. The other two-thirds are here today and gone tomorrow. When work is plentiful they seldom linger in the city more than a week at a time. In winter when jobs are scarce, and it takes courage to face the inclement weather, the visits to town lengthen to three weeks and a month. From 300,000 to 500,000 of these migratory men pass through the city during the course of a normal year.

A still larger number are wanderers who have spent their days and their strength on the "long, gray road" and have fled to this haven for succor. They are Chicago's portion of the down-and-outs.

> An investigation of 1,000 dependent, homeless men made in Chicago in 1911 indicated that 254, or more than one-fourth of the 1,000 examined, were either temporarily crippled or maimed. Some 89 of this 1,000, or 9 percent, were manifestly either insane, feeble minded,

From *The Hobo: The Sociology of the Homeless Man* (Chicago: University of Chicago Press, 1961), 3–15

or epileptic. This did not include those large numbers of borderline cases in which vice or an overwhelming desire to wander had assumed the character of a mania.

Homeless men are largely single men. Something like 75 percent of the cases examined were single, while only 9 percent admitted they were married.[1]

"Main Stems"

Every large city has its district into which these homeless types gravitate. In the parlance of the "road" such a section is known as the "stem" or the "main drag." To the homeless man it is home, for there, no matter how sorry his lot, he can find those who will understand. The veteran of the road finds other veterans; the old man finds the aged; the chronic grouch finds fellowship; the radical, the optimist, the crook, the inebriate, all find others here to tune in with them. The wanderer finds friends here or enemies, but, and that is at once a characteristic and pathetic feature of Hobohemia, they are friends or enemies only for the day. They meet and pass on.

Hobohemia is divided into four parts—west, south, north, and east—and no part is more than five minutes from the heart of the Loop. They are all the "stem" as they are also Hobohemia. This four-part concept, Hobohemia, is Chicago to the down-and-out.

The "Slave Market"

To the men of the road, West Madison Street is the "slave market." It is the slave market because here most of the employment agencies are located. Here men in search of work bargain for jobs in distant places with the "man catchers" from the agencies. Most of the men on West Madison Street are looking for work. If they are not seeking work they want jobs, at least; jobs that have long rides thrown in. Most of the men seen here are young, at any rate they are men under middle age; restless, seeking, they parade the streets and scan the signs chalked on the windows or smeared over colored posters. Eager to "ship" somewhere, they are generally interested in a job as a means to reach a destination. The result is that distant jobs are in demand while good, paying, local jobs usually go begging.

1. In the 1923 edition of *The Hobo,* Anderson acknowledges the use of several sources in this chapter, but does not indicate their association with specific quotations: Anderson, "Summary of a Study of Four Hundred Tramps" (summer 1921; reprinted as chap. 7 in this volume); R. N. Wood, *A Study of Eight Cases of Homeless Men in Lodging Houses* (December 1922); Henry M. Beardsley, "Along the Main Stem with Red" (unpublished paper; 20 March 1917); Sherman O. Cooper, *Chicago's Hobo Area* (December 1917); Melville J. Herskovits, *Chicago's Hobo District* (December 1919). *Ed.*

West Madison, being a port of homeless men, has its own character-istic institutions and professions. The bootlegger is at home here; the dope peddler hunts and finds here his victims; here the professional gambler plies his trade and the "jack roller," as he is commonly called, the man who robs his fellows while they are drunk or asleep; these and others of their kind find in the anonymity of this changing popula-tion the freedom and security that only the crowded city offers.

The street has its share also of peddlers, beggars, cripples, and old, broken men; men worn out with the adventure and vicissitudes of life on the road. One of its most striking characteristics is the almost com-plete absence of women and children; it is the most completely wom-anless and childless of all the city areas. It is quite definitely a man's street.

West Madison Street, near the river, has always been a stronghold of the casual laborer. At one time it was a rendezvous for the seamen, but of late these have made South Chicago their haven. Even before the coming of the factories, before family life had wholly departed, this was an area of the homeless man. It will continue to be so, no doubt, until big businesses or a new union depot crowds the hobo out. Then he will move farther out into that area of deteriorated property that inevitably grows up just outside the business center of the city, where property, which has been abandoned for residences, has not yet been taken over by businesses, and where land values are high but rents are low.

Jefferson Park, between Adams and Monroe and west of Throop Street, is an appanage of the "slave market." It is the favorite place for the "bos" to sleep in summer or to enjoy their leisure, relating their adventures and reading the papers. On the "stem" it is known as "Bum Park," and men who visit it daily know no other name for it. A certain high spot of ground in the park is generally designated as "Crumb Hill." It is especially dedicated to "drunks." At any rate, the drunk and the drowsy seem inevitably to drift to this rise of ground. In fact, so many men visit the place that the grass under the trees seems to be having a fierce struggle to hold its own. It must be said, however, that the men who go to Bum Park are for the most part sober and well behaved. It is too far out for the more confirmed Madison Street bums to walk. The town folks of the neighborhood use the park, to a certain extent, but the women and children of the neighborhood are usually outnumbered by the men of the road, who monopolize the benches and crowd the shady places.

Hobohemia's Playground

The thing that characterizes State Street south of the Loop is the burlesque show. It is here that the hobo, seeking entertainment, is cheered
and gladdened by the "bathing beauties" and the oriental dancers.
Here, also, he finds improvement at the hands of the lady barbers,
who, it is reported, are using these men as a wedge to make their way
into a profitable profession that up to the present time has belonged
almost wholly to men.

South State Street differs from West Madison in many particulars.
For one thing there are more women here, and there is nothing like so
complete an absence of family life. The male population, likewise, is
of a totally different complexion. The prevailing color is an urban pink,
rather than the rural grime and bronze of the man on the road. There
are not so many restless, seeking youngsters.

Men do not parade the streets in groups of threes and fours with
their coats or bundles under their arms. There are no employment offices on this street. They are not needed. Nobody wants to go anywhere. When these men work they are content to take some short job
in the city. Short local jobs are at a premium. Many of these men have
petty jobs about the city where they work a few hours a day and are
able to earn enough to live. In winter many men will be found in the
cheap hotels on South State, Van Buren, or South Clark streets who
have been able to save enough money during the summer to house
themselves during the cold weather. State Street is the rendezvous of
the vagabond who has settled and retired, the "home guard" as they
are rather contemptuously referred to by the tribe of younger and more
adventurous men who still choose to take the road.

The white man's end of the south section of Hobohemia does not
extend south of Twelfth Street. From that point on to about Thirtieth
Street there is an area that has been taken over by the colored population. Colored people go much farther south, but if there are any homeless men in the "Black Belt," they are likely to be found along State
Street, between Twenty-second and Thirtieth. The Douglas Hotel, in
this region, is a colored man's lodging house.

To the south and southwest are the railroad yards. In summer homeless men find these yards a convenient place to pass the night. For
those who wish to leave the city, they are more accessible than the
yards on the north and west. The railroad yard is, in most places, one
of the hobo's favorite holdouts. It is a good place to loaf. There are coal
and wood and often vacant spaces where he can build fires and cook
food or keep warm. This is not so easily done in Chicago where the
tramp's most deadly enemy, the railroad police, are numerous and in

closer co-operation with the civil authorities than in most cities. In spite of this, hobos hang about the yards.

"Bughouse Square"

On the north side of the river, Clark Street below Chicago Avenue is the "stem." Here a class of transients have drifted together, forming a group unlike any in either of the other areas of Hobohemia. This is the region of the hobo intellectuals. This area may be described as the rendezvous of the thinker, the dreamer, and the chronic agitator. Many of its denizens are "home guards." Few transients ever turn up here; they do not have time. They alone come here who have time to think, patience to listen, or courage to talk. Washington Square is the center of the northern area. To the "bos" it is "Bughouse Square." Many people do not know any other name for it. This area is as near to the so-called Latin Quarter as the hobo dare come. Bughouse Square is, in fact, quite as much the stronghold of the more or less vagabond poets, artists, writers, revolutionists of various types as of the go-abouts. Among themselves this region is known as the "village."

Bohemia and Hobohemia meet at Bughouse Square. On Sundays and holidays, any evening, in fact, when the weather permits, it will be teeming with life. At such times all the benches will be occupied. On the grass in the shade of the trees men sit about in little groups of a dozen or less. The park, except a little corner to the southeast where the women come to read, or knit, or gossip while the children play, is completely in possession of men. A polyglot population swarms here. Tramps, and hobos—yes, but they are only scatteringly represented. Pale-faced denizens of the Russian tearooms, philosophers and enthusiasts from the "Blue Fish," brush shoulders with kindred types from the "Dill Pickle," the "Green Mask," the "Gray Cottage." Free-lance propagandists who belong to no group and claim no following, nonconformists, dreamers, fakers, beggars, bootleggers, dope fiends—they are all here.

Around the edges of the square the curbstone orators gather their audiences. Religion, politics, science, the economic struggle—these are the principal themes of discussion in this outdoor forum. Often there are three or four audiences gathered at the same time in different parts of the park, each carrying on a different discussion. One may be calling miserable sinners to repent, and the other denouncing all religion as superstition. Opposing speakers frequently follow each other, talking to the same audience. In this aggregation of minds the most striking thing is the variety and violence of the antipathies. There is, notwithstanding, a generous tolerance. It is probably a tolerance growing out

A jungle camp. The "bos" hid from the camera.

of the fact that, although everyone talks and argues, no one takes the other seriously. It helps to pass the time and that is why folks come to Bughouse Square.

To the hobo who thinks, even though he does not think well, the lower North Side is a great source of comfort. On the North Side he finds people to whom he can talk and to whom he is willing to listen. Hobos do not generally go there to listen, however, but burning with a message of which they are bound to unburden themselves. They go to speak, perhaps to write. Many of them are there to get away from the sordidness of life in other areas of Hobohemia.

A "Jungle" on the Lakefront

Grant Park, east of Michigan Avenue, is a loafing place for hobos with time on their hands. They gather here from all parts of Hobohemia to read the papers, to talk, and to kill time. For men who have not had a bed it is a good place to sleep when the sun is kind and the grass is warm. In the long summer evenings Grant Park is a favorite gathering place for men who like to get together to tell yarns and to frolic. It is a favorite rendezvous for the boy tramps.

The section of Grant Park facing the lake shore is no less popular. Along the shore from the Field Museum northward to Randolph Street the homeless men have access to the lake. They take advantage of the unimproved condition of the park and make of the place, between the railroad tracks and the lake, a retreat, a resort, a social center. Here they wash their clothes, bathe, sew, mend shoes.

Summer resorting behind the Field Museum, Chicago.

Behind the Field Museum, on the section of the park that is still being used as a dump for rubbish, the hobos have established a series of camps or "jungles." Here, not more than five minutes from the Loop, are numerous improvised shacks in which men live. Many men visit these sections only for the day. To them it is a good place to come to fish and they spend hours gazing at the water and trying to keep the little fish from biting.

Why Men Come to Chicago

The hobo has no social centers other than the "stem" and the "jungle." He either spends his leisure in the "jungles" or in town. The "jungle" ordinarily is a station on his way to town. Life revolves for him around his contacts on the "stem," and it is to town he hies himself whenever free to do so.

Few casuals can give any reason for the attraction that the city has for them. Few have ever considered it. The explanations they give, when pressed for reasons, are more or less matter-of-fact and center in their material interests. Other motives, motives of which they are only half conscious, undoubtedly influence them.

The city is the labor exchange for the migratory worker and even for the migratory nonworker who is often just as ambitious to travel. When he is tired of a job, or when the old job is finished, he goes to town to get another in some other part of the country. The labor exchanges facilitate this turnover of seasonal labor. They enable a man to leave the city "on the cushins." This is the lure that draws him to the city. Hobohemia brings the job-seeking man and the man-seeking job together. Migrants have always known that a larger variety of jobs and a better assortment of good "shipments" were to be had in Chicago than elsewhere.

> Chicago is the greatest railway center in the United States. No one knows these facts better than the hobo. It is a fact that trains from all points of the compass are constantly entering and leaving the city over its 39 different railways. According to the *Chicago City Manual*, there are 2,840 miles of steam railways within the city limits. The mileage of steam railroad track in Chicago is equal to the entire railroad mileage in Switzerland and Belgium, and is greater than the steam railroad mileage found in each of the kingdoms of Denmark, Holland, Norway, and Portugal. Twenty-five through package cars leave Chicago every day for 18,000 shipping points in 44 states.

The termination of the seasonal occupations brings men cityward. They come here for shelter during the winter, and not only for shelter but for inside winter work. This is the hobo's only alternative, provided he cannot go to California or to one of the southern states. The dull routine of the inside job, which seemed so unattractive in the springtime, looks better with the falling of the temperature. We may add, also, that many of the men who are attracted to the city in winter are not particularly interested in work. There are, however, among the improvident tramp class, "wise virgins" who save in the summer in order to enjoy the life of a boardinghouse during the winter.

The hobo often goes to town for medical attention. For the sick and injured of the floating fraternity, Chicago is a haven of refuge because of the large number of opportunities found here for free treatment. The county hospital, the dispensaries, and the medical colleges are well known to these men. Many get well and go their way, others get no farther than the hospital—and then the morgue.

A man whose income is limited to a few hundred dollars a year can do more with it in the large city than in a small town. In no other American city will a dollar go farther than in Chicago. It is not uncommon to find men living in Hobohemia on less than a dollar a day. Large numbers make possible cheap service, and cheap service brings the men.

The Problem Defined in Terms of Numbers

Not only the extent, but the nature of the problem of the homeless man is revealed by a study of his numbers. In Chicago all estimates are in substantial agreement that the population of Hobohemia never falls below 30,000 in summer, doubles this figure in winter, and has reached 75,000 and over in periods of unemployment.[2]

These numbers, while large, are only between 1 and 2.5 percent of Chicago's population of nearly 3,000,000. Homeless men, however, are not distributed evenly throughout the city; they are concentrated, segregated, as we have seen, in three contiguous narrow areas close to the center of transportation and trade.

This segregation of tens of thousands of footloose, homeless, and not to say hopeless men is the fact fundamental to an understanding of the problem. Their concentration has created an isolated cultural area—Hobohemia. Here characteristic institutions have arisen—cheap hotels, lodging houses, flops, eating joints, outfitting shops, employment agencies, missions, radical bookstores, welfare agencies, economic and political institutions—to minister to the needs, physical and spiritual, of the homeless man. This massing of detached and migra-

2. Mrs. Solenberger's figures of more than a decade ago put the number of the various types of homeless men in this city at 40,000–60,000: "No exact census of the total number of homeless men of various types in the lodging-house districts of Chicago has been taken, but 40,000 is considered a conservative estimate by several careful students of the question who are closely in touch with local conditions. This number is somewhat increased at election times and very greatly increased when word goes out, as it did during the winter of 1907–8, that relief funds were being collected and free lodgings and food would be furnished to the unemployed. In December, January, February, and March of that winter all private lodging houses were filled to overflowing, and the Municipal Lodging House, its annex, and two other houses which it operated gave a total of 79,411 lodgings to homeless men as compared with 6,930 for the same months of the winter before, an increase of 72,481. The Health Department, which took charge of the municipal lodging houses and made a careful study of local conditions during the winter of 1907–8, estimated the number of homeless men then in Chicago to be probably not less than 60,000." —One Thousand Homeless Men, p. 9 n.

Nearly if not quite one-fifth of the 700 hotels in Chicago cater to the migratory and casual worker. The 63 hotels visited by investigators in this study had a total capacity for the accommodation of 15,000 men. On the basis of these figures, it seems safe to put the total capacity of the hotels in Hobohemian areas at 25,000–30,000. A like number of men are probably provided for in nearby boarding and lodging houses. Thousands of other men sleep at the docks, in engine rooms, in vacant houses, in flophouses, or in summer in the parks.

The returns of the 1920 United States census show that in the three wards of the city in which Hobohemian areas are located there are 28,105 more male than female residents. This figure indicates that the so-called home guard numbers about 30,000 the summer population of Hobohemia.

The Jewish Bureau of Social Service estimates that the number of homeless men in Chicago at any one time in the winter of 1921–22 was 120,000. This figure, which seems high when compared with estimates arrived at by other methods of calculation, assumes that the proportion of homeless men for the city is the same as that for the Jewish community.

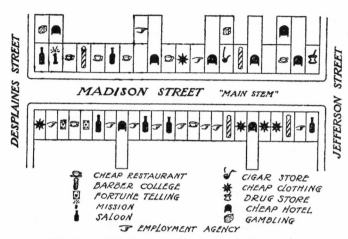

Hobo institutions on one street along the "Main Stem."

tory men upon a small area has created an environment in which gamblers, dope vendors, bootleggers, and pickpockets can live and thrive.

The mobility of the migratory worker complicates the problem of the missions, police, and welfare agencies. The mission measures its success not only in numbers of converts but in the numbers of men fed and lodged. The police department, on the contrary, alarmed by the influx of hobos and tramps in response to free meals and free flops, has adopted a policy of severity and repression for the protection of the community. Welfare agencies, opposing alike the demoralizing results of indiscriminate feeding and lodging, and the negative policy of the police, favor a program of organized effort based upon an investigation of the needs of each individual case.

3

The Jungles: The Homeless Man Abroad

In the city, under ordinary circumstances, the homeless man gathers with his kind. Even so he is very much alone and his contacts with his fellows are relatively formal and distant.

City life is interesting but full of danger. Even in a world where the conditions of life are so elementary, prudence dictates a certain amount of reserve and hence formality and convention in the relations of men. The flophouse and the cheap hotel compel promiscuity, but do not encourage intimacy or neighborliness. On the outskirts of cities, however, the homeless men have established social centers that they call "jungles," places where the hobos congregate to pass their leisure time outside the urban centers. The jungle is to the tramp what the campground is to the vagabond who travels by auto. It has for the hobo, perhaps, greater significance, since it becomes a necessary part of his daily life. The evening camp fire for the tourist, on the contrary, is a novelty merely, an experience but not a necessity.

Location and Types of Jungles

Jungles are usually located in close proximity to a railroad division point, where the trains are made up or where trains stop to change crews and engines. Sometimes they are located near a "tank town," where occasional stops are made for water or fuel. Not infrequently they are near the intersection of railroad lines. In the South, and on the West Coast, jungles are often located along the highways. This is due to the fact that many men go south in winter not to work but to escape the rigors of the northern climate. The railroad for the time being has no attraction for them and they are content to stroll abroad, seeing the country. In the West, where men frequently carry bedding and cooking equipment, they can camp anywhere. It is easier for them, therefore, to leave the railroad and venture along the highways.

Accessibility to a railroad is only one of the requirements of a good

From *The Hobo: The Sociology of the Homeless Man* (Chicago: University of Chicago Press, 1961), 16–26

jungle. It should be located in a dry and shady place that permits sleeping on the ground. There should be plenty of water for cooking and bathing and wood enough to keep the pot boiling. If there is a general store nearby where bread, meat, and vegetables may be had, so much the better. For those who have no money, but enough courage to "bum lumps," it is well that the jungles be not too far from a town, though far enough to escape the attention of the natives and officials, the town "clowns."

Jungle camps may be divided into two classes—the temporary and the permanent, or continuous. Temporary jungles are merely stopover or relay stations inhabited intermittently by the men of the road. Men temporarily stranded in a town usually seek a secluded spot at the edge of a village, not too far from the railroad, where they may while away the time without being molested. Men on the road look for places where other men preceding them have camped. There they are likely to find pots and kettles in which to cook food or wash clothes. At points where trains stop frequently, making it possible for men to get away at any time, the population of a temporary jungle is likely to be larger and more permanent.

The continuous or permanent jungles are seldom deserted, at least in summer. There is usually someone there to keep the fire burning and usually there are men or boys occupied at various tasks—cooking, washing or boiling clothes, shaving, sewing, bathing, and reading.

Women are often found in the areas of the cities where the homeless men congregate but not in the jungles. Here is an institution where the hobo is his own housewife. He not only cooks his own food, but has even invented dishes that are peculiar to jungle life. Chief among these is "mulligan" stew. "Mulligan," or "combination," is a "throw together" of vegetables and meat. There are certain ideal mixtures of vegetables and meat, but the tramp makes "mulligan" from anything that is at hand. Onions, potatoes, and beef are the prime essentials. Some men become adept at frying and roasting over campfires.

The hobo who lives in the jungles has proved that he can become domesticated without the aid of women. He has established the habit of keeping his clothes and person clean. It is not difficult to select from a group of transients the men who have just come from the jungles. Their clothes will be clean and even bear evidence of jungle sewing. Overalls that have seen service will be bleached almost white from numerous washings. The hobo learns here the housewife's art of keeping pots clean and the camp in order. The man who cannot, or will not, learn these few elementary principles of housekeeping is likely to fare ill in the jungle.

If it is a warm day some men will be sleeping. They may have been riding trains all night or have found the night too cold for sleep. A daily paper from an adjoining town may be going the rounds. There may be newspapers from different cities brought in by men traveling different directions. Travelers meeting this way have much of common interest to talk about and conversation is enlivened with discussions of questions of concern to "bos." The jungle is always astir with life and movement, and the hobo enters into this life as he does no other. Here he turns his back on the world and faces his fellows and is at ease.

Absolute democracy reigns in the jungle. The color line has been drawn in some camps, but it is the general custom, and especially in the North, for Negroes, Mexicans, and whites to share the same jungle. The jungle is the melting pot of trampdom.

The average man of the road has had a variety of experience and not a little adventure. In the jungles there is always an audience for anyone who wants to talk, whether of his thoughts, his experiences, or his observations. There is plenty of opportunity to tell stories. The art of telling a story is diligently cultivated by the "bos" in the assemblies about the fire. This vagabond existence tends to enrich the personality, and long practice has developed in some of these men an art of personal narrative that has greatly declined elsewhere. Many of them develop into fascinating *raconteurs* in the literal as well as the literary sense of the term. Talk in the jungle is of the open road and the day to come, and in that there is sufficient matter to occupy them.

Jungle populations are ever changing. Every hour new faces appear to take the place of those that have passed on. They come and go without ceremony, with scarcely a greeting or "fare-you-well." Every new member is of interest for the news he brings or the rumors that he spreads. Each is interested in the other so far as he has something to tell about the road over which he has come, the work conditions, the behavior of the police, or other significant details. But with all the discussion there is seldom any effort to discuss personal relations and connections. Here is one place where every man's past is his own secret.

Only in the case of very young boys or sick men and sometimes old men is there any effort to learn something of the individual's past. Men will brush elbows in the jungles for days and even weeks without ever learning one another's names. They live closed lives and grant others the same privilege.

The Laws of the Jungle

In every permanent camp there is likely to be a permanent group that makes the camp its headquarters. Sometimes these groups are able to take possession and exploit the transient guests. The IWW has at times been able to exclude everyone who did not carry the red card of that organization. As a rule, however, the jungle is extremely hospitable and democratic.

The freedom of the jungles is, however, limited by a code of etiquette. Jungle laws are unwritten, but strictly adhered to. The breaking of these rules, if intentional, leads to expulsion, forced labor, or physical punishment.

> Jungle crimes include (1) making fire by night in jungles subject to raids; (2) "hi-jacking" or robbing men at night when sleeping in the jungles; "buzzing," or making the jungle a permanent hangout for jungle "buzzards" who subsist on the leavings of meals; (4) wasting food or destroying it after eating is a serious crime; (5) leaving pots and other utensils dirty after using; (6) cooking without first hustling fuel; (7) destroying jungle equipment. In addition to these fixed offenses are other crimes which are dealt with as they arise. Men are supposed to use cooking cans for cooking only, "boiling up" cans for washing clothing, coffee cans to cook coffee, etc. After using, guests are expected to clean utensils, dry them, and leave them turned bottom side up so that they will not fill with rainwater and rust. They are expected to keep the camp clean. To enforce such common-sense rules, self-appointed committees come into existence.[1]

Exclusive camps are usually the result of the efforts of the older residents to enforce discipline. Most "jungle buzzards," men who linger in the jungles from season to season, take an interest in the running of things. For the most part they are parasitic, begging food from others, but they are generally on the alert to keep the place clean and orderly.

The following description of a day in the jungles was written by a migratory worker, a man who knows the life from years of experience. His narrative presents a faithful picture of an average day in an average jungle.

A Day in the Jungles

This jungle is on the edge of a strip of timber. A stream fed from a spring runs into the lake near by. The empty box cars on the railroad siding close by offer protection against rain and a place to sleep. Half

---

1. It is interesting here to note that there is a striking parallel between the rules of the jungles and the rules of cow camps and other camps of the hills. It is the custom of the cow men of the West to maintain camps in the hills which are stocked with provision and equipped with utensils and furnishings. These camps are usually left open, and anyone who passes is welcome to spend the night, provided he puts the place in order when he leaves.

a mile away is the junction of two railroads where all trains stop, and a mile and a half further on is a small town.

At one o'clock in the morning a few men step off a freight train. One speaks up: "Does anyone know if there is a jungle in this place?" "Yes," someone answers, "The jungle is up in that direction," pointing towards a woods, "but what's the use in going over there now? You can't build a fire at this time of night. I am going to hunt up a box car for a flop."

After a moment of silence someone else asks, "Any town close by?" "Yes, there it is," replies another, pointing to some lights showing in the distance. The men form groups according to acquaintance and talk in a low tone. "Come on, let us hunt up a place to flop till daylight." The different groups start off. One starts out for the town, one goes towards the box cars, and one makes for the jungles. I was with the group bound for the jungles.

A hundred feet from the railroad right-of-way under the darkness of big trees we see three or four dying camp fires. Around one fire we can see the shadows of men. Some are sitting on the butts of logs, smoking or dozing; others are stretched out on the ground sound asleep.

The new arrivals walk up to the fire, look over the bunch to find, perhaps, some old acquaintances. Then some of us find seats or lie down; others, with as little noise as possible, hunt up cans which they fill with water and place over the glowing coals. The men take ground coffee from packages in their pockets and pour it into boiling water. The feed is open to everybody. Bread and sausage are brought out; even sugar is passed around as long as it lasts. The men eat in silence. Each one takes the utensils he used and walks to the creek to wash them. Nearly all of the men then lie down, but some leave. Nobody asks anyone about himself and nobody says "hello" or "goodbye."

Daylight comes. The breaking of sticks for firewood is heard. Fires are started, cooking utensils are chosen. The law of the jungle is that no one can call a vessel his except at the time he uses it. Packages and receptacles are opened revealing food of all kinds. Eating commences. If any man with more than enough for himself sees someone else not eating, it is etiquette to offer to share with his neighbor. If the other man accepts the offer, he thereby takes upon himself the responsibility of cleaning the dishes.

At any time men will be seen leaving the jungles to hustle food, or to get wood, or to catch trains. Anytime is eating time in the jungles and someone is always bringing in "chuck" that he has bought or "bummed." Talking goes on as long as the daylight lasts. Heated arguments often develop. Papers and pamphlets are distributed, union cards are taken out; business meetings are held to decide policies and actions, how to get the next meal or how to win the battle between labor and capital.

About ten o'clock in the morning two townsmen displaying stars come into the jungle. One of them tells the men that they will have to clean out because people are kicking. A holdup has been committed in town the night before and they intend to prevent any more from being committed, "So you fellers have to leave."

One man in the jungles speaks up and tells the officers that we are not holdup men, that we are getting ourselves something to eat, and that we have got to have some place to do that. "We have paid for everything. What would you do if you was in our place; go into town and get pulled and let the town feed us?"

The officer looks nonplussed, but curtly replies, "Well, I am going by orders." After that he walks away. The timid men leave the jungle. The others reply by roundly cursing indiscriminately all their enemies. They are town clowns, sky pilots, Bible ranters, bulls, politicians, home guards, hicks, stool pigeons, systems, scissor bills, and capitalists. Incidentally they advocate strikes, rebellion, mass action, complete revolution of the political system, abolishment of the wage system.

It is close to twelve o'clock. Fires are replenished, cans, pots and pans are put into service. Plans are being made in anticipation of a coming raid by the police. At two o'clock, someone suggests a song. After a fiery song of the class struggle, a speech follows advising the men to organize.

By three o'clock only about fifteen or twenty are left in the jungle. The officer followed by townsmen armed with guns return. Some of the hobos retreat into the woods. Those remaining are ordered to hold up their hands with "You damn bums" added to the command. Some comply, others refuse. One even has the courage to shout, "Go ahead and shoot, you damn cowards." This starts a general shooting into every pot, pan and can in sight. The men scatter.

After the invaders leave, an inventory is immediately made to assess the damage. Since the utensils in best condition had been hidden in the brush, no serious loss to the jungle has resulted.

By four o'clock the story of the raid has traveled and men come in from all directions. The decision of the majority is to remain in the jungle over night. Food is brought in and preparations for supper begin. The men are doubling up to cook together. Those belonging to certain unions have as many as eight or ten in a bunch. There are from thirty to forty angry men in camp by now and more are coming in. There is some talk of revenge.

By six o'clock supper is well under way. Several fires are burning.

Containers of every description are used to cook in; broken shovels and tie plates are used to fry on, empty tobacco tins are used as cups, and tomato cans serve as fry pans, soup kettles, and soap dishes. Potatoes are roasted on the coals, wires are bent upon which to broil meat. All are still talking excitedly of the clash with the police.

While some of the men are busily engaged in cooking, others are sewing and mending their clothes or shoes, and still others are shaving. Now and then as at breakfast someone will shout, asking if anybody wants some spuds or a piece of punk or a piece of "gut" (sausage); and usually there is an affirmative answer. After supper, pans and cans are cleaned out, the paper is read and passes the rounds. Already it is growing dark, and the hunt begins for dry sleeping places.

Suddenly a commotion is started; a man is roughly rushed into the open. He is a hi-jack caught in the act of robbing a fellow who was sleeping, a greater crime in the jungle than an open hold up. Cries of "Burn the———" and "Let us hang him!" are heard from all sides. A council is hurriedly called, a chairman is selected, motions are made with amendments and substitutes. After a short discussion a vote is taken to give him a whipping. The man is tied to a tree facing toward it. His back is bared, and men are called for to apply punishment. No one steps forward; everybody declines to apply the strap or stick.

Another council is called but before they get started a young fellow has declared his willingness to fight the hi-jack to a finish because he knew him and didn't like him anyway. The proposition is accepted. The hi-jack is more than ten pounds heavier than the challenger; but whether from fear or not, for he knows that the challenger has the crowd back of him to a man, the hi-jack is slow to start. Perhaps he feels that the crowd will give him a beating whether he wins or not. He soon loosens up but he does not show the goods. The "bo" is more than a match for him but the hi-jack does not give up easily. He displays some courage but the "bo" fights like a madman and strikes the hi-jack blow after blow. The fight lasts more than ten minutes before the hi-jack is completely knocked out.

After he gets to his feet he is given a chance to wash his face and stick paper on the cuts; then he is "frisked," that is, ordered to donate all but one dollar to the jungle. Then he is sent out of camp with orders not to show up in any of the diggings along the line for it would be murder if anyone should spot him.

By eleven o'clock the excitement is over. Different men announce that they were headed for so and so and that the freight starts at such a time. To this someone replies that he is going that way too so they start off together. Others walk back among the trees to the places where they have prepared to sleep. Others who have insufficient clothes to stand the night chill bunch up around the glowing camp fires. Soon everything is quiet except for an occasional sound out of the darkness of men mumbling in conversation. Occasionally the sound of groans and snores or sighs, or curses are heard. These betray the dreams of men living like hunted animals.

I look at my watch and note that it is near midnight and that all is over for the night, so I curl up on some papers beside a bed of coals.[2]

The Melting Pot of Trampdom

The part played by the jungles as an agency of discipline for the men of the road cannot be overestimated. Here hobo tradition and law are formulated and transmitted. It is the nursery of tramp lore. Here the fledgling learns to behave like an old-timer. In the jungles the slang of the road and the cant of the tramp class is coined and circulated. It may originate elsewhere but here it gets recognition. The stories and songs current among the men of the road, the sentiments, the attitudes, and the philosophy of the migratory laborer are all given due airing. In short, every idea and ideal that finds lodgment in the tramp's fancy may be expressed here in the wayside forum where anyone who thinks may speak, whether he be a jester or a sage.

Suspicion and hostility are the universal attitudes of the town or small city to the hobo and the tramp. Accordingly, the so-called floater custom of passing vagrants on to other communities is widespread.[3] The net effect of this policy is to intensify the antisocial attitude of the homeless man and to release and accentuate criminal tendencies. The small town is helpless to cope with the situation. As things are, its action perhaps cannot be different. Agriculture, as it becomes organized upon a capitalistic basis, is increasingly dependent upon seasonal labor, in harvesting crops for example. The report of the Commission on Industrial Relations states:

> The attempts to regulate movements of migratory workers by local organizations have, without exception, proved failures. This must necessarily be true no matter how well planned or well managed such local organizations may be. The problem cannot be handled except on a national scale and by methods and machinery which are proportioned to the enormous size and complexity of the problem.[4]

2. Written by A. W. Dragstedt, secretary in 1922 of the "Hobo College" of Chicago.
3. For a discussion of the practice of "floating" with reference to the treatment of misdemeanants, see Stuart A. Queen, *The Passing of the County Jail.*
4. *Final Report,* 158.

4

The Lodging House: The Homeless Man at Home

Hobohemia is a lodging house area. The accommodations it offers the homeless man range from a bed in a single room for fifty cents to location on the floor of an empty loft for a dime. Lodging-house keepers take thin profits but they serve large numbers. There are usually more men than there are beds, particularly in winter. An estimate indicates that all hotels are full from December to May. During the rest of the year they are likely to be filled to two-thirds of their capacity.

Chicago has known three types of cheap hotels: the so-called "barrelhouse," the welfare institution, and the business enterprise. The first, the barrelhouse, was a rooming house, saloon, and house of prostitution, all in one. Men with money usually spent it in the barrelhouses. There they found warmth and companionship. They would join the circle at the bar, buy drinks for the crowd, and have a good time. Men who were afraid of being robbed placed their money with the bartender and charged against it the drinks purchased. As soon as they were overcome by drink they would be taken upstairs to bed. The following day the program would be repeated. A three- or four-hundred-dollar stake at this rate usually lasted a week. Not infrequently the barrelhouse added to its other attractions the opportunity for gambling.

The barrelhouse is a thing of the past. Its place has been taken in part by hotels like the Workingmen's Palace; the Reliance; the New Century, owned and operated by the Salvation Army; the Rufus F. Dawes, owned and maintained by General C. G. Dawes; the Popular Hotel, owned and maintained by the Chicago Christian Industrial League. In places of this sort, charges are small, usually not enough to cover operating expenses.

The Rufus F. Dawes and the Workingmen's Palace are both large, fireproof structures, clean and modern, constructed originally for other purposes. Like all paternalistic, quasi-charitable institutions, however,

From *The Hobo: The Sociology of the Homeless Man* (Chicago: University of Chicago Press, 1961), 27–39

they are not popular, although the charges for a room and bed are hardly sufficient to cover the operating expenses. This is the second type of lodging house.

The pioneers in the cheap hotel business in Chicago operated on a commercial basis were Harvey and McGuire, the founders of the well-known Harvey-McGuire hotel system. Harvey, an evangelist, in his work with the "down-and-outs" had learned the evils of barrelhouses. He went into a partnership with McGuire, a man acquainted with the rough side of life. After a number of years the Harvey-McGuire system went out of existence. McGuire went into the hotel business for himself and now owns a number of cheap lodging houses. Harvey sold his interests to his nephew and went back to evangelistic work. The nephew went into partnership with Mr. Dammarell. There are eight hotels in the present Harvey-Dammarell system with a combined capacity for lodging 3,000 men. The Ideal, opened in 1884 and probably the oldest men's hotel in the city, originally known as the Collonade, at 509 West Madison Street, is an example of the type. The Mohawk, the most modern men's hotel, is also the property of the Harvey-Dammarell system.

The men who run these hotels do not claim to be philanthropists. Mr. Harvey has defined the situation. He says,

> We are in the hotel business to make a living. We give the men the best service they can pay for. We give nothing away and we ask nothing. Consequently, we do not lay ourselves open to criticism. We insist on order and sobriety and we usually get it. We hold that the men have a right to criticize us and come to us if they are not satisfied with the service we give. That is business. The man who pays seventy-five cents for a bed has a right to seventy-five cents' worth of service. If a man can only pay twenty-five cents for a bed he is entitled to all that he pays for and is entitled to kick if he doesn't get it.

Different types of hotels attract different types of men. The better class of workingmen who patronize the Mohawk, where the prices range from forty to seventy cents, wear collars and creased trousers. The hotel provides stationary and desks. Hotels where the prices range from twenty-five cents to forty cents are patronized by a shabbier group of men. Few of them are shaven. Some of them read, but most of them sit alone with their thoughts. In some second-class places a man is employed to go the rounds and arouse the sleepers.

In the twenty-five-cent hotels, the patrons not only are content to sit unshaven, but they are often dirty. Many of them have the faces of beaten men; many of them are cripples and old men. The exceptions are the Popular and the Rufus F. Dawes, where the price is twenty cents or less to be sure, but the guests are more select. Since these places are semicharitable, they can force certain requirements upon their patrons.

The term "room" is a misnomer when applied to a sleeping apartment in a cheap hotel. These rooms have been aptly termed "cubicles," and among the patrons they are known as "cages." A cubicle is usually from six to eight feet in width and from eight to twelve feet in length. The thin walls, composed of steel or matched lumber, are usually about eight feet in height. A wire netting over the top admits air and prevents the guests climbing from one cubicle to another. The furnishings are simple; sometimes only a bed, sometimes a bed and a chair, and in more expensive places a stand. They are not constructed either for comfort or convenience; lighting and ventilation are usually bad. But they are all they were intended to be: places for men to sleep with a limited degree of privacy.

A canvass of the Hobohemian hotels has been made with a view to learning the approximate mobility of the hotel population. Few of these hotels are prepared to make any but general statements, though some of them have made an effort to get the facts. The consensus of opinion of hotel clerks is that the greatest turnover is in the cheapest hotels. Better-class places like the Acme, the Ironsides, and the Workingmen's Palace have a large proportion of permanent guests. The permanent guests, those who remain two or three months or more, range from a third to a half of the total number of roomers. Many of the older hotels have permanent patrons who are seasonal but regular. Others never leave the city.

The "Flophouse"

"Flophouses" are nearly all alike. Guests sleep on the floor or in bare, wooden bunks. The only privilege they buy is the privilege to lie down somewhere in a warm room.

> "Hogan's Flop" is known from coast to coast among hobos. A tramp who has been in Chicago long enough to learn of Lynch's place, the Workingmen's Palace, Hinky Dink's, or to eat doughnuts in missions has heard of Hogan's.
>
> The first "Hogan's Flop" was located on South State Street. Later it moved to the West Side and for some time was on Meridian Street. Since it left Meridian Street it has been located in several places. The original Hogan, who was a Spanish-American War veteran, has passed to his reward. Only his name remains. Every winter, however, someone starts a "flop" and it invariably inherits the name and fame of Hogan. Hogan is now a myth, a sort of eponymous hero. A tramp discussing this matter said: "Hogan may be dead but the bugs that were in business with him are still on the job. They follow this joint

wherever it goes. You know when they moved from Meridian Street it wasn't three days before the bugs got the new address and followed us."

The following account is adapted from a description of a night spent in "Hogan's Flop":

I spent the evening at the Bible Rescue Mission where sincere folks were pleading with men of the road to come forward and make things right with the Master. Two came forward and it was a time of rejoicing. They prayed and sang and fed us rolls and coffee, and to those who had no bed for the night they gave tickets to "Hogan's." They offered me a ticket but I thanked them and assured them that I still had a little money.

You have to know where "Hogan's" is to find it. In the spring of 1922, it occupied the second and third floors of a building at 16 South Desplaines Street. A narrow, shaky stairs, a squeaky door, a feebly lighted entrance, a night clerk who demands a dime and you are within. You may take your choice of sleeping on this floor or go on up to the third. There is no difference in the price. I chose the second floor. It was less crowded. The fire, from a large heater in the center of the room, was warmer.

The men around the stove had evidently been exposed to the elements. One was drying his shoes for it had rained all day. Another was drying his shirt. Two were engaged in listless conversation. Others were silent. The air was stuffy, the light dim. I walked around the room looking for a place to lie down. Dozens of men were sleeping on the floor with their heads to the wall. Some were lying on paper, others on the bare floor. Some were partly covered by their overcoats; some had no overcoats. It is an art to curl up under an overcoat. One man of fifty years or more had removed his shirt and trousers and was using the latter for a pillow. He had tied his shoes to his trousers which is evidence that he knew "flop" house ethics. When men sleep in box cars they sometimes use their shoes for pillows but this is not necessary in "Hogan's." A planking around the walls affords a resting place for weary heads.

A number of the faces here I had seen a great many times on the "stem." Two were old men in their seventies who had been in the city several years and were mendicants most of the time. There was a one-legged man whom I had seen chumming with another one-legged man on the streets. Both peddled lead pencils and shoestrings. On the only cot on the floor, two young fellows were lying. They were sleeping with their heads at opposite ends of the narrow bed and their bodies were entangled to prevent their falling off.

I found a vacant place on the floor where I could have about two feet between myself and my nearest neighbor so I spread my papers and lay down. I had more paper than I needed so I gave half to another man who was just circling about for a place to go to bed. I asked the man nearest me if the bugs bothered much. He answered in the richest of Irish brogues that Hogan's bugs were sure efficient. Another man chimed in. He said they were better organized than the German army. How well organized they were I can't say but I was not long in learning that they were enterprising.

Two men near me engaged in a discussion about the economic conference at Genoa. One man had very positive, orderly ideas of how things should go. The other interrupted occasionally only to agree. Someone wanted to know why he didn't hire a hall. Then there was silence, except for snores. I never heard such a variety of snores but none of them seemed to suggest peaceful slumbers or pleasant dreaming. Once the snores were broken into by some man bawling out, "Hey, you; quit spittin' over this way; you're gettin' it on my paper." "Well, dammit; How much room do you want to take up?" His neighbor retorted, "It's none of your————business how much room I take. You lay off'n that spittin', see."

More snores. A man got up, stretched, rubbed his legs, came to the center of the room to the stove. More snores. Some men came in, paid their dimes and looked for an opening on the floor. A man ran to the toilet to vomit. A wag called to him to "heave it up."

After an hour or so I felt something on my hand. I crushed it. There were others to be seen on the white papers. I lay down to try to sleep again. A second attack brought me suddenly to my feet. I lay down resolved a third time not to be disturbed. My companions seemed to be suffering more from the hard floor than anything else; and the floor was hard. I turned my thoughts to the hardness of the floor at "Hogan's."

How long I dozed I can't say but I awoke marveling at the endurance of the man of the road. While I pondered thus a man jumped to his feet and hastened out. He was cursing the bugs and saying that he knew an engine room that had this "place beat all hollow." I felt better. Someone else had weakened first. I got up and started home. It was two-thirty.

Restaurants and Lunchrooms

Hobohemian restaurants serve meals for a half or a third of the prices current in the Loop. In some of these lunchrooms the charges are so low that one marvels. However, the food is coarse and poor and the service rough and ready.

The homeless man is as casual in his eating as he is in his work. He usually gives all the restaurants a trial. If he has any money when mealtime comes he generally does a little "window shopping." He meanders up and down the street reading the bills of fare in the windows.

The Hobohemian restaurants know this and accordingly use window displays to attract the roaming patron. Food is placed in the windows, cooking is done within sight of the street, but the chief means of attraction are the menus chalked on the windows. The whole window is sometimes lettered up with special entrées of the day. Some of these bills of fare are interesting.

Gus's place on South Halsted Street near the Academy Theater, July 28, 1922, displayed the following:

Pig's Snouts and Cabbage or Kraut 15c	Pig's Feet and Potato Salad ...15c
	Beef Stew and Kraut 15c
Corn Beef Hash 10c	Sausage and Mashed
Hamburger Roast 10c	Potatoes 15c
Liver and Onions 15c	Roast Beef 20c
Hungarian Goulash 20c	Roast Pork 25c
Pig's Shank and Cabbage 15c	T-Bone Steak 30c
Spare Ribs and Cabbage 20c	

The same day the James Restaurant on Madison Street near Desplaines advertised the following under the caption, "A Full Meal for Ten Cents":

Veal Loaf 10c	Sausage and Mashed
Sardines and Potato Salad 10c	Potatoes 10c
Hamburger and One Egg 10c	Brown Hash and One Egg 10c
Baked Beans 10c	Liver and Brown Gravy 10c
Liver and Onions 10c	Salt Pork Plain 10c
Corn Beef Plain 10c	Salmon and Potato Salad 10c
Macaroni Italian 10c	Corn Flakes and Milk 5c
Three Eggs any Style 15c	Four Eggs any Style 20c
Kidney Stew 10c	

One eating-house on West Madison Street is "The Home Restaurant, Meals Fifteen Cents and Up." This is a popular appeal. Restaurants frequently advertise "Home Cooking," "Home Made Bread," "Home Made Coffee," "Doughnuts Like Mother Used to Make."

At mealtime, especially at noon, scores of men flock into these eating-houses. The men, a noisy and turbulent crowd, call out their orders, which are shouted by the waiters to the cooks who set out without ceremony the desired dishes. Four or five waiters are able to attend to the wants of a hundred or more men during the course of an hour. The waiters work like madmen during the rush hours, speeding in with orders, out with dirty dishes. During the course of this hour a waiter becomes literally plastered with splashes of coffee, gravy, and soup. The uncleanliness is revolting and the waiters are no less shock-

Leaders in the educational movement among the hobos.

A popular resort in Hobohemia.

A dining room on the Main Stem.

Employment bureaus offer opportunity for travel.

ing than the cooks and dishwashers. In the kitchens uncleanliness reaches its limit.

But what is the opinion of the patron? They know that the hamburger is generally mixed with bread and potatoes, that the bread is usually stale, that the milk is frequently sour. There are few who do not abhor the odors of the cheap restaurant, but a steady patron reasons thus: "I don't allow myself to see things, and as long as the eyes don't see the heart grieves not."

Outfitting Stores and Clothing Exchanges

The hobo seldom dresses up. If he does it is evidence that he is making an effort to get out of his class. When he does buy clothing, either rough clothing or a good "front," he finds his way to places where new clothes are on sale at astonishingly low prices. The seasonal laborer's outfitters handle a very cheap grade of goods. Much of it is out of date and either shopworn or soiled. Cheap clothing stores are not peculiar to Hobohemia, but here they cater to the wants of the homeless man.

Clothing exchanges, which is a polite term for secondhand clothing stores, are numerous in Hobohemia. There are many of them along North Clark Street and west of Clark on Chicago Avenue. These establishments make a specialty of buying slightly worn clothing, sample suits and overcoats from broken lots, which they sell at remarkably low prices.

Secondhand clothing stores are not entirely monopolized by the hobo trade, but the veteran hobo knows of their existence and he knows how to drive a bargain.

The cobbler who deals in shoes, both secondhand and new, as a sideline, gets his share of the Hobohemian trade. Coming off the road with a roll, the hobo is likely to invest in a whole outfit—shoes, suit, and overcoat—only to sell them again in a few days when he is broke. The secondhand dealer meets him both ways, coming and going.

Pawn Shops

Pawn shops are not typical of Hobohemia. They are usually located in that region just outside the limits of the lodging houses, a sort of border land between respectability and the down-and-outs. Not that the hobo is unwilling, when he is broke, to put anything valuable he happens to have in "hock," but usually he does not happen to have anything valuable. Still there are men who make a practice of carrying a watch or a ring upon which, in case of need, they can raise a few dollars.

Pawn shops are, to a limited extent, clothing exchanges. They are places where the hobo does much of his buying and selling of tools, firearms, leather goods, jewelry, and like articles of that sort.

Movies and Burlesques

Commercialized entertainment has had difficulty in getting a foothold in Hobohemia. The movie has firmly established itself on the border land, where it may be patronized by both the transient and the resident population. The movies put the admission fee at ten cents. As a matter of fact, there is one on South Halsted Street which charges only a nickel. The pictures shown in these houses have usually passed from the first-class theaters through the various grades of cheaper houses until finally they arrive here much out of date, badly scarred, and so scratched that they irritate the eyes.

Vaudeville and burlesque have become fully established on the South Side. Certain of these theaters cater to "men only." Advertisements of "classy girls," "bathing beauties," or "fancy dancing" have a strange attraction for the homeless and lonely men.

Many men in the Hobohemian population do not patronize either the movie or the burlesque. Those who do are sometimes merely looking for an opportunity to sit down in quiet for an hour. Some theaters, in recognition of this fact, extend an invitation to the audience to "Stay as Long as You Like." This draws a great many men, especially in cold weather.

Barber Colleges and Barbers

Chicago has several barber colleges in close proximity to the "stem." Four of them are located on West Madison Street and most of them are so situated that they can attract men who are willing to submit to the inexperienced efforts of students. Students must have practice, and here are men, who as they themselves say, can stand it.

The cheap rooming houses do not always offer facilities for shaving, so they are willing to sacrifice themselves in the interest of education and art. If they are fortunate they may be served by a senior, but they always are in danger of falling into the hands of a freshman. Haircuts cost ten or fifteen cents. This is governed by the law of supply and demand. The colleges must have patrons to keep the students busy. The lady barber flourishes in Hobohemia. The hobo, at least, seems to have no prejudice against a razor being wielded by feminine hands.

Bookstores

Hobohemia has its bookstores where new and secondhand books are sold. The Hobo Bookstore, sometimes called the Proletariat, located at

1237 West Madison Street, is the best known. This place makes a specialty of periodicals of a radical nature which are extensively read by the "'bos." A large line of books on many subjects are sold, but they are chiefly the paperbound volumes that the transient can afford. The Radical Book Shop, located on North Clark Street, is popular among the intellectuals who pass their time in Bughouse Square.

Saloons and Soft Drink Stands

The saloon still lives in Hobohemia, though with waning prestige. The five-cent schooner and the free lunch of prewar days have passed, but the saloons are far from being dead. One can still get a "kick" out of stuff that is sold across the bar, but the crowds do not gather as before Prohibition. Formerly, men who got drunk were kept inside, today they are hustled outside or at least kept out of sight. As the saloon has lost its prestige, the bootlegger has gained, and the "drunks" for which he is responsible parade the streets or litter the alleys.

Fruit and soft drink stands and ice cream cone peddlers are in evidence since Prohibition. Enthusiastic and persistent bootblacks swarm in the streets and Gypsy fortunetellers who hail every passerby for the privilege of "reading" his mind, and, perhaps, in order to turn a trick at his expense.

The Housing Problem

Standards of living are low in Hobohemia. Flops are unwholesome and unsanitary. Efforts have been made to improve these conditions, but they have not been wholly successful. The Salvation Army and the Dawes hotels have improved the lodging houses. But the municipal free lodging house has been opposed by the police on the ground that it was already too popular among casual and migratory workers. The same may be said of any other effort to deal with the problem from the point of view of philanthropy.

The only other alternative would seem to be to encourage the migratory workers to organize to help themselves. This is difficult but not impossible, but the history of these efforts is another chapter in the story of Hobohemia.

5
The Hobo and the Tramp

The term "homeless man" was used by Mrs. Alice W. Solenberger in her study of 1,000 cases in Chicago to include all types of unattached men, tramps, hobos, bums, and the other nameless varieties of the "go-abouts."

> Almost all "tramps" are "homeless men" but by no means are all homeless men tramps. The homeless man may be an able-bodied workman without a family; he may be a runaway boy, a consumptive temporarily stranded on his way to a health resort, an irresponsible, feeble-minded, or insane man, but unless he is also a professional wanderer he is not a "tramp."[1]

There is no better term at hand than "homeless men" by which the men who inhabit Hobohemia may be characterized. Dr. Ben L. Reitman, who has himself traveled as a tramp, in the sense in which he uses the word, has defined the three principal types of the hobo. He says: "There are three types of the genus vagrant: the hobo, the tramp, and the bum. The hobo works and wanders, the tramp dreams and wanders, and the bum drinks and wanders."

St. John Tucker, formerly the president of the "Hobo College" in Chicago, gives the same classification with a slightly different definition:

> A hobo is a migratory worker. A tramp is a migratory nonworker. A bum is a stationary nonworker. Upon the labor of the *migratory worker* all the basic industries depend. He goes forth from the crowded slavemarkets to hew the forests, build and repair the railroads, tunnel mountains and build ravines. His is the labor that harvests the wheat in the fall and cuts the ice in the winter. All of these are hobos.

M. Kuhn, of St. Louis (and elsewhere), a migrant, a writer, and, according to his own definition, a hobo, in a pamphlet entitled "The

From *The Hobo: The Sociology of the Homeless Man* (Chicago: University of Chicago Press, 1961), 87–95

1. *One Thousand Homeless Men*, 209.

Hobo Problem" gives a fairly representative statement of the homeless man's explanation of his lot.

> The hobo is a seasonal, transient, migratory worker of either sex. Being a seasonal worker he is necessarily idle much of the time; being transient, he is necessarily homeless. He is detached from the soil and the fireside. By the nature of his work and not by his own will, he is precluded from establishing a home and rearing a family. Sex, poverty, habits, and degree of skill have nothing whatever to do with classifying individuals as hobos; the character of his work does that.
>
> There are individuals not hobos who pose as such. They are enabled to do this for two reasons: first, hobos have no organization by which they can expose the impostor; second, the frauds are encouraged and made possible by organized and private charity. The hobo class, therefore, is unable to rid itself of this extremely undesirable element. With organization it can and will be done even if charity, which is strongly opposed by the hobo class, is not abolished.

Nicholas Klein, president of the "Hobo College" and attorney and adviser to James Eads How, the so-called hobo millionaire, who finances the "Hobo College," says:

> A hobo is one who travels in search of work, the migratory worker who must go about to find employment. Workers of that sort pick our berries, fruit, hops, and help to harvest the crops on the western farms. They follow the seasons around, giving their time to farms in spring, summer, and autumn, and ending up in the ice fields in winter. We could not get in our crops without them for the hobo is the boy who does the work. The name originated from the words "hoe-boy" plainly derived from work on the farm. A tramp is one who travels but does not work, and a bum is a man who stays in one place and does not work. Between these grades there is a great gulf of social distinction. Don't get tramps and hobos mixed. They are quite different in many respects. The chief difference being that the hobo will work and the tramp will not, preferring to live on what he can pick up at back doors as he makes his way through the country.[2]

Roger Payne, A.B. and LL.B., who has taken upon himself the title "hobo philosopher," sees only one type of the wanderer, and that is the hobo. The hobo to him is a migratory worker. If he works but does not migrate, or if he migrates but does not work, he is not a hobo. All others are either tramps or bums. He makes no distinction between them. The hobo, foot-loose and care free, leads, Mr. Payne thinks, the ideal life.

Although we cannot draw lines closely, it seems clear that there are

2. *Dearborn Independent,* 18 March 1922.

at least five types of homeless men: (*a*) the seasonal worker,[3] (*b*) the transient or occasional worker or hobo, (*c*) the tramp who "dreams and wanders" and works only when it is convenient, (*d*) the bum who seldom wanders and seldom works, and (*e*) the home guard who lives in Hobohemia and does not leave town.[4]

The Seasonal Worker

Seasonal workers are men who have definite occupations in different seasons. The yearly circuit of their labors takes them about the country, often into several different states. These men may work in the clothing industries during cold weather but in summer are employed at odd jobs; or they may have steady work in summer and do odd jobs in winter. One man picks fruit in summer and works as a machinist in winter. He does not spend his summers in the same state nor his winters in the same city but follows those two occupations throughout the year.

> Bill S. is a Scotchman and a seasonal worker. During the winter he is usually in Chicago. He works as a practical nurse. He is efficient and well liked by his patients and a steady worker during the winter. In summer he quits and goes to the harvest fields or works on a construction job. Since leaving his winter job (March to October, 1922) he has had several jobs out of Chicago none of which lasted more than a week or two. Between times he loafs on West Madison Street. He does not drink. He is well behaved. Seldom dresses up. When last heard of he was in Kansas City, Missouri, where he thought he would spend the winter.

> Jack M. works on the lake boats during the sailing season. When the boats tie up for the winter he tries to get into the factories, or he goes to the woods. Sometimes during the tie-up he takes a notion to travel and goes West or South to while away the time. He has just returned from a trip East and South where he has been "seeking work" and "killing time" a week or so before the season opened. He has already signed up for the summer. He is loafing and lodging in the meanwhile on West Madison and South State streets.

The seasonal worker has a particular kind of work that he follows somewhere at least part of the year. The hotels of Hobohemia are a winter resort for many of these seasonal workers whose schedule is relatively fixed and habitudinal. Some of these who return to the city regularly every winter come with money. In that case, they do not work until next season. Others return without money. They have some kind

---

3. The seasonal worker may be regarded as the upper-class hobo.
4. The first three types of homeless men are described in this chapter.

of work which they follow in the winter. The hobo, proper, is a transient worker without a program.

The Hobo

A hobo is a migratory worker in the strict sense of the word. He works at whatever is convenient in the mills, the shops, the mines, the harvests, or any of the numerous jobs that come his way without regard for the times or the seasons. The range of his activities is nation wide and with many hobos it is international. He may cross a continent between jobs. He may be able in one year to function in several industries. He may have a trade or even a profession. He may even be reduced to begging between jobs, but his living is primarily gained by work and that puts him in the hobo class.

> E. J. is a carpenter. He was at one time a good workman but due to drink and dissipation he has lost his ability to do fine work and has been reduced to the status of a rough carpenter. At present he follows bridge work and concrete form work. Sometimes he tries his hand at plain house carpentry but due to the fact that he moves about so much, he has lost or disposed of many of his tools. A spree lasts about three weeks and he has about three or four a year. Sometimes he travels without his kit and does not work at his trade. He never drinks while working. It is only when he goes to town to spend his vacations that he gets drunk. He is restless and uncomfortable and does not know how to occupy his mind when he is in town and sober. He is fifty-six years old. He never married and never has had a home since he was a boy.
>
> M. P. is interesting because he has a trade but does not follow it seasonally. He is a plasterer and he seems to be a good one. In his youth he learned the trade of stone mason. He came to this country from England in his twenties and he is past fifty now. He married in Pennsylvania where his wife died and where a daughter still lives. He became a wanderer and for many years did not work at his trade. He did various kinds of work as the notion came to him. As he is getting older he is less inclined to wander and he makes fewer excursions into other lines of work outside his trade. During the past year he has not left Chicago and he has done little other than to work as a plasterer. He lives in the Hobohemian areas and is able to get along two or three weeks on a few days' work. He seldom works more than a week at a time. He takes a lively interest in the hobo movement of the city and has been actively engaged in the "Hobo College." Recently he won a lot in a raffle. It is located in the suburbs of the city. During the summer (1922) he had a camp out there and he and his friends from Madison Street spent considerable time in his private "jungle."

The hobo group comprises the bulk of the migratory workers, in fact, nearly all migrants in transit are hobos of one sort or other. Hobos have a romantic place in our history. From the beginning they have been numbered among the pioneers. They have played an important rôle in reclaiming the desert and in subduing the trackless forests. They have contributed more to the open, frank, and adventurous spirit of the Old West than we are always willing to admit. They are, as it were, belated frontiersmen. Their presence in the migrant group has been the chief factor in making the American vagabond class different from that of any other country.

It is difficult to classify the numerous types of hobos. The habits, type of work, the routes of travel, etc., seem to differ with each individual. Some live more parasitic lives than others. Some never beg or get drunk, while others never come to town without getting intoxicated and being robbed or arrested, and perhaps beaten. One common characteristic of the hobo, however, is that he works. He usually has horny hands and a worker's mien. He aims to live by his labor.

As there are different types of homeless men, so different varieties of this particular brand, the hobo, may be differentiated. A part of the hobo group known as "harvest hands" follows the harvest and other agricultural occupations of seasonal nature. Another segment of the group works in the lumber woods and are known as "lumber jacks" or "timber beasts." A third group is employed in construction and maintenance work. A "gandy dancer" is a man who works on the railroad track tamping ties. If he works on the section he may be called a "snipe" or a "jerry."

A "skinner" is a man who drives horses or mules.

A "mucker" or a "shovel stiff" is a man who does manual labor on construction jobs.

A "rust eater" usually works on extra-gangs or track-laying jobs; handles steel.

A "dino" is a man who works with and handles dynamite.

A "splinter-belly" is a man who does rough carpenter work or bridge work.

A "cotton glaumer" picks cotton, an "apple knocker" picks apples and other fruit.

A "beach comber" is a plain sailor, of all men the most transient.

For every vocation that is open to the migratory worker there is some such characteristic name. In the West the hobo usually carries a bundle in which he has a bed, some extra clothes, and a little food. The man who carries such a bundle is usually known as a "bundle stiff" or "bundle bum." The modern hobo does not carry a bundle because it hinders him when he wishes to travel fast. It is the old man who went West "to grow up with the country" who still clings to his blanket roll.

The Tramp

While the word "tramp" is often used as a blanket term applied to all classes of homeless and potentially vagrant or transient types, it is here used in a stricter sense to designate a smaller group. He is usually thought of, by those familiar with his natural history, as an able-bodied individual who has the romantic passion to see the country and to gain new experience without work. He is a specialist at "getting by." He is the type that Josiah Flynt had in mind when he wrote his book, *Tramping with Tramps*. He is typically neither a drunkard nor a bum, but an easy-going individual who lives from hand to mouth for the mere joy of living.

> X. began life as a half orphan. Later he was adopted and taken from Ohio to South Dakota. In his early teens he grew restive at home and left. But for brief seasons he has been away ever since and he is now past forty-five. He has traveled far and wide since but has worked little. He makes his living by selling joke books and song books. Sometimes he tries his hand at selling little articles from door to door. A few years ago he wrote a booklet on an economic subject and sold several thousand copies. During the winter of 1921–22 he sold the *Hobo News* each month. He is able to make a living this way. Any extra money he has he loses at the gambling tables. He spends his leisure time attempting to write songs or poetry. He knows a great deal about publishers but it is all information that has come in his efforts to sell his songs. He claims that he has been working for several years on a novel. He offered his work for inspection. He tries to lead the hero through all the places that he has visited and the hero comes in contact with many of the things he has seen or experienced in many cities but nowhere does his hero work. He enjoys life just as X. endeavors to do now. During the summer (1922) he has taken several "vacations" in the country for a week or more at the time.
>
> C. is twenty-five years old. His home is in New York but he has not been home for more than ten years. He introduced himself to the "Hobo College" early in the spring of 1922 as "B-2." This name he assumed upon the conviction that he is the successor of "A-1," the famous tramp. He said that he had read "A-1"'s books and although he did not agree in every respect, yet he thought that "A-1" was the greatest of tramp writers. "B-2" claimed that he had ridden on every railroad in the United States. His evidence of travel was a book of post office stamps. When he comes to a town he goes to the post office and requests the postmaster to stamp his book much as letters are stamped. Another hobby he has is to go to the leading newspa-

pers and endeavor to sell a write-up. He carries an accumulation of clippings. He has an assortment of flashy stories that take well with newspaper men. He claims that he has been pursued by bloodhounds in the South, that he has been arrested many times for vagrancy, that he is the only man who has beat his way on the Pikes Peak Railroad. He always carries a blanket and many other things that class him among wanderers as an individualist. He has been in the Army, saw action and was in the Army of Occupation. He does not seek work. He says his leisure time can be better spent. He carries a vest pocket kodak. He says that the pictures and notes he takes will some day be published.

The distinctions between the seasonal worker, the hobo, and the tramp, while important, are not hard and fast. The seasonal worker may descend into the ranks of the hobos, and a hobo may sink to the level of the tramp. But the knowledge of this tendency to pass from one migratory group to another is significant for any program that attempts to deal with the homeless man. Significant, also, but not sufficiently recognized, is the difference between these migratory types and the stationary types of homeless men, the "home guard" and the "bum."

6

Summary of Findings and Recommendations

This study has pictured the life and the problems of the group of homeless migratory and casual workers in Chicago. It now remains to sum up the findings of the investigation and to outline the recommendations which seem to flow from the facts.[1]

Findings

1. The homeless casual and migratory workers, while found in all parts of the city, are segregated in great numbers in four distinct areas: West Madison Street, Lower South State Street (near the Loop), North Clark Street, and Upper State Street (the Negro section).
2. The number of homeless men in these areas fluctuates greatly with the seasons and with conditions of employment.
3. The concentration of casual and migratory workers in this city is the natural result of two factors: (a) the development of Chicago as a great industrial community with diversified enterprises requiring a variety of unskilled as well as skilled laborers, and (b) the position of Chicago as a center of transportation, of commerce and of employment for the states of the Mississippi Valley.
4. The homeless men in Chicago fall into five groups: (a) the seasonal laborer, (b) the migratory, casual laborer, the hobo, (c) the migratory nonworker, the tramp, (d) the nonmigratory casual laborer, the so-called home guard, (e) the bum. Groups b, c, d, and e constitute what are known in economic writings as "the Residuum of Industry." In addition to these groups of the homeless casual and migratory workers are the groups of seasonal laborers and the men out of work, which expand and contract with the periods of economic depression and of industrial prosperity.
5. The causes which reduce a man to the status of a homeless migra-

From *The Hobo: The Sociology of the Homeless Man* (Chicago: University of Chicago Press, 1961), 236–77

1. The findings and recommendations of this study were prepared by the Committee on Homeless Men of the Chicago Council of Social Agencies and its report accepted by the council.

tory and casual worker may be classified under five main heads as follows:

a. *Unemployment and seasonal work:* these maladjustments of modern industry which disorganize the routine of life of the individual and destroy regular habits of work.

b. *Industrial inadequacy:* "the misfits of industry," whether due to physical handicaps, mental deficiency, occupational disease, or lack of vocational training.

c. *Defects of personality:* as feeble-mindedness, constitutional inferiority, or egocentricity, which lead to the conflict of the person with constituted authority in industry, society, and government.

d. *Crises in the life of the person:* as family conflicts, misconduct, and crime, which exile a man from home and community and detach him from normal social ties.

e. *Racial or national discrimination:* where race, nationality, or social class of the person enters as a factor of adverse selection for employment.

f. *Wanderlust:* the desire for new experience, excitement, and adventure, which moves the boy "to see the world."

6. To satisfy the wants and wishes of the thousands of homeless migratory and casual workers at the lowest possible cost, specialized institutions and enterprises have been established in Chicago. These include

a. employment agencies,

b. restaurants and lodging houses,

c. barber colleges,

d. outfitting stores and clothing exchanges,

e. pawnshops,

f. movies and burlesques,

g. missions,

h. local political and social organizations, as the Industrial Workers of the World and the Hobo College,

i. secular street meetings and radical bookstores.

7. Chicago as the great clearing house of employment for the states of the Mississippi Valley naturally and inevitably becomes the temporary home of men out of work for the entire region. The following appear to be the facts in regard to the workers and the conditions of employment:

a. Fluctuations of industry, such as seasonal changes, and of unemployment, force large numbers of men into the group of homeless migratory and casual workers.

b. At the same time, the homeless migratory and casual worker develops irregular habits of work and a life policy of "living from hand to mouth."

c. Employment records indicate that the lower grade of casual workers prefer work by the day, or employment by the week or two, to "permanent" positions of three months or longer.

d. The Illinois Free Employment offices, efficiently administered with simple but well-kept records and with courteous treatment of applicants, placed 50,482 persons in the year ending September 30, 1922, mainly in positions in and near Chicago.

e. The private employment agencies dealing with the homeless man, about fifty in number, which are, in general, poorly equipped, with the minimum of record keeping required by law and with inconsiderate treatment of applicants, place about 200,000 men a year in positions, for the most part, outside of Chicago.

f. The law relating to private employment agencies as approved June 15, 1909, in force July 1, 1909, and as amended and approved June 7, 1911, in force July 1, 1911, appears not to be enforced in two points:

    i. the requirement that sections three (3), four (4), and five (5) of the law be posted in a conspicuous place in each room of the agency; and

    ii. the return to the applicant of three-fifths of the registration and other fees upon failure of applicant to accept position or upon his discharge for cause.

8. The health and hygiene of the homeless migratory and casual worker is of vital concern not only for his economic efficiency but also because of the relation of his high mobility to the spread of communicable diseases.

9. The homeless migratory and casual workers constitute a womanless group. The results of this sex isolation are

a. No opportunity for the expression and sublimation of the sex impulse in the normal life of the family.

b. In a few cases, the substitution for marriage of free unions more or less casual, usually terminated at the will of the man without due regard to the claims of the woman.

c. The dependence of the greatest number of homeless men upon the professional prostitute of the lowest grade and the cheapest sort.

d. The prevalence of sex perversions, as masturbation and homosexuality.

10. The attraction for the boy of excitement and adventure renders him peculiarly susceptible to the "call of the road."

a. Hundreds of Chicago boys, mainly but not entirely of wageearning families, every spring "beat their way" to the harvest fields, impelled by wanderlust and the opportunity for work away from home.

b. Of these a certain proportion acquire the migratory habit and may pass through successive stages from a high-grade seasonal worker to the lowest type of bum.

c. The boy on the road and in the city is constantly under the pressure of homosexual exploitation by confirmed perverts in the migratory group.

d. Certain areas of the city frequented by boys have been found to be resorts and rendezvous for homosexual prostitution.

11. While the majority of the homeless migratory workers are American citizens of native stock:

    a. They are in large numbers for practical purposes disfranchised because they seldom remain in any community long enough to secure legal residence.

    b. They constitute a shifting and shiftless group without property and family, and with no effective participation in the civic life of the community.

    c. According to statements from police authorities they contribute but slightly to the volume of serious crime.

    d. Both on the road and in the city, they are at all times subject to arbitrary handling and arrest by private and public police and to summary trial and sentence by the court.

    e. The attitude of Chicago, like that of other communities toward the homeless man, has been a policy of defense entrusted to the police department for execution.

12. Social service to the homeless migratory and casual worker has for the most part been remedial rather than preventive, unorganized and haphazard rather than organized and coordinated.

    a. Professional beggars and fakers exploit public sympathy and credulity for individual gain to the disadvantage of the men who need and deserve assistance.

    b. The missions and certain churches feed, clothe, and provide shelter for several thousand men during the winter months.

    c. The Dawes Hotel, the Christian Industrial League, and the Salvation Army hotels provide lodging at a low charge.

    d. The Salvation Army maintains the Industrial Home with workshops which accomodate a limited number of men.

    e. The United Charities and the Central Charity (Catholic) Bureau, although concerned mainly with family relief, give certain forms of assistance to the homeless man.

    f. The Jewish Social Service Bureau maintains a department for homeless men, which acts as a referring agency to two shelter houses.

    g. The American Legion and other patriotic organizations have provided assistance of various types to the ex–service man out of employment.

    h. The Municipal Lodging House, which closed its doors in 1918, has not been reopened, despite the evident need of the winters of 1920–21 and 1921–22.

    i. The Cook County agent provides free transportation to nonresidents to place of legal residence and refers residents to Oak Forest Infirmary.

    j. The county and city hospitals and dispensaries provide free medical care.

    k. Uncoordinated effort of the organizations for service to the homeless man has resulted in duplication of activities, a low standard of work, and the neglect of a constructive program of rehabilitation.

Recommendations

The findings of this study indicate conclusively (*a*) that any fundamental solution of the problem is national and not local, and (*b*) that the problem of the homeless migratory worker is but an aspect of the larger problems of industry, such as unemployment, seasonal work, and labor turnover.

National Program

The committee approves, as a national program for the control of the problem, the recommendations suggested by the studies on unemployment and migratory laborers contained in the *Final Report of the Commission on Industrial Relations* (114–15; 103):

1. The enactment of appropriate legislation modifying the title of the Bureau of Immigration to "Bureau of Immigration and Employment" and providing the statutory authority and appropriations necessary for
   a. The establishment of a national employment system,[2] under the Department of Labor, with a staff of well-paid and specially qualified officials in the main offices at least.
   b. The licensing, regulation, and supervision of all private employment agencies doing an interstate business.
   c. The investigation and preparation of plans for the regularization of employment, the decasualization of labor, the utilization of public work to fill in periods of business depression, insurance against unemployment in such trades and industries as may seem desirable, and other measures designed to promote regularity and steadiness of employment.
2. The immediate creation of a special board made up of the properly qualified officials from the Departments of Agriculture, Commerce, Interior, and Labor, and from the Board of Army Engineers to prepare plans for performing the largest possible amount of public work during the winter, and to devise a program for the future for performing, during periods of depression, such public work as road building, construction of public building, reforestation, irrigation, and drainage of swamps. The success attending the construction of the Panama Canal indicates the enormous national construction works which might be done to the advantage of the

---

2. The United States Employment Service, established in 1918, requires adequate appropriations for its efficient functioning.

entire nation during such periods of depression. Similar boards or commissions should be established in the various states and municipalities.

3. The Interstate Commerce Commission should be directed by Congress to investigate and report the most feasible plan of providing for the transportation of workers at the lowest reasonable rates, and, at the same time, measures necessary to eliminate the stealing of rides on railways. If special transportation rates for workers are provided, tickets may be issued only to those who secure employment through public employment agencies.

4. The establishment by states, municipalities, and, through the Department of Labor, the federal government, of sanitary workingmen's hotels in which the prices for accommodations shall be adjusted to the cost of operation. If such workingmen's hotels are established, the Post Office Department should establish branch postal savings banks in connection therewith.

5. The establishment by the municipal, state, and federal governments of colonies or farms for "down and outs" in order to rehabilitate them by means of proper food, regular habits of living and regular work that will train them for lives of usefulness. Such colonies should provide for hospital treatment of cases which require it.

The Chicago Plan for the Homeless Man

For the local situation and for such action as lies in the hands (*a*) of the citizens of this community, (*b*) of the city of Chicago, (*c*) of Cook County, and (*d*) of the state of Illinois, this committee recommends:

I. As a Program for Immediate Action
   1. The establishment of a Municipal Clearing House for Nonfamily Men.
      a. *Purpose:*
         i. To provide facilities for the registration, examination, classification, and treatment of homeless migratory and casual workers in order, on the basis of individual case study,
         ii. To secure by reference to the appropriate agency emergency relief, physical and mental rehabilitation, industrial training, commitment to institutional care, return to legal residence, and satisfactory employment.
      b. *Organization:* The Clearing House will maintain the following departments:
         i. *Information bureau:* to provide information in regard to employment, public institutions, social agencies, indorsed hotels, and lodging houses, etc.
         ii. *Registration:* by card, giving name, age, occupation, phys-

ical condition, reference, residence, nearest relative or friend, number of lodgings, disposition, and all other information.

   iii. *Vocational clinic:* to provide medical, psychiatric, psychological, and social examination as a basis of treatment.

   iv. *Records office:* to record findings of examination, to clear with other agencies, local and national, and to enter recommendations and results of treatment.

   v. *Social service bureau:* to provide for both immediate and aftercare service for the men under the supervision of the Clearing House.

c. *Personnel:* to consist of director, clerical force, interviewers, social workers, and experts, as physician, psychiatrist, psychologist, and sociologist.

d. *Intake of Clearing House:* registrants to be referred to the Clearing House by

   i. *Citizens,* to whom homeless men have applied for relief,

   ii. *Missions,* where food or lodging have been received by homeless men,

   iii. *Charities,*

   iv. *Travelers' Aid Society,*

   v. *Local organizations,*

   vi. *Police department:* closing of police stations to lodgers and provision for supply of such applicants with tickets of admission to the Clearing House; direction by police to the Clearing House of persons found for the first time begging.

   vii. *Courts, police stations, house of correction, and county jail:* provision to every homeless man or boy upon discharge with ticket of admission to Clearing House guaranteeing three days' liberty with food, lodging, and an opportunity for honest employment.

e. *Classification:* As a result of examination in the Vocational Clinic the men will be divided for treatment into three groups: (1) boys and youths, (2) employable men, and (3) unemployable men. The unemployable will be further divided into: (i) the physically handicapped, (ii) the mentally defective, (iii) alcoholics and drug addicts, (iv) the habitually idle, (v) the untrained, and (vi) the aged.

f. *Treatment:* Upon the basis of the preceding examination and classification, the men will be given the following services:

   i. Those in need of emergency relief, temporary lodging, meals and bath, by the agencies in the field and by the Municipal Lodging House (when reopened).

   ii. Those in need of clean clothes, free laundry work at the Municipal Laundry (to be established).

   iii. Those who are proper charges of other communities and

who may be better cared for there, transportation from relatives or from Cook County agent.

   iv. Those in need of medical service, treatment at the Cook County Hospital, Municipal Tuberculosis Sanitarium, or dispensaries, and observation at the Psychopathic Hospital.

   v. For the unemployable physically disabled, education as provided in the Chicago plan for the physically handicapped (under consideration by the state in cooperation with private agencies).

   vi. For the unemployable but physically able-bodied, individual arrangements for industrial education.

   vii. For the aged and permanently physically disabled, placement in the Oak Forest Home.

   viii. For the employable, references with vocational diagnosis and recommendation to the Illinois Free Employment offices and other employment agencies.

   ix. For persons under the supervision of the Municipal Clearing House, when desirable, individual case work and aftercare.

   x. For incorrigible vagrants and beggars for whom no constructive treatment is provided in the program for immediate action (see constructive treatment in "Program for Future Action") commitment to the House of Correction.

 g. *Administration:* The Clearing House to be administered by the city of Chicago under the City Department of Public Welfare; the director of the Clearing House to be also superintendent of the Lodging House and of the Municipal Laundry and the Municipal Bath House, a physician on full time to be assigned by the City Department of Public Health, a psychiatrist and psychologist by the state criminologist of the State Department of Public Welfare.

 h. *Advisory committee:* Under the auspices of the Chicago Council of Social Agencies, an advisory committee to the director of the Clearing House be organized to be composed of public and private agencies and civic, philanthropic, commercial, industrial, and labor organizations, cooperating with the Clearing House.

 i. *Financing:* An appeal to be made at once to the city council for funds to equip and maintain the Municipal Clearing House, Municipal Lodging House, Laundry and Bath House, to provide for the budget given in table 1.

2. *The reopening of the Municipal Lodging House* under the following conditions (adapted from "Program for Model Municipal Lodging House," by Raymond Robins):

 a. *Administration:* under the City Department of Public Health

TABLE 1

Tentative Annual Budget for Caring Adequately for Homeless Transient Men
in Chicago

Clearing House	Maximum*	Minimum
Rent of headquarters, including light and heat	$2,500.00	. . .
Heat and light in free quarters	. . .	$1,000.00
Equipment	1,000.00	1,000.00
Office supplies, stationery, printing, etc.	500.00	500.00
Staff:		
Superintendent	6,000.00	4,000.00
Assistant	2,500.00	. . .
Six interviewers and fieldworkers	9,000.00	. . .
Two interviewers and fieldworkers	. . .	4,000.00
Two stenographers	2,400.00	. . .
One stenographer	. . .	1,500.00
Physician (part-time)	1,800.00	. . .
Psychiatrist (part-time)	1,800.00	. . .
Director of vocational guidance	4,000.00	. . .
Janitors	1,800.00	1,800.00
Total	$33,300.00	$13,800.00

*The maximum budget represents expenditures in the event headquarters cannot be secured free of rent, services of physician and psychiatrist cannot be secured from the city and the Institute for Juvenile Research, and at a time when a full staff will be necessary.

in close affiliation with the Clearing House for Homeless Men.

b. *Purpose:* to provide free, under humane and sanitary conditions, food, lodging, and bath, with definite direction for such permanent relief as is needed for any man or boy stranded in Chicago.

c. *Registration and preliminary physical examination:* made in Clearing House a condition to admission.

d. *Standard of service:*
   i. sanitary building;
   ii. wholesome food;
   iii. dormitories quiet, beds comfortable and clean;
   iv. first aid treatment—vaccination, bandages and simple medicaments furnished free;
   v. isolation ward for men suffering from inebriety, insanity, venereal diseases, etc.;
   vi. fumigation of lodgers' clothing, including hat and shoes, every night;
   vii. nightly shower bath required.

3. *The establishment of a Municipal Laundry and a Municipal Bath House by the city of Chicago:* to be operated in close affiliation with the Municipal Clearing House.

4. *Utilization of existing facilities for industrial training:* Co-operation with existing educational institutions for the vocational training of boys and youths and of the physically handicapped, mentally defective, and industrially inadequate who are unemployable but willing to work. (See "Program for Future Action.")
5. *Employment agencies:*
   a. The extension of the service of the Illinois Free Employment office.
   b. The enforcement of the law relating to private employment agencies: the requirement that sections three (3), four (4), and five (5), of the law be posted in a conspicuous place in each room of the agency; and the return to the applicant of three-fifths of the registration and other fees upon the failure of applicant to accept position or upon his discharge for cause.
   c. The further study of private employment agencies and of labor camps in order to provide the homeless man with adequate protection against exploitation.
6. *Public health and housing:*
   a. The further building of sanitary workingmen's hotels with low charge for accommodations.
   b. The maintenance and raising of standards of cheap hotels in Chicago through rigid inspection and tightening of requirements.
   c. Medical examination, inspection, and supervision of men in flops, together with vaccination and hospitalization of needy cases.
7. *Vagrancy Court:* the reorganization of the Vagrancy Court for the hearing of cases of incorrigible vagrants and beggars on the basis of the investigations of the Clearing House.
8. *Protection of the boy:*
   a. Prevention of aimless wandering through the provision of wholesome and stimulating recreation, through the extension of all activities for boys, and through the further development of vocational education and supervision. The Vocational Guidance Bureau of the Board of Education should be removed to an area of the city free from unwholesome contacts.
   b. An educational campaign organized through the Midwest Boy's Club Federation should be carried on in all the boys' organizations in Chicago showing the danger of "flipping" trains and playing in railroad yards. The National Safety Council has a great deal of material which could be used in such a campaign.
   c. Cooperation with such organizations as the Brotherhood of Railway Trainmen, the special police organizations of the railroads, the Lake Carriers Association, and automobile

clubs, in a program to prevent boys wandering away from home. Pamphlets should be prepared for distribution, asking for cooperation and enforcement of working certificate regulations in this and other states, child labor laws, juvenile court laws, etc.

d. The enlistment officers of the army, navy, and marine should demand the presentation of a birth certificate in all cases in which they doubt the age of the applicant.

e. The cooperation of the managers of the hotels and lodging houses in an effort to keep boys under seventeen out of the hotels in the Hobohemian areas, or at least to use their influence in preventing boys and men from rooming together.

f. Because most of the contacts the boy has with tramps are unwholesome, the police should not permit boys to loiter or play in the areas most frequented by the tramp population; namely, West Madison Street, South State Street, North Clark Street, and adjacent territory. Parents ought to be made aware of the nature of the contacts the boy has with the tramp in these areas and in the parks.

g. The assignment of special plainclothes policemen experienced in dealing with vagrants to the parks and other places in which tramps congregate. They should be instructed to pick up and hold in the Detention Home any boy under seventeen years found in company with a tramp.

h. More strenuous effort should be made to occupy the leisure time of boys who frequent the districts in which the tramps congregate. It is the boy with leisure time who is the most susceptible to the unwholesome contacts. Supervised recreation should be carried on to an extent that boys who play in Hobohemian areas might be attracted to other sections. When school is not in session a more extensive program of summer camps might help.

i. Since the Juvenile Court of Cook County is equipped to investigate the cases of vagrant boys under seventeen in Chicago, and return them to their homes, all vagrant boys apprehended by anyone in the daytime should be reported to the chief probation officer, Juvenile Court. Vagrant boys over seventeen should be directed to the Clearing House.

j. After five o'clock vagrant boys under seventeen should be turned over to the police who will take them to the Detention Home, from which home they will be taken to the office of the chief probation officer the first thing in the morning.

k. Whenever a boy under seventeen is taken in custody by the police, because of contact with tramps, or whenever a boy is held as a complaining witness against a tramp, he should always be reported to the Juvenile Court. It is the responsibility of the court to put the boy in touch with some proper

individual or agency, so that he will be adequately supervised and befriended in the future.

9. *Publicity and public cooperation:* the education of the public
   through news items in the daily press and editorial comment;
   public cooperation through tickets of admission to the Clearing
   House providing food and lodging in the Municipal Lodging
   House constantly to be distributed through societies, institutions, hotels, business offices, churches, clubs, housewives, and
   other citizens.

II. A Program for Future Action

1. *That a bond issue* be submitted for approval to the voters of the
   city of Chicago providing for the erection of adequate buildings
   for a Municipal Clearing House, Municipal Lodging House,
   and Municipal Laundry and Bath House.

2. *That an Industrial Institute* be established by the state of Illinois
   in Chicago for the vocational training of the physically handicapped, mentally defective, and industrially inadequate, who
   are unemployable, but willing to work.

3. *That a State Farm Colony for Industrial Rehabilitation* be established by the state of Illinois for the compulsory detention and
   reeducation of unemployables, such as beggars, vagrants, petty
   criminals, who are unwilling to receive industrial training.

4. *That a Department of Industrial Training of the House of Correction*
   be opened, pending the establishment of the State Farm Colony
   for Industrial Rehabilitation, for the commitment and reeducation of unemployables, such as beggars, vagrants, and petty
   criminals.

7

Summary of a Study of Four Hundred Tramps, Summer 1921

This study was begun in Salt Lake City, in June 1921, and continued until the first day of September, when the writer arrived in Chicago. He started out with the intention of securing 1,000 cases, but due to the lack of time, was obliged to discontinue at the 400 mark. His personal expenses included only what he spent for food at the cheap restaurants, or for "jungle feeds" and a little for writing material and other such incidentals. For lodging, fares, and clothes, he spent nothing. He did not carry with him anything except what he could get into his pockets, which consisted of his razor, thread and needle, pen and ink, and his case card, which he carried in two special pockets inside his vest. He did not carry much money, and by his appearance and mien succeeded in giving the impression of being broke but not without hope.

About 250 of the 400 cases were taken at Salt Lake City, Ogden, or Pocatello. Ogden, which is sometimes designated as the "Hobo exchange" of the West, is on the junction of three railroads which constitute the "central route" east or west. During the summer there were thousands of transients who stopped for a brief season in Ogden, and so the major part of six weeks was spent by the writer at that point, where he loafed in the jungles, about the railroad yards, on the streets, and wherever he could engage transients in conversation.

At first the writer tried to gather his data by revealing his identity and purpose and asking the individual to fill out the case card, upon which were about twenty-five questions of a general nature. He was not long in learning that such a method was not practical, as the reactions of the men were generally negative. If he wasn't regarded as an impossible intellectualist he was shunned and pointed out with suspicion to other transients. Only eight men could be induced to fill out cards the first day, out of about twenty approached. No more than

From Burgess Papers, Regenstein Library, Department of Special Collections, University of Chicago (box 127, folder 2, document 115), unpublished document. Reprinted by permission.

fifteen of the four hundred cards were filled out by the men them-selves, and those were men who impressed the writer as being able to appreciate the nature of this survey.

The data were not so readily secured as the writer had anticipated. He found some men very ready to talk about themselves, and in the course of fifteen or twenty minutes would volunteer all the informa-tion desired. It was a slow process to obtain information from the most of them, however, and some of them he interviewed three or four times. Perhaps an hour and a half would be about the average time spent with each case, and he wrote up from four to seven cases a day, which was much slower than he expected to work. He tried to write men up as he chanced to meet them, though in several cases he must admit that he selected his cases because of something unusual about them that attracted him. This was true of two cripples and one man suffering from venereal diseases. Such information as was received was freely given, and in no case was he suspected of being an investi-gator, after he deemed it wise to conceal his purpose. One man noticed the cards in his vest pocket, and asked him if he was an IWW orga-nizer, but he assured his questioner that he was only getting unem-ployment information for a Salt Lake newspaper.

Although the writer met most of his cases in Idaho and Utah, the study was carried into nine states. With the exception of Salt Lake City, the men were all met in the smaller centers. None of them was interviewed in Chicago, though a great number were written up who were on their way to or from Chicago. The writer traveled about 2,200 miles, and all but fourteen miles on freight trains. The course of travel was over the following railroads: from Omaha to Chicago, over the Northwestern; from Chicago to Jackson, Michigan, over the Michigan Central, and by the same road to Grand Rapids, and from Grand Rap-ids back to Chicago over the Pere Marquette. He made two trips be-tween Ogden and Pocatello, Idaho, and three between Ogden and Salt Lake, on the Oregon Short Line.

In only one case was he molested by train crews, and but once by the police (railroad). He made no effort to avoid the train crews, though he found it convenient to dodge the police. He met thousands of men "on the tramp"; most of them were beating their way to the coast for the winter. It was a common thing to see from twenty to sixty men on one freight train. They rode on the top, or any place it was comfortable or convenient. As a rule, they were working men of the unskilled classes who carried very little on their backs, nothing in their hands, and seldom anything in their pockets. They were work seekers on their way somewhere—they knew not where—looking for a job for the winter.

The writer tried to get the general attitude of the men both by his observations and through the questions. He endeavored to write such observations on the case cards as they occurred to him. Most of the men were employable, though there were some who were work shirkers, and there were many irresponsible, purposeless individuals among them. It is surprising to note how few unemployables of the mentally and physically defective classes there were. It is equally surprising to note the large percentage of boys in their teens and early twenties.

The nationalities of the 400 tramps were as follows: native, 339 foreign, 61. The foreigners represented the following countries:

Austria,	4	Greece,	5	Sweden,	6
Canada,	5	Ireland,	3	Switzerland,	2
Denmark,	2	Italy,	2	Slavonica,	3
England,	9	Mexico,	4	Wales,	1
Finland,	4	Norway,	4	Peru,	1
Germany,	5	Poland,	1	Total,	61

The native-born represented the following states:

Alabama,	2	Louisiana,	3	Pennsylvania,	15
Arizona,	2	Maine,	2	Rhode Island,	1
Arkansas,	7	Maryland,	4	South Dakota,	2
California,	9	Michigan,	12	Texas,	9
Colorado,	12	Minnesota,	6	Tennessee,	5
Connecticut,	2	Massachusetts,	11	Utah,	14
Florida,	1	Missouri,	19	Virginia,	7
Georgia,	1	Montana,	5	Washington,	2
Idaho,	5	Nebraska,	8	West Virginia,	2
Illinois,	34	New Jersey,	11	Wisconsin,	7
Indiana,	16	New York,	20	Wyoming,	3
Iowa,	14	Ohio,	27	Not known,	7
Kansas,	15	Oklahoma,	4	Total,	339
Kentucky,	7	Oregon,	6		

This number included six Negroes, two Mexicans (American-born), and one Indian. It will be noted that industrial states and states traversed by the transcontinental trunk lines contribute the largest number of transients, especially along the Central Route.

Causes for being on the "road," as given by the men, and as observed by the writer:

Work reasons,	320	Mentally defective,	8
Wanderlust,	180	Physically defective,	35
Home trouble,	57	Age,	5
Drink,	34	Total reasons,	651
Women,	12		

TABLE 1
Conjugal Relation of 400 Tramps

No. and Condition		Age Group													
		14 to 19	20 to 24	25 to 29	30 to 34	35 to 39	40 to 44	45 to 49	50 to 54	55 to 59	60 to 64	65 to 69	70 to 74	74 and up	Not Known
Single	346	50	89	44	40	41	37	16	12	4	5	3	1	1	3
Married	19	1	1	3	2	2	3	6	1						
Divorced	15		1	1	1	4	1	3	1		3				
Separated	5		1				3						1		
Widowed	12						2	3		2	1	3		1	
Not known	3							1			1	1			
Total	400	51	92	48	43	47	46	29	14	6	10	7	2	2	3
Children	79		6	5	10	4	18	16	4	4	4	5	3	2	3

TABLE 2
Work Record for Past Twelve Months*

No. of Jobs Held	No. of Cases	No. of Jobs	No. of Quits	No. of Layoffs	% of Quits	% of Layoffs	Probable % of Discharges
1	31	31	11	19	34	36	6
2	58	116	33	77	28	66	9
3	67	201	61	122	30	61	13
4	47	188	69	96	36	51	13
5	24	120	47	49	39	40	21
Total	227	656	221	363	33.5	55.5	11.2

*By this is meant the twelve months preceding the interview. Too much importance must not be attached to these figures, as they are at best mere off-hand figures given by the men. The writer listed all men who reported more than five jobs as working at odd jobs, and classed them with the 173 unknown. Perhaps those reporting one, two, or three jobs have represented the approximate truth.

TABLE 3
Work and Earnings of 400 Tramps—Twelve Months

| Money Earned ($) | No. Cases | Time Worked Past Twelve Months (in months) | | | | | | | | | | | No. Cases |
		2	3	4	5	6	7	8	9	10	11	?	
100–200	3		3											3
200–300	10		3	5	5				1					10
300–400	21		3	6	5	1					1	1		21
400–500	22		3	2	5	10	1		1					22
500–700	54		1	1	5	19	17	9	1	1				54
700–900	75			1	1	5	26	23	16	2			1	75
900–1,100	65				2	8	21	14	15	4	1		65
1,100–1,300	41					1	1	11	21	7			41
1,300/up	22						3	3	5	10	1		22
Not known	87	2	4	3	3	16	9	11	4	6	5	24	87
Total	400	2	17	18	20	57	62	68	51	50	27	28	400

Table 1 is modeled after the one used by Mrs. Solenberger for the same purpose, on page 277 of her work, *One Thousand Homeless Men.* Table 2 reports work histories.

Some of these causes were not given, but they were so apparent that they were listed by the writer.

The figures in table 3 cannot be exact, as the average man had only his memory to rely upon and at best could give them only approximately. Perhaps this is as close as the average estimates are when the memory is wholly relied upon.

Occupations followed by the 400 tramps:

Auto mechanics,	12	Engineers,	6	Printers, etc.,	2
Bakers,	2	Electricians,	3	Painters,	1
Barbers,	1	Firemen	3	Sailors,	10
Blacksmiths,	1	Forgemen (drop)	2	Shoemakers,	1
Boilermakers,	3	Foremen (con)	5	Slate and tile	
Bookkeepers,	3	Farm, ranch, etc.,	23	repair,	1
Bookbinders,	4	Helpers,	5	Sheet Iron	
Bricklayers,	1	Hod carriers,	1	workers,	1
Business,	1	Laborers,	153	Switchmen,	3
Brakemen,	5	Lumbermen,	14	Tanners,	1
Butchers,	3	Machine		Tailors,	2
Cabinetmakers,	3	operators,	5	Teachers,	2
Candymakers,	1	Miners,	29	Teamsters,	14
Carpenters,	12	Machinists,	10	Tent and sail	
Car repairers,	3	Moulders,	4	makers,	1
Clerks,	5	Plumbers,	4	Textile workers,	2
Cooks,	10	Peddlers,	2	Tin workers,	2

| Toolmakers, | 2 | Typewriter repair, | 1 | Not known, | 9 |
| Truck drivers, | 4 | Upholsterer, | 1 | Total, | 400 |

The single business owner was an Italian who had owned a restaurant. Few of these men had been working at their trades for some time, or they had only worked intermittently at their trades.

Ages at which the 400 tramps entered the tramp body. These figures are gotten in each case by subtracting the number of years in the body from the present age as given by the individual.

Left home at 10 years,	1
" " " 11 "	1
" " " 12 "	2
" " " 13 "	4
" " " 14 "	7
" " " 15 "	4
" " " 16 "	12
" " " 17 "	16
" " " 18 "	23
" " " 19 "	37
" " " 20 "	34
Left home between 21 and 25 years,	69
" " " 26 " 30 "	81
" " " 31 " 35 "	36
" " " 36 " 40 "	14
" " " 41 " 45 "	10
" " " 46 " 50 "	8
" " later than 50	4
Not known..	17
	Total, 400

The number leaving home before 21 was 141. The military record of the 400 tramps is as follows:

Served in the United States Army,	71
" " " " " Marines,	2
" " " " " Navy,	15
" " " " " Army and Navy,	4
	Total, 92

Most of these were young men who had served in the late war (World War I).

Attitude of the 400 tramps on the IWW question:

Those who are IWW,	74
" " were IWW,	14
" opposed to the IWW,	96

TABLE 4
Time in the Tramp Body: Ages Given

Ages	Group Showing Years													Not Known	Total Number
	1Wk–6Mo	6Mo–1Yr	1–2	2–3	3–4	4–10	11–15	16–20	21–25	26–30	31–35	36–45	Over 45		
14–19	33	8	3	2		1								4	51
20–29	38	23	25	16	7	16	6	3						9	143
30–39	11	2	3	4	2	16	23	13	4					8	86
40–49	8	3		3	1	4	7	14	22	3	1			10	76
50–59	1					1		3	2	7	2	1	2	1	20
60–69						1		1	1	2	2	1	8	1	17
70–79											1	1			2
80									1				1		2
Not known				1		1		1							3
Total	91	36	31	26	10	40	36	35	30	12	6	3	11	33	400

"	favoring the IWW,	43
"	indifferent,	173
		Total, 400

Attitude of the 92 men who had seen military service, on the IWW question:

Those who are IWW,			24
"	"	were IWW,	2
"	"	are opposed to the IWW,	24
"	favorable to the IWW,		9
"	indifferent to the IWW,		33
			Total, 92

Report of the 400 men on the question "Did you vote at the last election?"

Answering no,	352
Answering yes,	48
	Total, 400

The 352 gave the following reasons for not voting at the last election:

No interest or residence,	28
Did not care,	54
No residence,	129
Too young,	88
Aliens,	38
In military service,	9
Disfranchised,	2
Not known,	4
	Total, 352

The two men disfranchised were dishonorably discharged from the navy, and both were under 21 years of age. Neither cared for voting privileges.

In response to the question "Do you expect to be on the road next year?" the men answered as follows:

No,	240
Yes,	100
Doubtful,	60
	Total, 400

Some of the men who answered yes did so because they followed transient occupations which kept them moving from place to place.

Physical and mental defects of the 400 tramps as observed by the writer (this is a survey only of apparent or admitted defects):

Age,	6
Maimed,	8
One eye gone, or partly blind,	5
Eye trouble,	5
Venereal disease,	1
Partly paralyzed,	2
Tuberculosis,	2
Feeble minded,	7
Chronic poor health,	4
Stuttered badly; other speech defect,	3
Hurt temporarily,	4
Oversized and undersized,	4
Total defects,	51
Total number of defective cases,	48

In answer to the question "In how many states have you been during the past year?"

33 had been in	1 state
33 " " "	2 states
68 " " "	3 "
41 " " "	4 "
20 " " "	5 "
21 " " "	6 "
13 " " "	7 "
20 " " "	8 "
16 " " "	9 "
15 " " "	10 "
7 " " "	11 "
19 " " "	12 "
6 " " "	13 "
5 " " "	14 "
18 " " "	15 "
2 " " "	16 "
2 " " "	17 "
4 " " "	18 "
1 " " "	19 "
12 " " "	20 or more states.
44 not known	
400, total	

8

How and the Hobos: Character Sketch of J. E. How, "Millionaire Hobo"

What is your opinion of a man who is content to live the life of a hobo, in spite of having a million dollars at his disposal? You needn't give it for it might not be essentially different from what many others have thought. The "Millionaire Tramp," as he has been dignified by the press for over fifteen years, is none other than James Eads How, a member of a prominent and wealthy St. Louis family. His grandfather was a contractor of note, and is better known as the builder of Eads Bridge, over the Mississippi River at St. Louis. The Eads fortune came to the How family through Eliza Eads How, the daughter of the builder and the mother of James Eads How. At the death of his parents, James and his brother Louis became joint heirs to the Eads millions. Louis became an artist and took to the gay Bohemian life, but James cast his lot with the "hobohemians."

How is a pleasant man to meet. He is not an imposing person—indeed, he is everything but that. He is a middle-aged man, and wears a short, shaggy beard, somewhat tinged with gray. He is generally garbed in rough and threadbare clothing, which for the most part is unkempt and tramplike. Sometimes it is more than tramplike, for there are times when an ordinary hobo would appear aristocratic beside him. How does not concern himself with appearances. If he can locate in a rooming house, he washes his shirt and sox, and permits them to dry during the night; but in spite of baths and clean clothes, he still looks tramplike. He does not make any studied effort to look the part—it seems to be second nature. He is a "pleb" to the bone, and doesn't care who knows it.

How has been a plebeian from childhood. At home, even in his youth, he lived the simple life, serving himself, and scorning the attention of valets. Much to the embarrassment of the family, he exiled himself from the luxuries and comforts which his wealth could afford him.

From Burgess Papers, Regenstein Library, Department of Special Collections, University of Chicago (box 127, folder 6, document 126), unpublished document. Reprinted by permission.

He never reconciled himself to being waited upon, nor was he able to understand how some people could be content with a string of porters and servants, while others had to make a desperate struggle to live at all. He tells the story of how he was brought to his present attitude toward wealth and poverty. One day in his early teens he picked up a purse containing some money. He made an effort to find the owner, and, not being successful, was told to keep the money—that it was his by reason of his having found it. Says he, "I reasoned in a small way— 'Whose money is this? Why am I entitled to it? Perhaps someone else is in need while I hold his money. I didn't do anything for this; I didn't even have to thank anyone for it. And then I thought of all the other money that had come to me without any effort on my part. What had I ever done for any of the money I had? Whose money was it?'"

This line of reasoning eventually drove him from home, and he found himself drifting into the tramp class. Among that grade of men he saw his life-work. To him, they were a great body of unorganized and uneducated workers drifting here and there, without plan or purpose. Here was a clear field for him—for his time, his talent, and, incidentally, his money. Here was a field in which he would not have to compete with other millionaire philanthropists. For more than fifteen years he has been traveling over this country and abroad, seeking out and organizing those restless and migrating men who travel here and there over the land doing seasonal work. The hobo who shears the sheep, harvests the grain, picks the fruit, cuts the timber and harvests the ice; who builds the railroads and pioneers the barren waste but does not linger to enjoy the fruits of his effort; these are the men that How is out to serve. No other interest holds him, not even matrimony.

How sees in the hobo an important factor in the industrial life of the country. He sees him as an economic factor, but he also sees him as a person closed out of the social life of the different communities in which he finds himself. How regards the hobo as a man who is driven out on the road by conditions over which he has little control, and by similar conditions is kept on the road. He is a man who is barked at by the dogs, snubbed by polite society, and man-handled by the police. He enters a town at his peril, and often leaves in haste. He is often misunderstood, even when he has the best intentions. When he works, he is generally obliged to take the hardest toil, with the meanest pay and the poorest fare. It is this man that How is out to serve.

Millionaire that he is, How has not failed to familiarize himself with every phase of tramp life. He knows the life better than many of the veteran hobos. He has become so thoroughly absorbed in the work of organizing what he terms the "migratory, casual, and unemployed," and sometimes "disemployed," workers that he practically loses interest in himself. He becomes so obsessed with some task at times that he will walk the streets all day without stopping long enough to eat. Sometimes he will order a meal, and then go away to perform some mission, forgetting for an hour to come back. In his personal living he is more frugal than many of the "bos." As soon as he gets to town he usually makes his way to the "main stem," or the district where the "bos" abound, and he engages a bed at a "flophouse," where the prices range from twenty to forty cents a night. He will give "flop" and coffee and money to a dozen men before he will take time to eat. This is his joy and his life.

A word about what How has been able to accomplish will not be amiss. The How organization is known as the "International Brotherhood Welfare Association" and has its headquarters in Cincinnati. There are local branches of the IBWA in more than twenty of the leading cities of the country. The IBWA is revolutionary, but not so red as it is sometimes painted. It is sufficiently anti-red to be opposed to the IWW, to which most of the radical tramps belong. The IBWA is primarily evolutionary; it is a labor movement, but it proposes reform through education. The two auxilliaries by which this end is hoped to be attained are the "Hobo College" and the "Hobo News."

The "College" is an effort to educate hobos in some of the rudiments of the social sciences, in public speaking, and in anything that may be adequately taught. It is an effort to bring to the hobo what he does not otherwise have access to. A hall is rented, and school is held on scheduled nights, for all who care to come. School usually consists of lectures on various subjects. The colleges usually operate only during the winter, when the men are in town after having spent the summer on some job. Whether a college is a success or not depends upon the officers who happen to be in charge, and their ability in getting outside speakers and lecturers. The Chicago branch of the "Hobo College" has been rather conspicuous. One year it debated with students from the University of Chicago. Most of the tramps who live in Chicago during the winter are proud of the fact that the "hobos" literally "tore 'em to pieces." If the college in Chicago has done nothing else, it has helped a number of "soap box orators" to find themselves.

The *Hobo News* is an interesting little magazine, dedicated to the interests of the "bos." Whether it is radical or not depends upon the man who happens to be editor, but the policy of the organization is to keep the reds out. It is a sixteen-page monthly, and carries no advertising. It prints a very well balanced assortment of poems, essays, and articles reflecting the tramp's life and representing his interests. The *News* is a sort of correspondence sheet, as well. In it are found communications to the editor, written by the hobos from different parts of the country. The maximum issue of the *Hobo News* ranges about twenty thousand copies. The minimum issue is usually reached during the summer months, when all the men are out of town, on the job. The paper prospers best when there are many tramps loafing about the town, as there are then more men to sell and to buy the paper. It is published in St. Louis or in Cincinnati, depending upon where the editor happens to be, but generally it has come from St. Louis, How's home.

How's favorite dream is to establish in each of the large cities a hobo college and a cooperative inn for the migrants. (He is not interested in any tramps but the workers.) He hopes these colleges will act as feeders to a grand central hobo university. The hobo stopping places or relay stations are calculated to care for the physical wants. Some of these "hotels de bum" are already established in certain of the cities of the East. The one in Cincinnati is typical. It is a two-story building, and is situated in a part of the city most frequented by the hobo. There are enough cots and blankets on the second floor to accommodate forty men. The lower floor is taken up by a lobby in front, while the rear is used as a washroom and kitchen. There is a stove, and utensils enough to accommodate a number of men who care to wash their clothes or cook a "mulligan" stew—the hobo's favorite dish. The only duty incumbent upon any man is that of helping to keep the place in order, and each man bears his share of the expense. The management is under the direction of a committee elected by the house. Few of these houses have ever succeeded, because of the inability of the average tramp to cooperate. These failures have not discouraged How.

In spite of How's democratic ideals, the IBWA does practically what he wants it to do. He insists that the sovereignty should rest with the rank and file, but due to the fact that he holds the pocketbook, the rank and file does about as he suggests. Indeed, there is always an effort to "feel him out" before a proposition comes up. This does not always happen, however. Sometimes How has opposition in his own organization, and sometimes he is voted down. When this is the case, he usually takes the decision as law. But being out-voted now and then does not alter the fact that How rules as long as he pays the bills. When a "college" in some city goes behind, How foots the bill. If the *Hobo News* does not make ends meet, he makes up the difference. He pays the bills of all the hobo conventions, and there have been three already, in 1922. The bills of the conventions usually mean the cost of meals and beds for the delegates. Sometimes he pays their transportation one way, usually to the convention; they beat their way back.

The problem of organizing about two million migratory workers into one big brotherhood is indeed stupendous, but How has never been daunted. He has met many defeats, and he has even endured persecution and ridicule, but his hopes are not less rosy, nor his enthusiasm less pronounced, than when he first had this vision. He declares he has made more progress than he even anticipated. It might be argued that his enthusiasm is due to ignorance, but that does not seem the case. Few men know the hobo better than How does. Perhaps not a day passes that he does not remark "We've got to organize these men; but first of all, we've got to educate them. Most of them have minds like children, and they don't know what organization means."

How is an educated man, having degrees from three universities. He is still studying. As he makes his way about the country, he is usually found spending his leisure time reading law. He still hopes to spend some time in a law school. He is also a religious man. His religion is probably the dominating motive for spending his life in the service of the "bos."

How never stops to learn what the hobo thinks of him. His worst critics are among the very men that he is most anxious to help. He is sometimes spoken of as the "doughnut" philosopher, because of the role the doughnut plays in his life. The average hobo considers How's method of organization as impractical, and this criticism is not without foundation for seldom does a local that he organizes last long. He spends most of his time going from town to town, not organizing new locals, but reorganizing old ones.

He has a few faithful co-workers, but most of the men who work with him soon despair of the effort of organizing the hobos, and withdraw from the movement. Said one man, "I've had my fill of How and his doughnuts. That's the only way you can organize the slum proletariat; as soon as How and his basket of doughnuts are gone, the organization falls."

The "bos" who know How have long ago given up the attempt to "work" him for cash donations. He is usually equal to the average panhandler. One man came to him on a cold day and plead, "Doctor, I haven't got any sox. Just look at this." "My! that is too bad," declared How, as he sat down on the curb and removed his shoes and sox. The "bo" thought he was taking off his shoes to get some money that might be hidden there, but when he saw that How was going to give him his own sox, he left, in disgust.

9

The Slum: A Project for Study

The word "slum" has come into disrepute. Having come into vogue with the wave of humanitarianism that swept the country in the eighties and nineties, suddenly, with the decline of slumming as a philanthropic pastime, the word became taboo, but the slum remains. In relative terms the slum differs from city to city as in any city it differs from time to time. In the organization and life of any city it is a changing and migrating fact. Yet it always remains the habitat of the socially and economically impotent folks; a retreat for the poverty-ridden and a last resort for the maladjusted. Every city has its worst area; its unkempt houses along the tracks, its shanties on the river bottom, its row of houseboats, or, if it is a metropolitan city, its East Side, its West Side or some other area of mediocrity. It is not poverty alone that marks the slum, nor is it the antiquated building. It is in addition an area of social disorganization, low morale, and high transiency.

The transiency of the slum is one with the transiency of the city. The city is the creature of movement and feeds upon it. People are constantly being sorted and shifted, and segregated spatially according to one or another set of interests, but chiefly they are distributed to the blocks and streets according to their abilities to pay rent. The slum *itself* is but an aggregate of smaller areas as varied in nature as the types that occupy them. Thus, to mention only a few, we have Chinatown, Greektown, Hobohemia, the rooming house slum, crime and vice areas, Black Belts and other areas of race, as well as a medley of family slums. Each tends to have its own social values, its own universe of discourse; in short, culture patterns of its own. But it is equally true that the life of the slum, regardless of the nature of the slum, if it is to function at all in the larger life of the entire city, must gear into that larger life or be an embarassment to it.

Origin of the Slum

The slum as we know it is no older than modern industrial society of which it is a part and into which it is anonymously integrated, though

From *Social Forces* 7 (1928): 87–90. Reprinted by permission.

superficially it may seem to be detached in its life from the rest of the city. We may say that while areas of the city become more highly integrated and bound together in their impersonal relations, in their associational relations they become more isolated. The extremes of society become strangers to each other, which is illustrated by the fact that before the industrial revolution had passed through one generation slumming had come into vogue. The poorest habitation areas had become so strange and removed from the general life of the city that visiting them was nothing short of adventure, and serving the slum was nothing short of heroic.

The slum was discovered to the rest of the city during the middle decades of the last century. It was brought to our attention by the newspaper seeking human interest stories and literature seeking fresh themes of life. That period which gave us a Dickens was followed by a period of more critical attention when people began to see problems and wrestle with cures. From philosophy they turned to social service, and out of this yearning to serve we got the beginning of social science. The conscience of the university was touched, and as a result a flood of intellectuals went into the slum establishing settlements. New York has no less than a dozen settlements that were started by the colleges and universities during those years. Students of society began to look for "laws" of social control. The social survey came into vogue; first as a sentimental investigation not unlike muckraking and gradually developing into painstaking factfinding. During the "humanitarian" eighties and nineties dozens of organizations for the "improvement," the "betterment," the "rescue," the "reform," the "correction," or the "protection" of the poor were set up. In half a century many of these old approaches to the slum have changed; old interests have been replaced by new ones. Crusading and slumming are yielding to science; all of which calls for a redefinition of the slum in more objective terms.

Known Aspects of the Slum

About the slum, its inhabitants, its relations to the city, its continuance and the problems it presents, there is much to be learned. Doubtless there is much to be unlearned as well. However, there are some things about which we are sufficiently certain that we may label them facts. We know, for instance, that the slum is not a thing apart but a segment of a larger arrangement; that whatever its nature it fits and functions in the life of the city. Obvious as this may be, housing reformers and slum removers have generally failed to recognize it. They have regarded the slum as a disease instead of the symptom of a disease. Take the poorest sixth of the population of any city, or the richest sixth, living at the opposite extremes of habitation areas. By isolating either, the life of the whole city would be paralyzed. Each segment of the population as well as each area of the city is a functioning part of the whole city. If we carry over to sociology the Gestalt concept, which is not new to psychology, we have difficulty in viewing any part of the city, whether Broadway, Park Avenue, the Bowery, Wall Street or Hester Street as detached unities.

Another significant fact is that the slum, like every other part of the city, is the creature of and derives its nature largely from shifting land values. Frequently it is a borderline residential occupancy wedged in between a retreating use of space for residential purposes and an advancing change of use. It is residential space the least in demand for residential purposes, though it may have a future for other types of occupants, depending upon its availability and demand. Like parts of the East Side in New York it may enter a new residential cycle, or like other parts of the East Side, it may be taken over by commerce or industry. In a rapidly growing city any residential area in the path of change may degenerate into a slum and any slum may be wiped out for more acceptable uses. The faster the city grows the faster these transformations take place.

This brings to our attention a third fact about the slum; that of movement and occupational succession. In the modern city changes pursue one another in disturbing procession. New occupants are constantly invading and old ones are being crowded out. Occupational succession is a fact not only of the slum but the whole city. No area is immune. Movement is both up and down the social scale, but generally the bulk of it is from areas of less advantage to areas of more advantage; from the slums at the heart of the city to the suburbs at the periphery. The slum is a point of invasion and hence a center of population increase. Most of the plain folks the city acquires come to it through this port of entry displacing the occupants they find in the slum. The displaced occupants move to a region of more advantage farther from the center there displacing some other occupants who in turn move farther out. The whole is a wave-like migration outward while any given residential area passes through as a result, a series of occupations; each occupation being of lower social and economic status than the previous. Ultimately there is in any given house a final and least occupant whose presence is tolerated until the situation permits or requires a change of use.

An Approach to the Study of the Slum

Any house in the city and any residential area in the city where the value is ultimately determined by the site value of the land and the improvements on the land, may experience such a succession of occupation and such decline in status. This is equivalent to saying that any residential area in a changing city may finally become a slum. The slum may then be regarded as a migrating phenomenon of the city. This is amply illustrated in our larger cities. In New York City the East Side is changing very rapidly. Settlements and community houses that established there three decades ago are now being stranded. The poor have gone to the Bronx and the Brooklyn shore of the East River. Many former East Siders have dared to move into Flatbush and former Flatbush residents have fled to the suburbs. They say that the East Side is becoming respectable. Certainly it is becoming colorful and there is plenty of evidence of building revival. It would be very interesting to find out how much this change has been brought about by the presence of hundreds of welfare agencies on the East Side and how much is it the natural result of changing land values and the shifting forces of city building. It would be interesting to find out if this area which we call the slum, the beggar area of the modern city, has been helped or hindered at any time by welfare moves against it or for its betterment. So long as we have a poorest population and relatively lowest rents and the least favored of social and economic classes may we expect to have slums? To press the queries on the other side: What can we hope for in the way of social direction and control from the social sciences? How can we so perfect the processes of human salvage so that, even though the slum continues in some form, the waste involved is reduced to a minimum? Finally, what resources and methods has sociology for arriving at a sane and scientific interpretation of the slum?

Obviously, this is a subject on which most thinking has been emotional. Nor are we helped much by the many books that have been written any more than we are helped in our study of the city by the many books that have appeared on that subject. The decks need to be cleared of a great deal of rubbish, and on this as on other matters with which sociology must deal we need to take our cue from the physical sciences and start at the beginning. And then we need to study it in relation to all other facts that incorporate it into the life of the city.

In ten years more than a third of the population moved out of the West Side of Chicago. They say that the East Side and the West Side are becoming respectable.

10

The Juvenile and the Tramp

The Problem

The United States has a peculiar tramp problem; a problem that has been largely the product of a peculiar set of historical circumstances and a peculiar industrial situation. For many reasons it is different from the tramp problem in any foreign country.

The American tramp class is practically a one-sex group. Few women ever enter it. Again, it is a young man's group. It is more mobile than any tramp class abroad. The American tramp is a traveling man, many of them migrating thousands of miles each year. While we have the inefficient and handicapped types which predominate in foreign tramp groups, we also have a large percent of workers. The greater proportion of the American tramp class are hobos or migrating and seasonal workers; perhaps the nonworkers of the class do not exceed 30 percent.

When we look for the explanation for the existence of an army of perhaps two million homeless, wandering men we are forced to the conclusion that the most significant reasons are to be found with the men themselves. Inadequate personalities, defective mentalities, or physical defects are exceedingly frequent among these men. To what extent these deficiencies exist cannot be said from the meager data at hand. But aside from the many who are the victims of habits and weaknesses or handicaps there are many who are in the tramp class for reasons largely external to themselves. These might be designated impelling forces as unemployment or crises in the person's life, and attracting forces such as the following:

1. *Pioneering attractions.* This country has always had a frontier which has attracted many footloose men, especially young men. Many of these have been unable to fit into the pioneering life and they continue to wander.

From *Journal of Criminal Law, Criminology and Police Science* 14 (1923–24): 290–312. Reprinted by permission of Martin Anderson.

2. *Work attractions.* Except when we have industrial depressions, there are in many industries yearly fluctuations in the demands for labor. At certain seasons the demand for workers in certain communities is greater than the local supply can satisfy. This always calls for the important of workers for a brief period, after which they must seek employment elsewhere.

3. *Climatic attractions.* The temptation to migrate to a warmer climate in winter has always been attractive to transient men.

4. *Transportation attractions.* The railroad has done much to bring the migratory worker into existence. He has played an important role in their construction and he has used them freely as a means of travel. It is difficult to think of the American tramp apart from the railroads.

Given these various inducements to travel, on the one hand, and the opportunity to travel, on the other, it seems only natural to expect men who are restless and footloose to take advantage of them. There is, we must admit, a real work reason for the existence of a certain migratory population, but little has ever been done to ascertain the approximate number needed in any community. The result of the lack of organization in this regard has been that there have been from two to three times the necessary number of migrants on the road. With many, work reasons serve as an excuse, and they drift aimlessly about doing a little work here and a little there as it comes convenient.

Regarded even as a working group, the tramp class is an exceedingly unwieldy and undisciplined body. The members of the group are always living anonymous lives, and generally they are shifting and moving to avoid responsibility. They are a group of men with no home attachments and few interests that would identify them with any community. They are not burdened with the moral problems of any group nor are they even put in a position where their own conduct gives them much concern.

Life, to the average tramp, is a problem of "getting by." He is out to get all the joy he can with the least effort, and he seldom puts himself into any position where he will be saddled with another man's load. Seldom does he linger long enough in any community to carry his own load. Being a tramp he is always in the position of an outcast and, feeling this, his hand is usually against anything that is established and regular in organized society. His becomes a negative attitude which, undesirable as it may be, is but natural.

On the other hand, whether the tramp is antisocial or not, he frequently drifts into conditions that react negatively toward him. In his work he is often taken advantage of. He is generally misunderstood even when he has good intentions. He is often abused and even beaten by the police. If he tries to rise out of the life he finds it difficult, for there is little help offered him by the upper strata. Under these circumstances the easiest thing to do, and the thing he does, is to drift along the path of least resistance, remaining in the class until he finally falls beside the way.

This is a life in which one comes into most intimate contact with vice and immorality. The tramp class spends its leisure in the cities, and usually in such sections of the city where the most undesirable conditions and influences exist. No other group comes closer to the bootlegger or the "dope" peddler; indeed, they are his fellow outcasts and for them the tramp develops a frank tolerance. Not only does he become tolerant, but he not infrequently indulges with them.

This is the life that tempts the boy.

The Attractions of Tramp Life

In spite of the hardships that tramps endure, and in spite of the bitter end at which most of them arrive, the life has its attractions. The boy who lives in a dream world where he is constantly building aircastles, only to see them toppled by the stern realities of the daily routine, is strangely attracted by the tramp's life. He sees in the life on the road a charm and fascination that no other offers. To him the tramp is a very interesting individual with a fund of information about life, and a man who goes where and when he pleases with no one to boss him and none to watch him. It is a life in which there are no daily tasks and no chores; it is a promise of escape from everything distasteful. He can only learn the bitterness and hopelessness of the life after he has spent years on the road.

Tramp life to the boy is a promise of all that he wishes. It promises him change of scenery and variety of experience. In it he can see prospects of wealth and fame and, best of all, it is an invitation to be off to gain a background of adventure. It is the ideal existence, and the tramp is the only person whom he regards as having the ideal philosophy. He sees him as does the poet:

> We are the true nobility;
>> Sons of rest and the outdoor air;
> Knights of the tide and rail are we,
>> Lightly meandering everywhere.
> Having no gold we buy no care,
>> As over the crust of the world we go,
> Stepping in tune to this ditty rare;
>> Take up your bundle and beat it, Bo!

—H. H. Knibbs

Who hasn't felt that urge to cast off all responsibility and strike out for parts unknown? No grownup can feel it more than the average red-blooded boy who has access to the railroad and who has confidence in his ability to do what other boys do. It is some unusual expression he yearns for; to prove himself in some unusual way. He may want to go to sea, to fight Indians, to dig gold or be a cowboy or movie actor. He may only have visions of seeking work in the city. Whatever his ulterior motives may be, somewhere in his plans is the resolve to play to some degree the role of a tramp.

Types of Boy Tramps

Perhaps one-fourth of the tramp class in the United States are boys under twenty-one. This would be considerable when we remember that various estimates place our tramp population at about two million. Anderson found fifty-one boys, nineteen and under, among the four hundred tramps he interviewed.[1] Other observers have estimated the number of boys in the tramp body as nearer one-third. Boys are not numerous in the areas most frequented by the tramp population in the cities. In Chicago's Hobohemia one finds more old men than boy tramps. When conditions are favorable the boy becomes tired of life on the "stem" and moves on.

The boy tramp must be met on the road where there is movement and change. If he is a normal boy and does not become frightened by the dangers and uncertainties he is almost sure to develop into a daring and clever tramp—the type of tramp who will travel more miles in a day than the average man. He will take more chances; he will go longer without food. When he begs he goes about it with more energy and tact than the adult "moocher" or "panhandler." He is out to learn the game and nothing escapes his observation. This is the behavior to be expected from the normal, intelligent boy who finds his way into the tramp class. There are many exceptions.

1. These 400 tramps were interviewed while in transit between Chicago and the west coast during the summer of 1921. There were 143 under 25 years; about 60% were under 35 years, and but 70 were over 45. These men left home at the following ages. Given number and age at which they left home:

Four left home before 12 years.	Thirty-four left at 20 years.
Four left home at 13 years.	Eighty-nine left before 25 years.
Seven left home at 14 years.	Eighty-one left before 30 years.
Four left home at 15 years.	Thirty-six left before 35 years.
Twelve left home at 16 years.	Fourteen left before 40 years.
Sixteen left at 17 years.	Ten left before 45 years.
Twenty-three left at 18 years.	Eight left before 50 years.
Thirty-seven left at 19 years.	Later than 50 and not known, 21.

There are many boys on the road who are not seeking variety. Many of them are away from home because of crises or misfortune. Some have had home trouble, while others may have become offenders and are avoiding the law. Many are mentally or physically handicapped, while others have personalities that will not permit them to fit into any group. They have gone away because they were not wanted or to start anew elsewhere. These mentally defective boys and otherwise psychopathic boys who find their way into the tramp class do not often become successful tramps.

The following cases illustrate some of the many types of boy tramps.

Wanderlust Type

At the age of fourteen M. S. got tired of things at home. One day he became disgruntled because his father would not permit him to go to a fireman's carnival in a near-by town. He had been to the town many times to play ball. He had ridden there on the freight trains. He sulked when his father told him to mow the lawn. This caused his father to tell him that if he didn't like it at home that the world was big. He had been humbled before by this retort, but never again. It was a challenge.

He and a chum got their things together and left. They went to the carnival, stayed a few hours and lost interest. They had made up their minds to go west and they caught a freight to Omaha; worked in Omaha a few days; saw a man from their hometown, got frightened and went to Denver; from Denver to Ogden, back to Denver and then to Pueblo, where the chum had some relatives.

In the fall they returned home and went to school; had much to talk of during the winter. Left again in the spring. The following are some of the things they did during the two summers they were away. Went to Ogden to visit the gambling halls where they heard that the gold was stacked on the tables. Went to Cripple Creek, got job in gold mine expecting to see gold and get some; became frightened of mine and quit. Went to Rocky Ford, Colo., to pick melons because they wanted to see fields of melons and to eat their fill. Walked from Colorado Springs to the foot of Pikes Peak to see the soda springs; stayed all day, drank themselves sick. Made a trip to Wyoming to pick potatoes.

They worked only when forced to it or to get variety. Begged without fear. Begged for each other. Rode only fast trains.

Egocentric Type

Age 19, active, intelligent, robust. Left home two years ago (about 1920). Since that time he has traveled a great deal. His home is in Wisconsin and his folks are farmers. He became restless and his parents permitted him to go away to work, thinking he would be glad to return after a while. He returned after six months or so, but he could not get along with them. He had learned to smoke, which they objected to, and he had learned to take an interest in girls. He would take no advice from his parents. "They were always trying to make me think I was a damn fool, but I know what I'm doing." He has ceased to write home because they still endeavor to advise him.

He likes to tell of his affairs with girls. This is how most of his affairs ended. "A red-headed girl got stuck on me, and not caring for her I let her go. The other girl got jealous of the red-head and I let her go, too." He does not admit having ever been jilted.

When asked how he got about the country, if police bothered, etc., he said that he could ride any train he wanted to and that the police only made fun for him. He told of several affairs he had had with railroad police and in all of them the police had got the worst of it.

How he got his money was a question. It was evident that he did very little work. During the last year he has been arrested three times. Once in Los Angeles in connection with a robbery: "Proving myself innocent, I was released" is his verdict. He was also arrested in Chicago for begging on the street—"the police, not liking my looks, run me in for 'stemming.' The judge did not like me so he gave me fifty dollars and costs." This he worked out in the House of Correction at fifty cents a day.

He likes to tell about his experiences gambling. He claims that he always wins. Investigator gave him fifty cents and followed him. He went into the gambling house at 732 West Madison Street.

Mentally Defective Type

Age 19. This boy came from farm in Minnesota. At home he was very much imposed upon. It was hard for him to make his grades. He was truant from school. His parents had so much trouble that they found it easier to permit him to remain at home than to force him to go to school. Finally they reached the conclusion that it was useless to send him to school. This suited him and he remained at work. He was even imposed upon at home, for he was given tasks that really should have been done by his brothers.

He was large for his age and during the war someone told him that he might get a job in town, so he went to Minneapolis. He got a job and things went fairly well. Of a sudden he developed considerable confidence in himself. During his first year away from home he had several jobs. He learned to like to move. He spent money like the other migrants with whom he came in contact. He learned to play fast and loose with work as they do. He learned to ride freight trains, to beg on streets; but he was not a good beggar.

He left home largely because he had been imposed upon. The neighbor boys teased him and he could find no companions. This cause enters into his moving from job to job. After he has been on the job for some time he becomes the object of much teasing. When it becomes unbearable he moves. He prefers to work alone and his favorite job is unloading coal cars. He likes this kind of work if he can work by the ton, and then, he can work as hard as he likes.

Winter of 1921–22 he was in Chicago most of time. Dirty and ragged. He spent much time in missions. Worked some, but not enough to pay his way. When spring came he got a job and cleaned up. He does not care to go home. He says the people in his hometown are "Hoosiers."

Home Trouble

M. is the product of a broken home. He is fifteen years old and has traveled considerable both by train and automobile. He has developed into an efficient tramp and a good beggar. His parents divorced and later both remarried. His mother and her husband moved to Colorado. His father and stepmother remained in his home state, Oklahoma.

M. elected to live with his father and stepmother. For some time he got along fairly well, but soon trouble arose and he decided to go to his mother and stepfather. His mother sent for him, but he was not with her long when he found that he could not get along with his stepfather. He ran away and beat his way back to Oklahoma. This trip gave him a measure of himself. He learned what he could do. When he arrived at his father's home he found that he was still not in the good graces of his stepmother, so he "hit a freight" for Kansas City. He kept it up for two or three months until he finally drifted into Chicago, where he was picked up by the police and sent to his father. While traveling he was begging his food and having a good time.

Work

N., age 16, lived in a little farming community in Michigan where he could find little to do aside from farm work, which he did not like. He had visions of being a mechanic. He tried to get a job near home in a garage, where he hoped to learn something about automobiles, but there was no chance. He tried to take a course by correspondence, but that was not satisfactory. Finally he got restless and ran away to get the kind of work he wanted.

He came to Chicago, but he was too young and too small and no one cared to hire him, so he left town and beat his way to Kansas City where he got a job. But he could not get a job that suited him so he began wandering again. He discovered that he could get over the country very well and that he could live very well from odd jobs here and there. But he couldn't save any money for his purposes.

When last seen he was in Chicago. He didn't want to go home because he felt that it would look like he had given up. He left to get work and to save money to learn auto mechanics, though he was getting lukewarm on his resolution to be a mechanic.

Concerning the homes the boy tramps come from we can say little. Many do come from broken homes or homes in which there is a bad influence. Boys often leave good homes for the road. Home trouble, being misunderstood or in some way antagonized are not uncommon factors in making boy tramps. Most of the normal boys in the tramp body come from good homes or at least average homes. It is not uncommon to find them keeping in touch with their folks. They may not remain in one place long enough to get mail, but at least they write home occasionally.

The Adaptability of the Boy Tramp

The boy on the road is an apt student of tramp lore. Every situation common to the life he learns to meet in a regular fashion. He learns to outwit the police, and, like all veterans, he likes to tell of his escapades. If he can ride one passenger train from five hundred to a thousand miles in spite of the opposition he has something to talk about. He makes a studied effort to absorb everything that he should know; the slang, the habits and all the tricks of the road; anything that will give him the air of an old-timer. The following was written by a fifteen-year boy tramp who had been held in the Chicago Detention Home for a few days. No corrections have been made.

Two Months' Adventures of a Road Kid

"My folks sent me to P. C. on a visit. I hit P. about eight-thirty in the morning. About fifteen minutes later I hit the blind of a fast passenger bound north.

"I held it until I got into the yard limit of Arkansas City, Kansas. I jumped off it there, walked over to the elevator about a block away and caught a ride uptown on a truck, when I hit the main drag I thought I'd better throw my feet (that is, bum a meal). I mooched me set-downs in many restaurants and then hit up some fellows for a light piece (a quarter). As it happened I hit a bull (off duty). He grabbed me and started around the corner to take me to the can, but I wasn't of any mind to be pinched and pay for my board making little ones out of big ones for the county roads.

"We stepped down from the sidewalk to the pavement and I stuck my foot in front of the flatfoot. He fell and I ran. I beat it about four blocks down the alley before I hit the main drag again. I tried to rustle for a light piece and I had such good luck that in about an hour I had two dollars and fifteen cents, so I caught a ride in a car to the next town, for the railroad dicks and the special officers in Arkansas City were hostile."

It is not difficult to see that here is one boy who is at least familiar with the slang of the road. Some of it, of course, was used for display, but it came without effort. He was one of the many boys who could get over the country as well by automobile as by train.

Recently, and especially in summer, the automobile has become a popular means of transportation for transient boys. The following is typical of certain types of boy automobile tramps.[2]

> David S. in office on Sept. 1921. States he never applied to a social agency before, but that he is compelled to do so today because of the inclement weather, which makes it impossible for him to pick a ride westward out of Chicago. He came here from New York City. With the exception of a short stretch of rail riding on the Pennsylvania out of New York, he claims to have made the whole trip by automobile. This is not his first adventure. He estimates that in his career as a wanderer he has used up at least $500 worth of tires and an equal amount of gasoline for neither of which he has paid. He has made a mental note of the fact that besides having gotten over a thousand lifts from sympathetic automobilists, he has also received from about half of them a meal in the next town in which they landed.
>
> David states that he never knew how many good natured people there were in the world until he took to the road and found that he never had to walk more than a half a mile a day between various lifts to get to his destination. He recalls only on one occasion when he was picked up by highway police, whom he approached for a ride.
>
> David claims that he did not have to tell any imaginary tales to get a lift or a meal at the end of his lift. When he gets to a large city he usually walks around the main highway towards the city limits and there he gets his pick-up. He carries no baggage and has with him only the clothes that he wears. When he came here from New York he stated that upon leaving he had $2.00 in his pocket.

David is representative of a great many boys who get over the country in this manner. Perhaps this practice is indulged in more frequently on the West Coast and in the East than in the Middle West where the towns are so far apart. It is a kind of travel at which a lone boy will succeed better than a man. Autoists fear to give a lift to an adult and they will generally pass if two men are in company.

The sea has always been an attraction for the boy. There have always been opportunities to work on ships for boys who cared to go to sea.

---

2. Submitted by Mr. Wirth, Homeless Man Department, Chicago Jewish Charities.

Even the lake traffic has a tendency to attract boys of tender years, as shown by the case of R. B.[3]

> Rub. B. came to the attention of the Boys Dept. of the JSSB July 1920. Father complained that R hangs around State and Harrison Streets with gang, often coming home after midnight. The boy was then fifteen years of age. He left home in Feb. 1920, and had begun to work in the post office, giving his age as 18. The boy was sent to various prospective employers for work, but invariably failed to report.
>
> One day, late in July, R's father appeared in our office with a card from the boy reading, "Am working as a gunmate X on this ship and getting $87.50 a month." The card bore the name of S.S. Jimmie of Brein of Milwaukee. In a card received a few days later he stated that he had been promoted to the same job (gunmate!) on the Steamship Columbus of the Goodrich Transfer Company. Upon investigating the purser's book of the "Columbus" which docked the next morning, we found that R had worked as cabin boy for one trip. Upon leaving this job the boy informed the purser that he intended joining Barnum and Bailey's Circus in Grant Park. We lost track of the boy until September 1920, and then we learned that he had enlisted in the United States Army at the South State Street Recruiting Office.

This boy later deserted the army and has not been heard from since.

It is important to keep in mind the roles played by the boat and the automobile as means for facilitating the wanderings of the boy tramp, but both these modes of travel taken together are not of so much consequence as the railroad. The railroad can be used throughout the year, whereas the highways and the steamship lines are in operation only part of the year.

The boy tramp seldom carries anything except what he wears unless it be a pair of overalls to protect his clothes while he rides the trains. The most that he carries is what will go into his pockets without inconveniencing him. He may carry matches to build a fire and a roll of paper to lie upon in case he gets into a dirty car. Sometimes, after the fashion of the veterans, he may carry a small bag of coffee and a little sugar which come in handy when he cooks in the jungles. Often, if he is the kind of tramp who rides the trucks and the tops of passenger trains, he may have a pair of goggles.

The boy usually travels with a partner who is sometimes an adult, but more often some other boy. As we shall see later, this is partly for protection, but it is chiefly because boys get along better. Their interests are more in common. They dare to do many things together that they would be slow to do in the company of older men. The boy who

---

3. Also submitted by Mr. Wirth.

likes to ride passenger trains is more apt to travel in the company of another boy than a man, for the older tramps are content to ride the freights. Boys want fun and they can have it better when together. Sometimes they will travel several in a group.

> These two boys came from Boone, Iowa. They left home together at the close of the school term (1921). They went into the northwest, visiting Washington, Idaho, Oregon, and coming back they traversed Utah, Wyoming, and Colorado. They traveled a long ways to see Pueblo, Colorado, where a flood had devastated the town. They went here and there at will, but they always went together. Even when they quarreled they remained together.
>
> If they were riding on top of a freight train and one wanted to sleep the other would watch that he did not roll off. They used to beg food and meet some place to divide up. They would fight and wrestle a great deal. Each had a list of stories to tell about the other, about being chased by police and dogs, about getting good meals, etc. They would read each other's letters and when they wrote home they would sometimes put two letters in the same envelope. Their folks were neighbors. They said that their folks didn't care what they did so long as they got back in time for school in the fall. They were both about fifteen.

The Boy's Contacts with the Tramp

From their contacts with seasoned tramps we may say that most boys get their first stimulus to travel. The tramp with his tales of adventure and travel (and most of these types recommend themselves highly) is able to thrill the average boy; at times the boy stands in awe of the old-timer.

Boys need not go on the road to meet the transients. There are a hundred points of contact in the parks, the railroad yards and in the areas to which the tramp population gravitates when in the city. In Chicago the places of contact are not essentially different than in many other cities, though they are probably more numerous. The principal section of Chicago's Hobohemia is along West Madison Street, a few blocks west of the river. Here may be found the bulk of the labor exchanges which make of Chicago the greatest hobo labor market in the country. The next important area is South State Street between the loop and Roosevelt Road. A great many of these men live in the lower North Clark Street area. Jefferson Park or "Bum" Park, Union Park, Washington Square or "Bughouse" Square, Grant Park and the docks are also favorite rendezvous for the homeless men, as well as for boys.

Once a boy breaks home ties and gets out on the road he is in company with the tramp most of the time. As we have pointed out, if he is inexperienced, he seeks the company of the tramp who knows the game. A boy and a man may become partners and travel together; however, this is not frequent, for they do not seem to agree. They certainly do not agree very well after the boy has begun to get some confidence in his own ability.

Most boys found in the Hobohemian areas have had experience on the road. Many of them are not Chicago boys, but are only temporarily stopping in the city. Some of the local boys found there are runaways; others live in the neighborhood and are only there to pass the time. Many of them, however, follow some of the street trades such as peddling papers or shining shoes. Some have jobs that take them into these localities. In the South State Street area of Chicago's tramp section there are the cheap burlesque shows and movies that attract many boys.

The Boy's Relations with the Tramp

Not infrequently the tramp is an easy-going, devil-may-care man of pleasing personality. Generally he has the "gift of gab" and likes to be listened to. Out in the country when he has more leisure and can sit with his fellows about the fire he is apt to have a number of the local boys in his audience. The boys make themselves generally useful by giving information about the trains or the police, in gathering wood, furnishing potatoes, water, and such necessities. There is a spirit of fellowship here; a spirit that seldom enters into the relations of the tramp and the boy in town. There is less opportunity in the city where each man faces alone the problem of getting a living. Each man becomes a rank individualist. Partners may cling together a year, but separate when they come to the city.

There are intimate contacts between the tramp and the boy in town, but they are usually relationships that revolve about sex. Sex perversion is very prevalent among the tramp population. How extensive it is cannot be said. Tramps who indulge maintain that "they all do it," while many others feel satisfied that perversion is rare. At least one need not be in the class long before he learns of the existence of the practice, and any boy who has been on the road long without having been approached many times is an exception.

Officer M. F. Kelly, Police Probation Officer with the Juvenile Court, has been especially diligent in apprehending perverts in his district, which includes the South State Street section of Hobohemia. During 1921 he brought before the courts 186 adults on charges of contributing to juvenile delinquency. Out of this number there were 164 convictions and more than 50 percent of these were cases of perversion. This is the record of one man working in one of the homeless man areas. There is, perhaps, an equal amount of homosexuality in the West Madison Street district.

In addition to the comradeship relations and the sex contacts between boys and tramps there are many cases where they associate for economic reasons. That is, a man of the road may exploit a boy or several boys. A "road kid" who has not been away from home very long will find himself being taken advantage of in many ways. Men, on the pretense of being sick, will have boys beg food or money for them. Until they learn to stand alone they will find many persons at hand to share anything they might accumulate. One old man on West Madison Street seldom begs anyone but boys and young men. Another man got money from two boys for a week on the strength of a promise to pilot them west when the weather got warm. They were Chicago boys and planning on going to California. He knew the way. He could get them there "without a scratch." When the spring came and the boys were ready he was missing.

The Boy and the Pervert

Homosexuality is a subject as much talked of and joked about among the tramp population as among men in jails and prisons or the men of the sea. It was in existence centuries before there was a tramp class in this country. Whenever men have been segregated apart from the association of women, whether as soldiers, sailors, or as inmates of penal institutions, there has been sex perversion. The tramp body is such a womanless group, closed out from most ideal associations with women and without the funds to patronize the prostitute.

Given the idea that men must have sex expression in order to be healthy, and this is not more generally believed among the tramps than some other strata of society, and add to this the fact of the absence of women and we have a partial explanation of the practice.[4] The professional prostitutes who do cater to the small purse of the tramp are generally women who have not been able to compete in better paying circles. They are women who have seen their best days and are not even attractive to the average tramp. Thus isolated he must seek elsewhere for his sex expression, which is substantially what all womanless groups have done. He substitutes the boy for the woman.

Says one pervert, who is known among his friends as "Mother" Jones: "I never saw a boy I couldn't get next to." Jones is a man in his fifties. He makes his living by catering to the wants of homosexuals

---

4. We are aware that perversion frequently exists in well-to-do and intellectual circles where there is no sex isolation.

who are willing to pay for it. He plays either the female or the male role. He always dresses well and looks attractive. He spends his time in Grant Park in summer and in the hotel lobbies in winter. He used to be a tramp and while on the road was initiated to the practice. He saw in it a means of livelihood and he left the tramp class.

Many perverts will corroborate "Mother's" statement, but in spite of that it seems to be an exaggeration. Many boys may be potential perverts, but not all boys may be approached with such a proposition. Many boys fear the practice and for that reason resent any such advances. Many boys will not travel in company with men because of their fear of being suspected of having improper relations with them. Boys sometimes travel alone to avoid men, as the following cases illustrate:

> James F. (taken from his narrative). He was loafing in the jungles in Aurora. Some men were cooking food and asked him to join them. He desired to but said that he had to catch a train. He missed the train and came back to the jungles. Dinner was over. One of the men asked him, "Why didn't you stay and eat? You can catch a train here as well as in the yards. Are you hungry? Here take this lunch I put up. I had all I wanted." He gave him three egg sandwiches. "They were still warm."
>
> They loafed around the fire for a while and when the train came going towards Chicago, they all got aboard. The lad and the man who gave him the egg sandwiches got into the same car. There was plenty of straw in the car and when they got in Chicago they decided to remain there for the night.
>
> "Sometimes during the night I woke up and he was trying to roll me over. So that's what you gave me that feed for. You ———, I'm sorry I took it now." The man coaxed him to sleep, but he said he would not sleep any more that night. "I got a club and went over to the other end of the car and lay down."
>
> M. Guy came to Chicago on his way to Texas where his brother lived. He had not tramped much, but was sufficiently familiar with the road to catch trains and ride in a safe place. When asked why he traveled alone he said he "tried to get another kid to go along," but no one was going to Texas. Investigator followed him about the streets and saw two men approach him. One gave him money to get something to eat and watched for him when he came out of the lunch room. Both men tried to get him to go with them, but he went his way. Both advances were made on West Madison Street.
>
> Later when the investigator talked with the boy he admitted that the men wanted him to go to a room. He said that he got rid of one of them by promising to meet him at five o'clock. He said that he had been approached by several men during the two or three weeks that

he was away from home, but he kept out of their way. He was a small, handsome lad of sixteen.

But not all boys take this opposing attitude. Many resent such approaches at first but later yield to them. A case in point is that of Doug.

> (Taken from case record.) He had a fellow tramp arrested in Sacramento, Cal. "He was a wolf and tried to get fresh with me." Later it was found that he was living with two men in a room here in the city. He was serving both of them and one of them was "going 50–50" with him. That is, they would take turns playing the female role. His story was verified by the day clerk of the blank hotel to which the men with whom he had these relations had been forbidden to come. He also talked with a boy.
>
> W. B. is a man, about 21, who is now prostituting himself among the well-to-do perverts. In his teens he ran away from home and fell in with a group of tramps who virtually raped him in a box car. Since then he has become reconciled to the practice and at one time even enticed another boy to leave home. This boy became so attached to him and behaved in such a manner that W. B. was afraid that the police might suspect them so he ran away from the boy. W. B.'s rendezvous is in Grant Park in summer.

Getting into the Game

Granting the pervert his contention that every boy is a potential homosexual, he still faces the problem of getting the boy into a mood and a position where it is safe to make such advances. There are many ways of doing this. If he is a talkative boy it may be done by listening to him and agreeing with him which is indeed flattering. Many men put themselves into the position of a protector, or they may win favor by making presents. Anything serves their purpose that puts the boy under obligation to them. The boy who is away from home without money and who has not the courage to beg is easiest approached and won over.

> This man worked on a boat plying between Chicago and Michigan ports. He met a boy in Michigan who had run away from home and wanted to come to Chicago. He took an interest in the boy and promised to bring him here and help him to get a job. He took him to a hotel on South State Street where he used him for immoral purposes for three days. When he got tired of the boy he turned him over to a Frenchman for the same purposes. The boy and Corrig. were arrested but the Frenchman got away.
>
> He and a boy chum played a great deal in the South State Street area. They met an Italian there who took them to shows and bought

candy for them. He took them behind State Street under the "L" tracks, where he had improper relations with them. This was not the first experience for either boy, but it was the charge under which they were arrested. The Italian was convicted.

In neither of the above cases were the boys forced to submit. They were persuaded after receiving favors. Their yielding was perhaps as much of their own choosing as to please the men.

It must be borne in mind that the pervert is not a popular person even among the tramps. He is not popular in the penal institutions where so much perversion exists. Perverts speak disparagingly of the "wolves" and "jockers" who indulge in these practices, and the boy who is known as a "punk" or a "lamb" or "fairy" has no better status among even the perverts than has a prostitute. This indignation and opposition is more apparent than real. It is the individual's defense. It is probably safe to put this interpretation to most of the claims of perverts who say that their initiation into the practice was a forced one.

One man claims that he was sleeping with a number of tramps in a jungle camp and that he was forced to submit to the group. He is a "wolf" now and whenever he is in town with money to spend he stands on the street corner watching for approachable lads. Before he became a "wolf" and while he was yet a boy tramping about the country he used to put himself in the way of men if he thought it would get him a meal and a bed. It was his way of getting along. Another case in point:

> The investigator spent several days getting acquainted with "Shorty," who is a pervert living on West Madison Street. He claims that he has lived on that street for thirty-nine years. He did leave the street long enough to marry and live with his wife for several years, but for eight years he and his wife have been separated. He is often found in company with some boy. Sometimes he has two or three boys with him. Generally they are boys who have just drifted into town and are loafing about Madison Street. He claims that he has never forced a boy nor has he been brutal to one. He usually wins their esteem by doing favors. He claims there are plenty of boys and it doesn't pay to take a chance. He succeeds best with a boy who is without money and who has not the courage to beg. He is an excellent beggar and he will work hard at odd jobs for a few days until his interest or the interest of the boy wears out.
>
> He tells of being arrested on this account twice, though he has been arrested many times for drunkeness. He was caught with a boy in Sherman Park. They were locked in the same cell and he had relations with him there. Again he was in an alley while submitting to another man. Both were drunk. Each time he was released. He has had many fights over boys.

There are many cases on record of boys having been forced. There would probably be many more, but this is such a delicate subject that boys do not care to appear before a court. The contention is that fewer boys are initiated to the practice by force than is commonly supposed. It cannot be said that a boy was altogether a victim of force if he reconciles himself to the practice and indulges in other clandestine company for months. This is especially true where the boys have reached their late teens and their being together is less liable to arouse suspicion. It is the young boy that the tramp fears to travel with. Once in town these attachments tend to break up and any others that are formed are passing. The fear of being conspicuous is greater in the city and men and boys who are interested in each other will keep apart on the street.

Dangers of Perversion

The greatest danger the pervert faces is that of being ostracized. So long as one is in the tramp class this danger does not worry him. The tramp is not identified with any community or any social group. He is ever surrounded with the cloak of anonymity. Not even arrest reveals his identity. It is not easy to get this class of men into a position where they fear any stigma, for they only need to pass on and start anew elsewhere without reference to their past. Each lives in his own world, and this promise of security is often taken advantage of.

It has been believed that there is less danger of venereal infection from perverted than normal sex practices. This is probably true, but even for the pervert there is no guarantee from infection if he exposes himself. There are many cases on record in our hospitals and dispensaries which assure us that there is no security in perversion. It is not easy for one infected thus to apply for treatment. It is much easier to seek treatment if he can trace his infection to a woman.

The Welfare Agencies

The chief agency that comes into contact with the boy on the road is the police department. The private police come into more frequent contact with boys on the road than do the civil authorities. The special police on the railroad say that the boy tramp is the most difficult problem they have because of his versatility and daring. But the private police seldom bring the boy to the courts. Their jurisdiction ends with the right-of-way; their efforts cease when they have driven these trespassers off the railroad property. Only when they find that a boy or man has stolen or destroyed some property do they venture to arraign him. Where the tramp is only guilty of trespassing their only weapon is to frighten him and at times they even manhandle him. After he has learned to avoid them, the boy on the road does not take the "dicks" seriously. They furnish just enough opposition to make train riding interesting.

The civil police do not make a practice of picking up juveniles unless they are told to look for a certain boy. In such cases many boys are taken in on suspicion. Runaway boys when they come before the authorities are generally brought in by the city police, but a boy tramp may come to Chicago many times without ever being molested unless he disturbs the peace or loafs in a forbidden place. The unusually young boy, because he is conspicuous, is most apt to be taken into custody.

The welfare agencies have many opportunities to come into contact with boys. Often boys who are stranded are referred to these agencies by the police or the citizens. Often boys go to the agencies of their own accord. Some boys make a practice of going from city to city "working" the welfare agencies. Some of these boys are so familiar with the workings of such organizations that they usually know beforehand what questions they will be asked and how best to answer. They have ways and means of learning the kind of treatment each place will give and what is best to ask for.

The missions have more frequent contact with boy tramps than any other type of organization. This may be because in the mission no questions are asked. No record is taken. The audience comes and goes at will. Missions that feed give the food out indiscriminately to whomsoever may be present. In winter the men go to the missions for shelter from the cold as much as to get the food. When they are in need boys will sometimes even become converted, but in this they only imitate the older tramps.

Labor agencies are not supposed to bid for the patronage of boys, but many boys who are able to pass as men buy jobs with long rides thrown in. To go from Chicago to South or North Dakota or Kansas for a fee of two dollars, or to St. Louis or Omaha for the same price is a great temptation. Another temptation is to ship south in the winter time. When the days shorten and the nights get cold the old-timers begin to scan the boards for a job in a warmer clime, and the boy who has never traveled is no less attracted by these offers.

But the man on the street comes closer to the homeless boy than any institution. Among the tramps it is far more honorable to "panhandle," or beg on the "stem," than to go to the welfare agencies, unless the agencies can be "worked." Seldom does the man of the road like to talk about receiving bread in the missions. The mission beggar or "mission stiff" is a very unpopular person in hoboland, and the boy does not care to do anything that will bring him into disrepute. He only goes to the missions when in dire need or when he does not know the stigma attached to such begging. The most creditable kind of begging he can do is "stemming," and he can usually do this better than a man. There is no red tape to "panhandling"; there is when one approaches a welfare agency.

In winter when he cannot sleep outdoors the boy becomes a regular patron of the cheap hotels and rooming houses. In these places he makes many acquaintances and has many opportunities to indulge in the intimacies which we have described. The price of a room in many of these places ranges from twenty to thirty-five cents a night. In some of them the beds are arranged in large rooms in dormitory style and may be had for as low as fifteen cents a night. Also, there are places where the patrons are permitted to sleep on the floor or on bare bunks for ten cents a night. These are called "flop" houses or "scratch" houses and boys frequently find their way into them.

Conclusions and Recommendations

The organizations and institutions described above are a few of those that touch the life of the boy on the road. They should be considered in any program to deal with the problem presented by the boy tramp. Since he is such an elusive and mobile individual it would seem futile for any community to adopt any measures to apply to a problem that is interstate in its dimensions. But there are things that the community can do for its own protection and convenience in handling local boys and boys who drift into town. There are many things that such a center as Chicago, located as it is on so many railroads and highways, can do to halt juvenile tramping.

A single community can take the stand, if it seems advisable, that the contacts boys have with tramps are not desirable and should be prevented as far as practicable. A local community can initiate a movement on the part of the agencies and organizations to prevent such contacts. It may even start an educational campaign that would reach other places.

As the problem has presented itself from this brief study it would seem that the following recommendations are feasible. They are recommendations that are made in the light of the problem as it looms up in Chicago and in terms of the institutional facilities of Chicago, but the problem is not essentially different here than in other large cities. These recommendations fall into three groups: (1) recommendations to prevent boys coming in contact with tramps and becoming tramps; (2) recommendations for handling vagrant and runaway boys; and, (3) recommendations for dealing with boys who have become tramps. These recommendations represent in part the findings of the Committee on Homeless Men of the Chicago Council of Social Agencies.

1. Recommendations to prevent boys coming in contact with tramps and becoming tramps.
   a. An educational campaign should be carried on in all the boys' organizations in Chicago showing the danger of flipping trains and playing in railroad yards. This program should be organized through the Mid-West Boys' Club Federation. The National Defense Council has a good deal of material which could be used in such a campaign.
   b. An effort should be made to secure the cooperation of such organizations as the Brotherhood of Railway Trainmen, the special police organizations of the railroads, the Lake Carriers' Association and automobile clubs in a program to prevent boys wandering away from home. Pamphlets should be prepared for distribution asking for cooperation and the enforcement of working certificates regulations in this and other states, child labor laws, juvenile court laws, etc.
   c. The enlistment officers of the army, navy, and marine corps should demand the presentation of a birth certificate in all cases in which they doubt the age of the applicant.
   d. The cooperation of the managers of the hotels and lodging houses should be sought in an effort to keep boys under seventeen out of the hotels in the Hobohemian areas. At least they should be prevailed upon to use their influence to prevent boys and men from rooming together.
   e. An effort should be made to prevent boys from working or playing in the areas most frequented by the tramp population, namely, West Madison Street, South State Street, North Clark Street and adjacent territory, and some of the parks. The dangers of frequenting these areas should be made known to the parents.
   f. Special plainclothes men should be assigned to the parks and other public places in which the tramps congregate, especially Grant Park. These men should be experienced in dealing with vagrants and should be instructed to pick up and hold in the Detention Home any boy found in company with a tramp, where their behavior is suspicious.
   g. More strenuous effort should be made to occupy the leisure time of boys inclined to visit the districts frequented by tramps. Supervised recreation should be carried on to an extent that these boys will be attracted to other places. When school is not in session a more extensive program of summer camps might help.

2. Recommendations for handling vagrant and runaway boys in Chicago.
   a. The Juvenile Court of Cook County is equipped to investigate the cases of vagrant boys under seventeen and return them to their homes. It is, therefore, recommended that all vagrant boys apprehended by anyone in the daytime should be reported to the Chief Probation Officer.
   b. Vagrant boys apprehended after five o'clock should be turned over to the police who will take them to the Detention Home from where they will be taken to the office of the Chief Probation Officer the following morning.
3. Recommendations for handling vagrant and runaway boys who have already entered the tramp group.
   a. Whenever a boy under seventeen is taken in custody by the police, because of his contact with tramps, or whenever a boy is held as a complaining witness against a tramp he should be reported to the Juvenile Court. It is the responsibility of the court to see that he is put in touch with some proper individual or agency, so that he will be adequately supervised and befriended in the future.

11
An Old Problem in New Form

Migrants Are Marginal People

The problem of the modern migrant is modern only in the sense that it is currently urgent. Something should be done about it. It is, however, no more modern than the problem of technological change, which is modern only in relation to its current phase and the speed with which the changes are now brought about. Today, as always, migrancy and technology have gone hand in hand.

New methods for making a living, new techniques for doing the work of the day, and new tools or machines serve to dislocate people. Whether it be the introduction of money payments for labor in the fourteenth century, which led to Wat Tyler's rebellion, or the inclosures of the sixteenth century, by which little farms in England were turned into sheep pastures and peasants were dispossessed, the causes and consequences had much in common with the current situation. People had to move and work out some other economic adjustment. The process was repeated when the hand factories, using new methods, invaded the ancient guild system and again when machines began to replace hand tools. There have been many such general economic dislocations which resulted in a general shifting and dislocation of the population. The present situation is different only in detail and extent, but it is not different in its general implications.

Whereas the great economic and technological forces may account for mass migrations such as have occurred from time to time, they do not account for all the migration between these periods. Down through the years and the world over, the migrants have been with us. Migrants have gone abroad in prosperous years as well as hard times, for personal reasons as well as because of economic forces. For a review of this phase of the subject, the reader would find much of interest in a

From *Men on the Move* (Chicago: University of Chicago Press, 1940): 41–68. © 1940 by The University of Chicago.

monumental work by Charles J. Ribton-Turner, *A History of Vagrants and Vagrancy and Beggars and Begging*, published in 1887.

Whether migrancy is brought about by such natural forces as droughts, floods, or whether change or because of economic conditions or whether migrancy is the result of social change, the people called on to move are confronted with difficulty. Go where they will, they receive no welcome, unless they are fortunate enough to find a land frontier.

About 1348 Europe was visited by the Black Death, and in some places up to 50 percent of the population died. Most of those who died were poor people; thus there was created in some sections a labor shortage. Prices and wages rose, and bound men were wont to leave their masters. A law was passed by Parliament to prevent people from wandering about. There were social as well as economic reasons for the Ordinances of Labourers of 1349. The resident people were afraid of the wanderers, and the masters wanted to prevent their workers from leaving for higher wages.

Depressions and migrancy have appeared together often, which may explain why the Ordinances of Labourers in England were confirmed or modified from time to time, usually when circumstances stimulated people to start wandering. At times the Ordinances were used to keep people at home. That was when the workers in good times wandered in search of better-paying jobs. At times the Ordinances were used to send people back home. That was when they could not find work in their home parishes and wandered in search of jobs, begging along the way.

These Ordinances and laws passed in England were in time repeated in the United States when resident people in the communities felt they needed safeguards against too many indigent strangers coming around. In early Colonial times, for example, an ordinance was passed in New York City which required householders not to give lodging to strangers, especially sailors, without so reporting to the proper officials.

In those times when the migrant was the immigrant, there were no regulations for the bringing-in of aliens. One of the first efforts to deal with this problem was "A Law to Prevent Strangers from Being a Charge to This Corporation," an ordinance of New York City passed in 1731. The purpose was to bring under control the masters of ships who indiscriminately brought in their passengers and dumped them on American shores. The law required an accounting of these passengers, thus to prevent the influx of alien dependents.

Ten years before the above ordinance was passed, the colony of New

York passed its first poor law. One of the objectives of the law was to control the migration of indigent persons or families. This law was revised in 1788 and titled "An Act for the Better Settlement and Relief of the Poor." As reported by David M. Schneider in his *History of Public Welfare in New York State*, the purpose was to prevent the transiency of indigents. The constable of the town was charged with the task of passing the migrant back to his last residence. If such an indigent returned, he was to be whipped, "if a man, not exceeding 39 lashes, and if a woman, not exceeding 25 lashes, and so as often as he or she shall return" (Schneider, 113).

New York's settlement and relief law of 1788, however cruel, was far more humane than the laws of early England from which it was derived. We quote from the vagrancy law of 1531 (22 Henry VIII, c. 12); wherein it was written that when vagrants or idle persons were arrested they would be taken to the court. If found guilty, they were to be taken to the marketplace,

> and there to be tied to the end of a cart naked and be beated with whips through the same market town or other place till his body is bloody by reason of such whipping; and after such punishment and whipping had, the person so punished . . . shall be enjoined upon his oath to return forthwith to the place where he was born or where he last dwelled before the same punishment by the space of three years, and there put himself to labour as a true man oweth to do.

In that old ordinance can be seen the roots, not only of early American laws for dealing with strangers, but the antecendents of present-time "border patrols," three-year-residence laws, and severe "passing-on" policies. But the American civilization had to feed on the migration of strangers. From the Atlantic Seaboard, over the eastern mountains, across the plains, and beyond the western mountains, building up the nation had to wait on the migrants. They were brought in and absorbed except here and there and in general were needed except in periods of economic depression.

Just as migrancy was essential to the growth and expansion of the American civilization in good times, it was the source of embarrassment in hard times, when people followed the same roads which were temporarily barren of opportunity. Under such circumstances the migrants were marginal people, circulating about the country but for the time not a part of its economy. Migrants who might have been very welcome at other times were very unwelcome during those periods when they were surplus.

Generally, in the development period of the American civilization, especially in the eastern states, a good share of the surplus migrants were immigrants. There were times when skilled workers from abroad were in great demand, but unskilled workers were not so much in demand, unless they could find the guidance and means for getting inland. Emigrant societies were formed for the guidance of these groups. One such organization was the Shamrock Society, which in 1817 (Schneider, 138) issued a pamphlet for unskilled workers.

> There are not many of the laborious classes, whom we would advise to reside or loiter in the great towns, because as much will be spent during a long winter as can be made through a toilsome summer, so that a man may be kept a moneyless drudge for life. But this is not perhaps the worst; he is tempted to become a tippler, by the cheapness and plenty of liquors, and then his prospects are blasted forever.

These societies, in behalf of the immigrants, pressed Congress to open the unsold public lands. Largely as a result of this pressure for settlement Congress passed the Pre-emption Act of 1841, which provided for the purchase of public lands at reasonably low rates, and the Homestead Act of 1862, which opened up vast areas of the public domain for settlement. Many of the immigrants passed on through the eastern ports of entry to the open frontier to occupy vacant lands or to take part in building up the new industries.

From time to time there were periods of unemployment. Families and individuals who normally would have gone their way without notice became temporary relief cases. But generally these seasons of economic distress passed. During the unemployment period following the Civil War the larger eastern cities were temporarily distressed with the influx of great numbers of persons seeking work; it was also claimed that the soup kitchens, bread lines, and shelters were being preyed upon by the hordes of "vagrants, bummers, and revolvers."

Then came the crisis of 1873 when for five years unemployment again enveloped the land. Again there were the soup kitchens, the bread lines, and the shelters. Again the unemployed from the towns and villages flocked to the cities or migrated from city to city. Thousands of immigrant families and individuals wandered from state to state or were "passed on" by the civil authorities and welfare agencies from one city to another. Those who had been encouraged to migrate inland tried to return to the Eastern Seaboard. Many immigrants who had landed in New York for employment in the factory towns of New England were shipped back to New York. But this period of migrancy, job hunting, and poverty passed, and again there was a shortage of labor. The roads to opportunity were again cleared, and there was employment in the industrial cities. The frontier opened wider, and thousands of homeseekers and job seekers turned inland following the roads into the new country.

The first coast-to-coast depression came in 1893, when the roads to opportunity were again closed, when again an economic drought settled over the whole country. Thousands of families who were known as workers or settlers the previous year suddenly became unemployed migrants or vagrants. Resident people again set up the barriers. The migrant again became the marginal man, not needed around and noticed mainly because he was in the way. Soup kitchens, "potato patch" projects, make-work programs by private charity, and other temporary but inadequate services were resorted to. In most communities again the police power was invoked, and families were passed on, told to return to the places from whence they came, or were not permitted to come into town.

Thousands of disemployed persons or families migrated from town to city or from city to city or set out for the West without finding anything there and returned again to the East. This was the first depression in which a great transcontinental movement of jobless men was known, and about that migration more will be said in a moment.

Pattern of Frontier Expansion

At this point we turn our attention to some of the pertinent elements of the extension of American civilization. These are as pertinent now as they were in previous depressions. In response to certain dominant social and economic forces the frontier expansion appears to have developed as a pattern. The trails that grew into roads turned out in some cases to become broad highways. These highways and roads, when studied in relation to one another, appear to have developed as they were used differently in the development of the frontier.

It was no accident, for example, that the bulk of the early migration to California followed the middle course over the states. Nor is it merely coincidental that the bulk of the migration to California today moves over the southern route followed by the Joad family, as portrayed in Steinbeck's *The Grapes of Wrath*. Migrant men made up the work gangs so necessary in the westward spread of industry, but this migration was across the northern half of the United States. For many years the so-called slave market cities, where the migratory workers found their job shipments, were northern cities: Cleveland, Chicago, Minneapolis, Omaha, Kansas City, Denver, Salt Lake City, Seattle, and Portland.

In this northern section the building of railroads, the growth of the lumber industry, mining, and manufacturing moved faster than in the southern half of the United States. It was the northern tier of states that was most in the news during the depression of 1893. That was the zone of the great strikes, the marches of the jobless, the emergency relief programs, and distress among dislodged people.

William H. Yarbrough studied the relation of slavery to the westward migration of the southern states. He has shown that the migration in the southern half of the United States was different in several respects from that of the northern half. It was a nonindustrial migration. It was, moreover, a migration in which the emigrants from abroad had very little part. White people as workers did not figure greatly in the westward expansion in the South. White mechanics, unable to compete with slave labor, migrated to the North rather than to some slave state farther west.

We have heard how Daniel Boone moved westward when he could no longer stand in his doorway and shoot a deer. When small farmers moved in, he moved away. Most of the small farmers who followed the frontiersmen into Kentucky and Tennessee were economic refugees from the Piedmont states east of the mountains. In the Carolinas, Virginia, or Maryland they had been cotton and tobacco growers, but when those crops depleted the soil they migrated to find more productive soil (Yarbrough, 5–7).

Some of the small farmers who migrated from the settled states over the mountains were slaveowners, but most of them did not own slaves. They were frontier farmers who lived by their own labor, and they moved from the Piedmont region because they could no longer survive against the plantation economy. The land they were forced to abandon was soon taken over and added to the plantations. The planters, some of them owning as many as three hundred slaves, continued to grow cotton and tobacco and to deplete the soil. They did not know how to fertilize the land or did not care. Perhaps land was too cheap. These planters soon encountered difficulty, but their slave population was increasing, and they managed for years to balance their budgets by selling surplus slaves.

Slaves marketed by the planters were shipped over the mountains into the developing western and southwestern regions, where new plantations were rapidly being formed. Some planters with their slaves also migrated. The farmers who followed the frontiersmen were forced again to sell and move. The farmer economy was again overwhelmed by the plantation economy. If the small farmer who lived by his own labor did not move farther west, he escaped to the North. In this way, in three waves of settlement and development, the agricultural economy of the South continued westward until it reached the Great Plains where the slave economy could not survive. From that point on to the

Former slave and his wife sitting on the steps of a crumbling plantation house, Greene County. (Photo: Farm Security Administration, by Lange.)

West Coast the country was taken over mainly by great ranches for cattle or sheep. It was not developed by small farmers.

Such was the southern pattern of settlement. It was different in the North where the small, self-sustaining farm was typical. Slave labor so cheapened all labor in the South that it was difficult for craftsmen and mechanics to live there. Most of these people migrated also, many of them to the North. Hence there was in the southern half of the nation a great dearth of competent labor, which was not conducive to industrial development and not inviting to skilled migrants (Yarbrough, p. 61).

Thus in the western expansion there were in the United States two frontiers, two systems of economy, and two patterns of migration. The southern pattern, while it changed somewhat with the passing of slavery, was sufficiently well established to retain its distinct character for at least three more decades. The North and the West developed differently, and in those regions migrating labor continued in demand. When periods of unemployment came it was in the North or the West where the bread lines formed and where the roads were lined with migrants.

The westward migration in the northern half of the United States was also characterized by waves. This is illustrated in the migrations of the Mormons. Many of the founders of the church in New York were people who migrated westward from Massachusetts or Vermont. From New York the Mormons moved to Ohio. The roads they followed were the same over which many other families and individuals traveled to Ohio or Indiana. Next they went to the Mississippi Valley and finally over the plains and mountains to the Great Basin. The Mormons were not trailblazers. They followed beaten roads and continued to do so until they arrived at their place of final settlement.

It was the western migration of the northern half of the United States that overflowed most rapidly, stimulated largely by the great influx of immigrants and the development of industry. The booming of industry in these states tended to attract migrants from the South, and the routes that tapped the regions below the Mason and Dixon Line were mainly roads to the North, not to the West.

This observation is pertinent to the present discussion because now at last there is a westward movement from the southern states. Here is a new phase of migration, and, while it is not the entire problem of migration, it is the most immediate and challenging phase. For the first time, California, a state that has always had a migrancy problem, is concerned about migrants from Texas, Oklahoma, Arkansas, Louisiana. In these states the small farmers are being dispossessed by natural forces or by mechanized farming with the same relentless insistence that southern farmers of two generations ago were dispossessed by the plantation-slave economy. There was new land to go to then, but there is no new land waiting for them now.

March of "Coxey's Army"

On March 25, 1894, Easter Sunday, an aggregate of unemployed men gathered at Massillon, Ohio, to begin a march to the nation's capital to ask the president and Congress to launch a program of public works. It was then a radical idea to ask the government to appropriate funds for public roads, and it was much more shocking for such a request to come from the ranks of the unemployed.

This group of jobless men, enlisted under the banner of the "Commonweal of Christ," was led by Jacob S. Coxey, who still lives and who was then a well-to-do contractor of Massillon. For some time prior to the march Coxey had been making speeches and gaining support for his proposal for a federal bond issue to build roads. The time had come for something more substantial. He would take to Washington "a petition in boots."

"General" Coxey with his "army" started something which was then as disturbing to the nation as the present influx of "Oakies" and "Texies" is to the residents of California.

In 1850, the year of greatest gold-rush migration to the "diggings" of California, no less than fifty thousand persons, mostly men, crossed the country to share in the wealth of that great bonanza hunt. Hundreds died en route. Some found gold, but all who reached the West found work. The country stirred with visions of prosperity. Coxey's march was the antithesis. Jobless men were returning over the same roads.

Never before or since has there been such a demonstration of the unemployed. For days and weeks "General" Coxey and his migrant band were front-page news. As the army proceeded from town to town, en route east, it was met by crowds of the curious or greeted by marching committees of the unemployed. In some cases they were escorted through town by the police.

As the news of Coxey's march reached the western cities, crowded with unemployed workers, the country began to hear of other armies and of other leaders calling themselves "General." Within a few weeks, mainly from the states west of the Mississippi, companies and battalions of men took to the road, walking or riding the trains, bound for Washington to join the "petition in boots." Literally thousands of men who had migrated to the West to the lumber camps, the mines, or the construction camps, now turned their faces eastward on a determined mass job hunt.

From California came two armies of "industrials." "General" Charles T. Kelly, with fifteen hundred men, left San Francisco on April 1, 1894. The other, commanded by "General" Lewis C. Fry, left earlier from Los Angeles with eight hundred men. Lesser aggregates emerged from other frontier states: Oregon, Washington, Idaho, Montana. As far as police and public officials were concerned, the country was confronted with a problem in mass vagrancy. The railroads called for protection when bands of a hundred men or more took possession of freight trains. In Utah the railroads demanded police or military aid to clear the freight trains. Public officials replied in effect: "You brought these men here. After we have fed them, you will take them away again." So in every division point along the lines, railroad officials had to bow to public officials. No town cared to fill its jails with unwanted "industrials."

Most of the homeless men converging with so much ado on Washington from all points west had traveled those routes previously without being noticed. During the prosperity years they had migrated toward the frontier, "bumming" their way on the freight trains, but they went singly or in small groups. Their moving caused no alarm. They were not then a foraging mob but were accepted as migrating workers going where work had to be done.

In his book *Coxey's Army* Donald L. McMurry reminds us that the marchers who traveled under direction of Coxey, Fry, Kelly, Galvin, or other leaders were in the main orderly and respectful. The semimilitary character of the groups served to exclude those characters not amenable to discipline. Nonetheless, the people in the towns through which the bands passed were uneasy. While respecting generally the avowed good purposes of the marchers, they were relieved to see them move on. The *Pittsburgh Press* printed the following under a cartoon, a fair reflection of what many thought:

> Hark Hark! Hear the dogs bark!
> Coxey is coming to town.
> In his ranks are scamps,
> And growler-fed tramps,
> On all of whom workingmen frown.

"General" Charles T. Kelly, en route from San Francisco, was forced to go into camp for several days at Des Moines. It was with this contingent that the novelist and reporter Jack London traveled and concerning which he has written. We are informed also by McMurry in his story of Coxey that the students of Drake University at Des Moines interviewed a good share of Kelly's "industrials" (McMurry, 187–89). The students questioned 763 men as to their nationality and found that 549, or 72 percent, were American born, a higher percentage of natives than could have been found among the adult males of the frontier states. From the *Iowa State Register* for May 4, 1894, McMurry has included the following additional information regarding the findings of the study made by the students from Drake:

> Of the foreign-born, two-fifths came from the British Isles or British colonies, and more than a fourth from Germany. Most of the remainder were from western Europe, the list being completed by three Poles, one Russian, one Greek, one Turk, and one from the Argentine Republic. Eighty-three trades and occupations were represented among the 425 men examined who claimed to have any, the miners being more numerous than those of any other occupation. As to politics; 240 were Populists, 218 were Republicans, 196 were Democrats, 81 were undecided, and 11 were independents. There were 358 Protestants and 280 Catholics with 114 who said they had no religion. The average time since the men had been last employed was six months.

Perhaps it was not surprising that so many of Kelly's army were Populists, although the Populist party had not yet been in existence two years. The Coxey crusade, his "Commonweal of Christ," with its program for public works, was quite in harmony with the share-the-wealth purposes of populism. Why disemployed, homeless workers should lean toward this brand of politics is understandable from the following excerpt from the Populist platform, adopted at the first national convention of the party, which met at Omaha, Nebraska, July 4, 1892:

> We meet in the midst of a nation brought to the verge of moral, political and material ruin. Corruption dominates the ballot-box, the legislatures, the Congress, and touches even the ermine of the bench. The people are demoralized. . . . The newspapers are largely subsidized or muzzled; public opinion silenced; business prostrated; our homes covered with mortgages; labor impoverished; and the land concentrated in the hands of capitalist. . . . The fruit of the toil of millions is boldly stolen to build up colossal fortunes for the few, unprecedented in the history of mankind; and the possessors of these, in turn, despise the republic and endanger liberty. From the same prolific womb of governmental injustice are bred the two great classes of tramps and millionaires.

While "commonwealers" continued their march toward Washington, a number of the lesser groups became disorganized before reaching the seat of government. Many a migrant, after breaking away from one or another of the bands, went his way to Washington alone. The groups began arriving in May and June, having started most of them in February and March. Coxey entered the capital with banners flying. The town was his for the day until he attempted to present his petition to Congress. He was arrested as a trespasser on the Capitol grounds and for disorderly conduct. His army readily demobilized itself. Prosperity very soon provided jobs for all.

During the months when the thousand commonwealers were riding the freight trains or marching the highways toward the East, there was great uneasiness in the land. Had the panic of 1893 continued much longer, it is not unlikely that certain states, if not many, would have tried to stop the marchers at their borders as certain states did following the panic of 1929. But the 1893 depression was brief. The migrants found work and very soon were circulating as before to all parts of the nation.

Migrancy and the Road

Coxey's army was made up of disemployed workers who had originally gone into the West as frontier industrial workers. It was their sudden unemployment that transferred them from the work army to the army of the Commonweal. Like the soldiers mustered out in the wars of the Middle Ages, they turned homeward, foraging on the country as they went. They returned over the same routes whereon they had previously traveled to the West. They traveled the same routes that are traversed by the migrants of today.

This observation is generally true of migrants; they follow the well-used routes, and in this country there are definite roads over which the bulk of the migrants move. Most of this movement is to the East or to the West. There are three general routes between the North and South. One of these up-and-down routes follows the Atlantic Seaboard, reaching from the southeastern states to New England. The second route follows north and south along the valley of the Mississippi. The third route reaches from border to border along the Pacific Coast. Most of the east-west migration crosses the northern tier of states.

Another observation regarding the march of Coxey's army concerns the speed with which the contingents traveled. They were a generation of migrants who learned to use a new mode of transportation. When the "Bonus Army" marched on Washington in 1932, there was a repetition of the exploit of the Commonweal. Great numbers of veterans piled on trains and set out for the nation's capital. The migration of the bonus marchers was speedy and less interfered with than the march of the Commonweal. The bonus marchers had the added advantage of another mode of travel, the automobile, which was not available in 1894.

American migrancy had always been responsive to changes in the modes of travel. It had been said that the character and extent of the vagrancy problem are determined by existing modes of travel. The minstrels, craftsmen, even the scholars and beggars of the Middle Ages who wandered the highways encompassed in their travels very small areas. It was the railroad that helped take the migrant off the wagon road in the period of our westward expansion. The migrant responded to the railroad as readily as he is now responding to the new mode of transportation, the automobile, by which he is being changed from a railroad to a highroad traveler.

The transfer from boxcar to automobile is not by any means complete. Many migrants still ride the freights or the blind baggage. Some alternate between train riding and hitchhiking. The important implication is that today the migrant is more mobile than ever before. He has more facilities for travel, and more places are made easily accessible to him.

Another consideration which reflects the influence of the new facilities for travel relates to the increase of families and women migrants. While the number of unattached female migrants does not exceed 3

Migrant, old style—the "bundle stiff," a vanishing species. (Photo: Farm Security Administration, by Lange.)

percent of the single migrants, that is a much greater proportion of women than could have been found among the migrants in the palmiest days of the boxcar hobos. But the automobile has also helped to detach families. It has facilitated a considerable amount of family migrancy that was not possible before (see map).

There is a fourth consideration which concerns the realism of American people respecting travel. Even the untraveled American has extensive information about the roads that converge in his community. He knows where each road leads and what may be found at the other end. It is true that some families still migrate to California, expecting to

Migrants, new style—called by some "rubber tramps" because they travel on tires. (Photo: Farm Security Administration, by Lange.)

find there plenty of work and good wages, country boys still migrate cityward expecting to get rich, but these cases are not typical. The average American gets over the road without much difficulty, and when the sum total of all migrations is considered it develops that the flow of travel tends to be from the areas of least advantage to areas of more advantage.

Most efficient of migrants in his heyday was the hobo who moved with ease from state to state, sometimes traveling thousands of miles in a year. He managed to get around whether he had cash or not. That tradition appears still to be with us, in fact road-mindedness assumes the proportions of an institution of the American civilization. The aver-

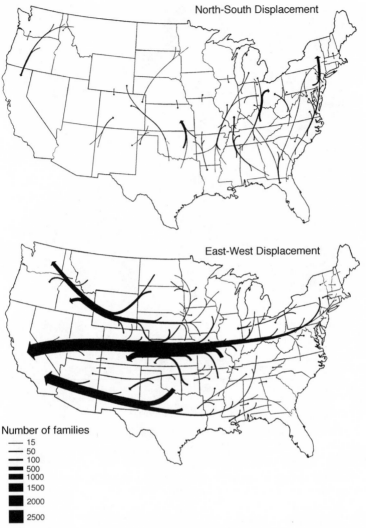

Net displacement of migrant families, 30 June 1935. Net interchange of fewer than fifteen families between states excluded. Source: Division of Transient Activities, Quarterly Census of Transients under Care (Washington, D.C.: Federal Emergency Relief Administration, 30 June 1935).

age adult in this country knows that the road in front of his door leads to any other door in any other state, and it is no great adventure for him to break loose.

E. G. Ravenstein, in 1885 and again in 1889, published the findings of his studies of migration for England and Continental Europe. He con-

TABLE 1

Distance Traveled	Percent
400 miles or less	38
401–1,500 miles	40
1,501–2,100 miles	19
2,101 miles or more	3

ceived certain "Laws of Migration," of which one of the principal generalizations was that people who move are more likely to travel short distances than long distances. The implication is that people migrate for practical reasons, and the extent of their migrancy is also determined by practical considerations. They travel known routes rather than strange routes (Ravenstein 1889) and to places with which they are somewhat familiar rather than to strange places.

Webb and Brown, in their study *Migrant Families,* found some confirmation for the Ravenstein thesis respecting distance traveled. For the families studied at the federal transient shelters they found the distribution in percentages for distances migrated as shown in table 1.

Distances are greater in the United States than in the countries studied by Ravenstein. Roads are better and longer here, and the facilities for travel are more advanced. Although the distances of migration today in this country are relatively greater, Ravenstein's observations still appear to have some applicability.

According to the report of the Federal Transient Service for the first quarter of 1935, a total of 293,716 cases received shelter in the camps and stations of all states where the federal program was in operation. This figure included both individual cases and families.

Tables 2 and 3 show the sources of migrants for two of the top states reported in the census of migrants in federal shelters for the first quarter of 1935. For these two states are shown the ten states from which the largest number of migrants have been received. They also show the number of migrants in the states reported who came from California or from New York.

While many Oklahomans went to California, not many migrants from California were located in Oklahoma. It should be noted that nearby states contributed in greater proportion to their population than far states. Table 3 gives similar information regarding migrants reported in New York.

According to table 2, California received about 35 migrants for each 10 who migrated from California. Table 3 shows that New York received 16 migrants for each 14 who migrated elsewhere. Also, California received 1,660 migrants from New York, while only 526 migrants

TABLE 2

State	No. of Migrants to California	No. of Migrants from California
Oklahoma	3,944	211
Texas	3,107	679
Washington	2,113	1,198
Missouri	2,050	439
Illinois	1,989	589
New York	1,660	526
Oregon	1,644	767
Colorado	1,524	570
Arizona	1,318	661
Ohio	1,216	658
Total migrants in California, quarter ending March 31, 1935	35,288	. . .
Total California migrants in other states, same date	. . .	10,255

TABLE 3

State	No. of Migrants to New York	No. of Migrants from New York
Pennsylvania	2,724	2,617
New Jersey	1,602	893
Massachusetts	1,233	427
Ohio	1,013	1,216
Illinois	797	802
Connecticut	692	450
Michigan	584	292
California	526	1,660
Virginia	384	249
Maryland	269	435
Total migrants in New York, quarter ending March 31, 1935	16,244	. . .
Total New York migrants in other states, same date	. . .	14,229

from California were reported in New York. Similar analyses for other states based on the same source of information bear out this observation—that the greater volume of the cross-country movement is westward.

According to the Federal Transient Service census for the first quarter of 1935, Texas had received 9 migrants for each 12 migrants from Texas reported in other states. On the basis of total population in the states of origin, the greater proportion of the migrants from elsewhere found in Texas came from the southern states. These migrants were moving westward over southern routes or moving southwestward mainly from the central states.

Concerning the Number of Migrants

Nobody knows how many migrants there are in the United States. This has ever been the case. There have always been estimates, but these have not been in very close agreement. Perhaps there are at present a million people on the move. That would depend on which classes of moving people would be classified as migrants.

According to the 1930 census, 25,400,000 native-born Americans were living in states other than the states of their birth. Many of these have lived in several states since leaving their places of birth. Some moved only recently, others several years or many years ago. Some moved in poverty, others in relative security. This means that in a generation about 20 percent of the people have migrated. Many of these people now living in their states of birth have from time to time lived in other states. Possibly as many as 50 percent of the people in this country have lived in other states than those in which they now reside. This would, of course, include the 14,200,000 persons of foreign birth, for these people are also migratory.

John N. Webb of the Work Projects Administration has estimated that about 2,000,000 workers cross state lines each year in search of jobs. How much migration would that amount to? How many of these workers migrated with their families?

The 1939 *Report* for the Social Security Board in the section on old age insurance contains information regarding the 30,000,000 workers employed in 1937 in the industries covered by the law. During that year, according to the records of the board, 2,155,207 workers in the covered industries crossed state lines to other jobs. While many of these interstate moves did not include a change of residence, it is apparent that the amount of migration is great, even if half the number reported merely commuted over state lines, as, for example, from Kansas City, Kansas, to Kansas City, Missouri, or from New York City to Jersey City.

Of the millions of people who travel or migrate over state lines each year, the percentage not self-supporting must be small and would probably include about half of the 2,000,000 estimated by Webb as the annual number of interstate worker migrants.

On March 22, 1933, the Committee on Care of Transient and Homeless, which committee was made up of representatives of agencies giving service to migrants, conducted a one-day census. This enumeration

TABLE 4

Persons sheltered in private agencies	. . .	120,798
Salvation Army	40,189	. . .
Young Men's Christian Association	3,580	. . .
Travelers' Aid Societies	1,142	. . .
Jewish Welfare Agencies	959	. . .
Young Women's Christian Association	808	. . .
Other private agencies	74,120	. . .
Persons sheltered in public agencies	. . .	32,914
Jails and police stations	11,487	. . .
Other public shelters	21,427	. . .
Persons in poverty camps or without shelter	. . .	33,697
Shantytowns	15,658	. . .
Jungles, boxcars, etc.	18,039	. . .
Persons included in 3,155 homeless families (these include families receiving case-work care from public or private agencies and are not otherwise counted)		14,187
Total		201,596

was conducted by volunteers in private agencies in 765 cities and towns. At that time the public agencies were not very active. The count is shown in table 4.

In addition to the 201,596 who were counted in 765 towns and cities on March 22, 1933, how many others were not counted? Thousands in the same cities were living by begging on the streets. Who can estimate how many on that date were riding the freight trains or moving over the highways in their dilapidated automobiles?

There have been other estimates. For example, Mayor Frank L. Shaw of Los Angeles, speaking to the Conference of Mayors at Washington on November 16, 1937, said: "Today it is probable that somewhere between 500,000 and 600,000 persons, including many family groups, are wandering through the country without ample means of support." The mayor of that city so harassed by migrants spoke of the plight of the children of the homeless families, but he also implied that a good share of the migrants had criminal records, a generalization not confirmed by other reports.

Viewed in the most practical terms, the overall number of migrants is probably not the major consideration. The challenge of this problem is in relation to spots. If California gets 200,000 migrants, most of them in family groups, and these are concentrated in certain areas, the immediate problem may be very acute. It is a problem involving work and wages and the tensions relating thereto. It is a problem of health, of education, and of relief. Each year at certain spots in California,

Arizona, and Texas the residents see the gathering of the migrants. A thousand migrant workers arriving in a locality where only 500 jobs may be had offers many possibilities of misunderstanding and conflict.

The tension spots at the moment are in agriculture, on the Pacific Coast, in the South, along the Atlantic Seaboard. Some years ago the tension spot for migratory-labor conflict was in the lumbering industry of the Northwest or in the wheat belt of the Midwest. There are more such problem areas now than ever before in the American labor market, and the situation for the migrant is serious, because whichever way he turns he finds there are already too many other migrants. The road leads nowhere.

12
The Unattached Migrant

Migratory-Casual Workers

When the federal government in 1933 assumed partial responsibility for extending financial aid to the staggering and overloaded relief programs in the states, provision was made for transient care. In September of that year the Federal Transient Bureau was established. This program for migrants, of which more will be said in a later chapter, continued in operation for two years. In addition to whatever benefits were received by the migrants from the Federal Transient Program, it was the source of considerable new information about the problem.

Every month, once the program got under way, a census was taken of the persons under care in 13 selected centers. In these federal shelters approximately 25,000 cases received service each month. John N. Webb has compiled from this source considerable information about migrants not before available. For example, it was news to learn how few of the migrants were seasonable hobos. Of the single migrants he found

57 percent had been migrating less than 6 months,
19 percent had been migrating from 6 months to 1 year,
12 percent had been migrating from 1 to 3 years,
12 percent had been migrating more than 3 years.

Less than 10 percent of the unattached persons (Webb, *Transient Unemployed*, 118) could be classified as "constant" migrants, and this percentage did not increase from month to month, which appears to support the conclusion that most "depression" migrants gave up their migrancy after a period of a few months.

As a sample study Webb selected 500 cases of seasonal workers. These were of the hobo type and were described by him as "migratory-casuals." They were selected on the basis of (1) their distribution

From *Men on the Move* (Chicago: University of Chicago Press, 1940): 69–98. © 1940 by The University of Chicago.

TABLE 1

Seattle, Wash.	90	Jacksonville, Fla.	24
Denver, Colo.	79	Kansas City, Mo.	21
Memphis, Tenn.	62	New Orleans, La.	20
Minneapolis, Minn.	61	Boston, Mass.	17
Los Angeles, Calif.	56	Chicago, Ill.	12
Dallas, Tex.	30	Pittsburgh, Pa.	4
Phoenix, Ariz.	24	Total	500

among the 13 cities, and (2) their lines of employment. There were 200 migrant agricultural workers, 100 migrants of industry, and 200 who worked in both agriculture and industry. The cities from which they were selected and the numbers are shown in table 1.

These migratory casuals were most numerous in the West and Southwest. The purpose of the study was to learn how they lived and how their way of life was compared with that of the short-time, short-distance, or amateur migrants. The main distinction was that the migrant seasonal or casual worker had established a pattern or habit; perhaps it might be called a technique for getting about with less lost motion.

Webb concluded that the chronic migrant is the product of a complex of factors: the economic forces without and the personal qualities within which tend to keep him on the move. He found some to be of the militant type who feel their condition is due to the malfunctioning of the economic system. Others proved to be apathetic workers who drift gradually from regular to casual employment (*Migratory-Casual Worker*, p. xvi). Others appear to be moved by what Webb might have called "wanderlust": "Perhaps it can only be said that, in general, it is essential to the migratory-casual worker that he move, that no one environment claim him long, that scenes be new and persons different. These desires, expressed or only vaguely felt, are the core of his existence and the governor of his activity."

The 500 migratory-casuals reported for the whole number a minimum employment in winter of 600 man-weeks per month and a maximum employment of 1,200 man-weeks in July of each year. For the period covered by the interviews, 1933 and 1934, these men reported the average length of job as two months. About half of the men found their jobs within one state, one-fourth found their jobs in two states. About half of the 500 workers had crossed 1–10 state lines during the two years. An average of 41 weeks out of each year had been spent in the migratory work or travel.

Migratory agricultural workers employed in packing houses at Homestead, Florida. These young migrants came from Tennessee and Alabama. (Photo: Farm Security Administration, by Post.)

TABLE 2

Group	1933	1934
The agricultural migrants	$110	$124
The industrial migrants	257	272
Those in agriculture and industry	223	203

Webb found that the reported annual earnings of the migratory-casuals were low, but they were no doubt in excess of the sums earned by the less experienced migrants (table 2).

If the earnings as shown here are computed for the year in terms of daily income, the result is shocking, ranging from 30 to 75 cents per day. It was obviously less for the occasional migrants not so expert in getting from job to job.

During 1933 and 1934 the 500 workers reported a total of 2,297 jobs, which totaled 21,128 man-weeks of employment. Of the total jobs held,

TABLE 3

Group	Median Age (Years)	Percentage 45 Years and Over
Unattached transients	27–30	12–16
500 migratory-casual workers	37	29
Local homeless persons	42–45	40–49

957 were in agriculture, 433 in industry, and 907 were of the combination type. The principal sources of agricultural employment were cotton, fruit, grain, sugar beets, vegetables, and berry picking. The principal sources of industrial employment were construction, logging, gas and oil, railroad maintenance, and mining.

Approximately one-half of the migratory-casuals had been on the road 10 years or more, 12 percent had been migrants from 15 to 20 years, and 18 percent had been migrants 20 years or more. Webb found the different homeless types differed greatly in their ages (*Transient Unemployed*, p. 29), as shown in table 3.

Regarding color and nativity, 77 percent of the 500 migratory-casuals were native white, 8 percent were foreign-born white, 5 percent were Negroes, 9 percent were Mexicans, and 1 percent were of other groups.

Two Migratory-Casuals

Webb included in his report a number of case stories of migratory-casuals showing their year-after-year movement from job to job—agriculture, lumbering, construction, fishing (*Migratory-Casual Worker*, pp. 91–92). The "Autobiography of John McClosky" begins in Illinois in 1889. He was one of five children. His father was a coal miner, horse trader, fish peddler, and handy man.

In 1893 McClosky's mother died. The father migrated with his children to Seattle, Washington. He bought a small farm near Bellingham, and there it was that the boy John learned to work. He labored in the fields and helped his father chop stove wood, which they hauled to town and peddled from door to door.

But John wanted work that was less arduous and more exciting. He got a job as bellboy in Bellingham. Next he worked as a Western Union messenger. That bored him, and he ran away. Here Webb quotes McClosky:

> I went to Seattle and got a job as deckboy on steamship that went to San Francisco. I got paid off there, got taken in by sights of the big city. Came to my senses, my boat had sailed. I had 5¢ left in my

pocket. I spent it for a newspaper and looked through the ads. Porter wanted, restaurant. Convinced the boss I could do the work. $5 a week and board. Stayed there 10 days, had fight with cook, got fired.

Got a job on a steamer to San Diego. Worked 3 months then quit. Got a job in a family hotel in San Francisco as bellboy, stayed about 3 weeks and got fired for pulling a boner. Went back to San Diego. Left after short time. Got job in Hotel San Rafael, San Francisco, bellboy $15 per month.

About this time I began to think of home for the first time. After 4 weeks I wrote home. Dad had moved to near Blaine, Washington, on 40 acres of unimproved land. Headed for home. Went to Aberdeen on a lumber schooner, Seattle on train, to Blaine on the boat.

John could not be domesticated so readily. Jobs were easy to get. A few months at home, and he hied himself to Seattle, thence to a logging camp, and back to Seattle to spend his "pile." Occasionally, he went home to stay a week or so; then he was gone again.

I finally got work in a shingle mill near my father's ranch. I worked there in the woods cutting shingle bolts, and learning to saw and pack shingles. Then I went to Everett, Washington, and lived around there cutting shingle bolts, sawing and packing. Worked in shingle mills up and down Puget Sound. Never stayed long in one place. I put in three years on Vancouver Island sawing shingles.

In 1918 I married. Wife and I came to Seattle and I longshored up to the general strike in 1919. Drove a car for my brother-in-law for 18 months. Went east of the mountains logging. Back to Seattle. Peddled handbills from house to house. Worked for junk company. Cut wood on the beach. Worked on a paving job wheeling sand and gravel to the concrete mixer.

My wife's health was poorly, and they said the mountain air would help her. I went up to Lake Wenatchee to cut shingle bolts and took my wife. Stayed there two years while my wife's health greatly improved. Picked apples in Wenatchee Valley for the first time. Wife wanted divorce. Started same then changed mind. After another year took another notion for divorce. I went to San Juan Island and cut cordwood from January to August. When I came out to Bellingham I found I was divorced.

I worked two months mucking on the Cascade Tunnel. Sawed shingles at Quilcene, Washington. Worked one winter for a coal company in Seattle. Made cedar shakes one summer at Kerriston, Washington. Was married while there. Wife and I parted same year. Since then I have been knocking around Washington working here and there at odd jobs, mostly in Wenatchee Valley, but I have only averaged four month's work per year since 1928.

Thus, going around the circle of many jobs, McClosky ended up at the age of 45 in a transient camp. Would he remain in a camp? One needs only to look at his record, but in his case it was a record of home-guard migrancy. The next job was never far away; that was the case before 1929.

California is the land of industrial agriculture and employs many workers like the man whose labor journal follows. This case shows the brevity of the jobs and the "scatter" of jobs; how a worker must go many places and turn his hand to many tasks in the round of the seasons (Webb, *Migratory-Casual Worker*, pp. 3–4).

July–October, 1932. Picked figs at Fresno, California, and vicinity. Wages 10 cents a box, average 50-pound box. Picked about 15 boxes a day to earn $1.50; about $40 a month.

October–December, 1932. Cut Malaga and Muscat grapes near Fresno. Wages 25 cents an hour. Average six-hour day, earning $1.50; about $40 a month.

December 1932. Left for Imperial Valley, California.

February 1933. Picked peas, Imperial Valley. Wages one cent a pound. Average 125 pounds a day. Earned $30 for season. Also worked as wagon man in lettuce field on contract. Contract price, 5 cents a crate repack out of packing houses; not field work. This work paid 60 cents to $1 a day. On account of weather was fortunate to break even at finish of season. Was paying 50 cents a day room and board.

March–April, 1933. Left for Chicago. Stayed a couple of weeks. Returned to California two months later.

May 1933. Odd jobs at lawns, radios, and Victrolas at Fresno. Also worked as porter and handyman.

June 1933. Returned to picking figs near Fresno. Wages 10 cents a box. Average $1.50 a day, and earned $50 in two months.

August 1993. Cut Thompson's seedless grapes near Fresno for seven days at 1½ cents a tray. Earned $11. Picked cotton one day, 115 pounds; earned $1.

September–November, 1933. Cut Malaga and Muscat grapes near Fresno. Wages, 25 cents an hour. Made $30 for season.

December 1933. Picked oranges and lemons in Tulare County, California.

January 1934. Picked oranges for 5 cents per box for small jobs and 25 cents per box for large jobs, Redlands, California. Earned $30. Picked lemons at 25 cents an hour.

January 1934. Went to Brawley, California. Picked peas at one cent a pound. Picked 125–40 pounds a day for 15-day season.

February 1934. Picked grapefruit at 25 cents an hour, Koehler, California. Worked 8 hours a day on three jobs for a total of 22 days. Also hauled fertilizer at 25 cents an hour.

March 1934. Worked as helper on fertilizer truck at $2 a day for 20 days, Brawley, California.

June 1934. Worked as circus hand with Al G. Barnes Circus for four weeks at $4.60 a week and board, Seattle to Wallace, Idaho.

July 1934. Tree shaker at 25 cents an hour, averaged $2 a day for 25 days near Fresno.

August–October, 1934. Picked oranges and lemons at 25 cents an hour, working an average of six hours a day, for 60 days, near Fresno.

December 1934. Houseman in hotel, Fresno. Received 50 cents a day and board for one month, and 25 cents a day and board for two months.

The migrant-casual goes in search of his work, "wearing out" one poorly paid job after another. The only difference between his life as migratory-casual and the life of a newcomer to the migrant life is that for him there is no more adventure or new experience. He travels a "beat," which for the temporary transient may in time also become a way of work and living. For the chronic migrant the road leads to some blind alley eventually, the "skid row" of some city to be a home guard in Hobohemia.

The Unattached Migrants

Migrants of the hobo species were far less numerous among the unattached persons registered with the Federal Transient Program. They were outnumbered ten to one by the novices of the road. The depression transients probably became disillusioned and gave up their migrancy, but for each class that graduated there were many more recruits. We turn now to some of the available information about the unattached occasional migrants.

The Federal Transient Program gave shelter to approximately two hundred thousand unattached transients, and this number is estimated on the basis of various sample studies. Since this program served a moving population, allowance must be made for those who, en route to their destinations, stopped at a number of shelters. On the basis of the information received from the 13 selected cities, as reported by Webb, the newcomer migrants were younger than the seasonal, constant casual workers. He also found that they were generally migrating with a settlement objective.

A review of the month-to-month enumerations from May 1934 to April 1935 showed a median age for the unattached migrants ranging from 25 to 29 years. These ages varied from one to another of the 13 selected cities. The median ages in the West were lower, and summer migrants were younger than the winter migrants. The age distribution for September, 1934, a typical month, is as shown in table 4 (*Transient Unemployed*, p. 101).

It should be kept in mind that the federal program would show

TABLE 4

Total number registered	26,898
Median age	27.1
All persons (percentage distribution)	100
Under 16 years	1
16–19 years	17
20–24 years	26
25–34 years	28
35–44 years	15
45–54 years	9
55–64 years	3
65 years and over	1

TABLE 5

Age Groups	Federal Transient Service (October, 1934)	Central Registration Bureau, New York City (1931–32)	Emergency Relief Bureau, Buffalo (1934)
Total in each group	25,160	19,861	9,052
Approximate median age	29	41	29
All persons (percentage)	100	100	100
Under 25 years	40	8	33
25–34 years	28	22	32
35–44 years	17	30	21
45–54 years	10	24	10
55 years and over	5	16	4

lower median ages because the federal government tried to limit its services to the transients, leaving resident homeless to the local agencies. Table 5 is compiled and adapted from these additional sources: records of the Central Registration Bureau of New York City for October 1931 to February 1932 and Herman J. P. Schubert's study of *Twenty Thousand Transients* for 1924, in Buffalo.

An unpublished study of homeless and transient persons made by the Welfare Council of New York City showed that in some of the private agencies that served transients only the median age of applicants was generally about 30 years, but in other private agencies that served mainly resident homeless the median age ranged from 40 to 50 years. For October 1934 (*Transient Unemployed*, 101), there were, among the 25,160 transients registered, 1,317 resident homeless persons in six of the cities in which the occasional census was taken. The median age for this group was 43.7 years.

A Chicago study of *Twenty Thousand Homeless Men*, made in 1934 by E. H. Sutherland and H. J. Locke, revealed that the average age of the "shelter man" (p. 37) was 45 years. The Buffalo study revealed that the median age of transients varied (Schubert, p. 14) from 28 years in

TABLE 6

Group	Number	Percentage
All persons	26,898	100
Native white	22,954	85
Foreign-born white	1,321	5
Negro	2,340	9
Other (Mexicans, Filipinos, etc.)	283	1

TABLE 7

Group	New York City	Chicago	Pittsburgh
All persons	19,861	6,009	10,294
Native	10,730	2,695	8,205
Foreign-born	9,131	2,314	2,089
Percentage foreign-born	46.0	38.5	20.3

March to 34 years in January. Young transients are more likely to strike out on the road with the spring and try to be settled during the winter.

Studies of the transient and homeless are in general agreement that the preponderance of both groups is native white. For those enumerated in the count of September 1934 in 13 cities (*Transient Unemployed*, p. 105) the distribution was as shown in table 6.

If foreign-born persons or Negroes are found among the migrants, they are in smaller proportion than among the resident homeless. Table 7 shows the native and foreign-born for three cities before the advent of the Federal Transient Service. For New York City the information was taken from an unpublished study by the Welfare Council from the records of the Central Registration Bureau for October 1931 to February 1932. The figures for Chicago were obtained from a report of the Clearing House for Men of the Illinois Emergency Relief Commission, 1931–32. The figures for Pittsburgh were obtained from a report of the Central Application Bureau of that city for 1932.

The foreign-born types found among the migrants and resident homeless in each of the three cities reflect the dominant nationality groups within each of the metropolitan areas and adjacent regions. New York City, like other northeastern cities, contains many Irish; they were top in the five principal nationality groups reported (table 8).

Of the foreign-born among New York City's transient and resident homeless, 27.6 percent were Irish, and 9.7 percent were Poles, while Germans comprised 7.5 percent. The array of nationality groups in Chicago was different.

In the Chicago Clearing House for Men the Irish comprised but 10.7 percent of the foreign-born homeless and transients, whereas the Poles

TABLE 8

Ireland	2,517
Poland	889
Germany	687
Russia	674
Italy	434

TABLE 9

Poland	427
Ireland	247
Austria	206
Sweden	202
Germany	178

TABLE 10

Poland	340
Austria	306
Ireland	205
Italy	157
Russia	151

topped the list with 18.4 percent, and the Swedes were third with 8.9 percent (see table 9). For the Pittsburgh Central Application Bureau the distribution was different still.

At Pittsburgh the Poles comprised 16.3 percent and the Austrians 14.6 percent (see table 10). In 1932 the Employment Stabilization Institute of the University of Minnesota conducted a study of 287 homeless casual workers in the city of Duluth. These were mainly resident homeless men of the state who had worked in the iron mines or the lumber industry. Among the foreign-born the four principal nationalities represented were Finns, 67; Swedes, 41; Norwegians, 30; and Poles, 26.

Of approximately 200,000 unattached migrants served by the Federal Transient Program, no more than 2 or 3 percent (*Transient Unemployed,* 32) were females. To quote Webb:

> The wanderings of the unattached women were beset with more difficulties than was the case with unattached men. Travel without resources, as practiced by unattached transients, was largely a matter of riding freight and passenger trains illegally, and the solicitation of rides in automobiles and trucks. For the former means of travel women are less fit physically, and even success at the latter was not free from hazards. Moreover, women are novices at unattached wandering, and in addition are likely to encounter both suspicion and prejudice from citizen and police alike.

TABLE 11

Marital Status	Male	Female
All persons	26,306	592
Percentage distribution	100	100
Single	81	39
Married	6	14
Widowed or divorced	9	31
Separated	4	16

Migrancy is a man's way of life, and migrants mainly are men without women. Table 11 (Webb, 103) shows the marital status for both male and female unattached transients for the enumeration of September, 1934, sheltered in the federal bureaus of 13 cities.

It may be true, as often charged, that the homeless wanderer does not correctly report his marital status, but the difference between the truth and the tale is probably not great enough to warrant much consideration. At the public agencies there is little incentive to falsify answers on these matters. The incidence of marriage or having been married would naturally be higher among the resident homeless. These men are older and less migrant and have greater opportunity for exposure to marriage. Of 18,010 men studied by the Welfare Council of New York City at the Central Registration Bureau from October 1931 to February 1932 75.4 percent were recorded as single.

Of the transients studied in Buffalo in 1934 (Schubert, p. 77) there were 6,997 whites and 1,962 Negroes reported for marital status. The whites were 86.5 percent single, and the Negroes 88.7 percent single. Schubert found that the transients interviewed at Buffalo came from fairly large families. The younger transients came from families of four or five children. It could be safely added that they came mainly from very poor families.

> The transient over 40 is more likely to be the eldest among his brothers and sisters than to hold any other position in the family. This fact is by no means as clearly set forth for those under 40, but there is a definite indication that more of the transients are eldest than would be expected from a random sample. This may be due to the fact that the eldest is more likely to be the burden bearer and therefore suffers more in times of economic insecurity.

Other Characteristics of Transients

Schubert found in his study of transients at Buffalo that 68 percent of the white persons had completed the eighth grade, 13 percent had completed high school, and 6 percent had attended college. He found

TABLE 12

Rating	Resident Homeless	Draft Army
Superior (A, B)	.4	12.0
Average (C+, C, C−)	37.7	61.5
Inferior (D, D−)	61.9	26.5
Total	100.0	100.0

that about 4 percent of the whites and about 30 percent of the Negroes were illiterate (p. 54). He found, too, that a considerable number of the transients were retarded at the time they left school.

The Buffalo study of transients concerned men having a median age of about 29 years. A study conducted by Sutherland and Locke of a group of resident homeless men having a median age of about 45 years showed that the average schooling for the Chicago group was 5.5 years. Less than 1 percent of the Chicago group reached college, only 13 percent reached high school, and less than 40 percent finished grammar school (Sutherland and Locke, pp. 35–36).

Sutherland and Locke gave the Army Beta Mental Test to 740 resident homeless. Table 12 shows the percentage distribution of intelligence scores of resident homeless men in comparison with the draft army.

As a class the shelter men were at a disadvantage (Webb, pp. 43–44) because of the preponderance of older men, laborers, and foreign-born. The mean Beta score for men over 45 years of age was 34.6, whereas the score for the men under 45 was 49.9. For 27 youths in their teens the score was 66.7.

Webb, reporting on the education of transients sheltered in the federal transient bureaus for September 1934 also found a considerable difference between transient and resident homeless. His figures for the latter group, both colored and white, were taken from only 6 of the 13 cities (*Transient Unemployed*, pp. 106–7) and are shown in table 13.

Younger transients are likely to have more education. This is evident when the native whites of the Transient Bureau group are compared with a special group of migrant boys sheltered by the Boys' Welfare Department of Los Angeles between December 1933 and November 1934. Most of these boys were between the ages of 16 and 21 (table 14).

Although the median age of the transients at the federal bureaus was higher, the median degree of education attained was lower. It was a little above the eighth grade for the Federal Transient Service group and a little in excess of the ninth grade for the migrant boys.

Boys from the northern and eastern states were more than a grade

TABLE 13

Schooling Completed	Transient Homeless	Resident Homeless
All persons	26,898	1,539
Percentage distribution	100.0	100.0
No schooling	2.0	6.1
Less than eighth grade	29.8	43.2
Completed eighth grade	26.3	27.9
Attended high school	25.1	13.2
Completed high school	12.9	7.0
Attended college	2.8	1.6
Completed college	1.1	1.0

TABLE 14

Schooling Completed	Native White (Federal Transient Bureaus, September 1934)	Migrant Boys (Boys' Welfare Department,* Los Angeles, December 1933–November 1934)
All persons	22,954	9,919
Percentage distribution	100.0	100.0
No schooling	1.0	0.5
Less than eighth grade	26.1	17.2
Completed eighth grade	27.6	22.3
Attended high school	27.0	42.0
Completed high school	14.1	15.9
Attended college	4.2	2.1

*See article in Bibliography by Outland.

ahead of boys from the southern states. States in which the annual average expenditure per pupil in school is less than $50 were at the bottom of the list, whereas states spending annually on education from $75 to $100 per pupil were at the top of the list. Among the top states in order from the highest were South Dakota, Utah, Iowa, Michigan, Indiana, New Hampshire, Minnesota, Ohio, Wisconsin, Nebraska, and Wyoming.

At this point, however, it is pertinent to include some descriptive information about the work transients can do and the work they get to do. There may be a difference between the transient's occupation and his job. So often these workers set out to find one kind of work but end up by doing something else. Webb found that 92.2 percent of the transients served by the federal bureaus were employable (*Tran-*

TABLE 15

Usual Occupation	Transients in 13 Cities, April, 1934*	Gainful Workers[†] (1930 U.S. Census)
All persons, percentage distribution	100.0	100.0
Professional persons	2.2	6.1
Semiprofessional persons	0.3	0.4
Proprietors, managers, officials	4.2	18.9
Clerical workers	4.8	8.6
Sales persons	5.9	7.3
Telephone, telegraph, radio operators	0.3	0.7
Skilled workers	16.3	13.4
Semiskilled workers	23.6	16.6
Unskilled workers	31.8	21.1
Servants and allied workers	10.4	6.9

*Includes unattached persons and family-group heads.
[†]*Fifteenth Census*, vol. 5: *Population*, table 5.

sient Unemployed, pp. 43–48). About 5 percent of these transients had no work history. They were probably in search of work experience. About 80 percent of the unattached transients claimed a usual occupation. The classification by Webb of the transients by occupation and comparison with workers in the general population is shown in table 15 (*Transient Unemployed*, p. 110).

In order of size the three chief semiskilled occupations were found to be factory-machine operators, sailors and beach workers, and truck, tractor, or automobile drivers. About half of those classed as unskilled were farm laborers. This group of migrants, with widely separated exceptions, did not find in migrancy the solution to their unemployment or to their desired occupation.

Some Reasons for Migration

When a young man leaves home are his reasons for migration different from those which motivated the migration of a family? Jeff Davis, who calls himself "King of the Hobos," is convinced that many young men migrate because they are moved by the wanderlust. Various observers of this phenomenon have come to similar conclusions; recent students of the problem, however, give little credence to the "inner urge" reasons for migrancy. There is a trend toward explaining transiency in terms of social or economic pressures upon the individual.

Dr. Robert C. Van Riggle, a psychiatrist associated with the Florida Transient Service, wrote in a publication of that agency in January 1935:

Street scene in Jackson, Kentucky. What should they do, loaf around the hometown or migrate? (Photo: Work Projects Administration.)

Transiency is the result of a deep inner need to escape from a known condition into an unknown condition, to remove the old and discover the new, to break restraining bonds and find freedom, to renounce the too obvious "real" for the more glitteringly "unreal." Stability in life has always meant sacrifice. Stability exists because the ways of life upon which we have placed the ultimate value (i.e., marriage, children, position, recognition, property, etc.) all demand that quality of life as a fundamental basis for existence.

Dr. Van Riggle argued that a closing of the stabilizing ways of life may press people out and they then become transients; that, in the process of seeking escape, these detached people present baffling problems for the stable people to solve. Traditionally, since the Code of Hammurabi, the stable groups have attempted to control the unstable by the vagrancy laws. He adds: "Those transients who had money were called travelers . . . were scorned or secretly envied; the transients who had no money were automatically thrown into jail or sent to far away colonies."

Thomas Minehan, who roamed the country in 1932 and 1933 to gather the material for his *Boy and Girl Tramps of America,* found a variety of reasons for leaving home, but in the main they related to crises in the family. He made an effort to classify these reasons as quoted in table 16 (p. 260).

As far as the boys were concerned, Minehan found mixed or mul-

Drought refugees from Glendive, Montana, en route to Washington or other points on the Pacific Coast. (Photo: Farm Security Administration, by Rothstein.)

TABLE 16

Reasons for Leaving Home	Boys	Girls
Hard times	384	3
Trouble with girl	26	0
Liked to travel	23	5
Hated high school	19	4
Going to get married anyway	3	4
Miscellaneous	17	4
Total	450	16

tiple reasons for migration. The facts do not reveal single or simple reasons for such complex action as leaving one's home and community. This interpretation is expressed by Sutherland and Locke in their report of *Twenty Thousand Homeless Men* in the public shelters of Chicago during 1934 and 1935. They concluded that homeless and transient men reached the shelters in the course of a series of related experiences which they described as "roads to dependency" (pp. 70–92).

Without attempting to classify the homeless or to count them in relation to the roads by which they reached shelter life, Sutherland and Locke concluded: "For many men the descent to the shelters began years ago. The factors which were involved in this long-term descent to dependency were varied and interrelated. They include economic transitions, marital and sexual problems, alcoholism, physical injuries or illness, cultural conflict and detachment." Most important of these factors was the first-named, the economic.

They found also that homeless men differed in their economic experiences, but in general they fell into general classes: (1) those who chronically fluctuated back and forth across the line of dependency, or between stability and instability; (2) those who had been fairly stable until depression reverses overtook them, when they became dependent, often migratory, and sometimes unstable; and (3) those who at one time were unstable, later achieved stability, but finally through reverses again became dependent if not also unstable. It was found that skilled and professional persons, falling into dependency, were more subject to personal deterioration than unskilled workers.

Concerning marital and sexual problems, Sutherland and Locke found that occupational instability, family disorganization, and general dissipation were closely related. Alcoholism was found to be both cause and effect in a process involving many interacting factors. While alcoholism was not found to be itself a general cause of dependency, it contributed in pulling men down from the level of steady workers to casual workers. Physical injuries and illness contributed to dependency and homelessness mainly as it reduced a worker's ability to compete in the labor market. Men who had reached the shelters for reasons described as "detachments" were, in the main, persons who were already migrants or unattached. They were on their own without family or community ties in the localities where they happened to be. Being so detached, they were also without the usual social and economic resources of persons attached to the communities and were less able to withstand economic reverse.

The analysis of "roads to dependency" and homelessness used by Sutherland and Locke might be applied to migrant families as well as to unattached persons. Families, much like individuals, become migrants, not because of some single impelling situation, but because of various experiences leading up to the situation or condition causing them to start moving.

Information gathered by the Federal Transient Program showed that the reasons given by unattached transients for their migrancy were mainly economic (*Transient Unemployed*, p. 117). In table 17 are given the reasons as reported for a selected month, April 1935; and it should be noted that this group is more transient than the "shelter man."

TABLE 17
Reasons for Beginning Migration

Number of unattached migrants	24,268
Percentage distribution	100
Seeking work	75
Promised a job	2
Adventure	8
Ill health	2
Migratory occupation	3
Domestic difficulty	3
Inadequate relief at home	1
En route on visits	4
Personal business	1
Other reasons	1

Granting that these reasons are approximate, they are also suggestive of the material objectives of unattached migrants. It is significant that only 3 percent of the persons reported were regarded as chronic migrants. The rest were depression migrants seeking work, and a minor number, 8 percent, without apparent work reasons were considered as traveling for "adventure."

It has been suggested that migrants in applying for public aid are likely to give "pious" reasons for their migrancy, but that observation probably would apply with less force to the Federal Transient Service. Related information seems to confirm the economic reasons for migrancy as reported by the transients.

Youth and Labor Relocation

It was found in the study of 20,000 homeless men in Chicago (Sutherland and Locke, p. 36) that the typical homeless man left school at the age of 13 and at about 19 years of age he left home, but 16 percent of this number left home before reaching the age of 15. For any man who is now 40 years of age or over, having left home at the age of 15 or even up to 19 is a matter of proud recollection. They were able to find jobs.

But the story of teenage migrancy during the late 1920s and through the 1930s is far from rosy, yet the great proportion of migrants—the unattached migrants—were of younger ages. A. W. McMillen, during the depth of the depression, visited several southeastern and western states. He wrote his observations, "An Army of Boys on the Loose," for the *Survey* of September 1, 1932. Some of his most pertinent findings can be summed up briefly.

1. Phoenix, Arizona—10,000 homeless transients sheltered; 1,529 or 15 percent were under 21 years.

2. El Paso, Texas—45,150 homeless transients sheltered; estimated about 25 percent were under 21 years.
3. Oklahoma City, Oklahoma—13,047 homeless transients sheltered; 2,358 or 18 percent were under 21 years.
4. Memphis, Tennessee—10,870 homeless transients sheltered; 2,885 or 27 percent were under 21 years.
5. Ogden, Utah—919 homeless transients sheltered; 164 or 18 percent were under 21 years.

For the year ending March 31, 1932, the Central Bureau for Transient Men in Washington, D.C., as reported by the Travelers Aid Society, showed a total of 4,317 men given service. Of this number 876, or 20 percent, were under 21 years. Quoting this report: "A small proportion inevitably will join the ranks of the permanent wanderers because of low mentality, lack of education and training and unfortunate backgrounds. The majority, however, were those mentioned previously who are ready for the world, but find the world has no place for them."

During its two years of operation, ending September 1935, the Federal Transient Service reported 40 percent or more of the unattached migrants as being under 25 years of age and about 18 percent under 19 years of age.

Migrancy is now and will be for some time to come a youth problem. Youths in their teens and twenties outnumber all other migrants. The family migrants are young too. At the present time, if the number of unemployed totals 10,000,000, we may be sure that 3,000,000 are persons under 25 years of age. The greater number of these jobless young workers are located in the villages and open country, the usual source of the nation's supply of surplus labor.

Between 1930 and 1935 there was in the United States an increase of youth (16–24 years) from 20,126,800 to 20,786,700 (Melvin and Smith, p. 18), but the increase was mainly rural. There was an actual decrease in the cities. In percentages, between 1930 and 1935, all youth 16–24 years in the United States increased 3.2 percent; urban youth decreased by 4.3 percent; all rural youth increased 13 percent, but farm youth increased 19 percent.

Since agriculture is on the decline as far as the need of labor is concerned, it is imperative that rural youth migrate. It is not economical that the farms should have two hands to do the work of one. If there is not an outlet for this surplus of young farm labor, according to Melvin and Smith (1938) the number of potential migrants will climb to more than 2,000,000 before the end of this decade.

At this point the population problem of the future and the unemployment problem of today meet. There are too many youths mainly because jobs are too few, but, if and when jobs are available, there must

Cannery workers in Polk County, Florida. Many of the workers in this occupation are migrants. (Photo: Farm Security Administration, by Rothstein.)

be more jobs and a considerable migration of youth from areas of less advantage. This has been described as the problem of "delayed migration" in a study of *Farm-City Migration and Industry's Labor Reserve,* by Francis M. Vreeland and E. J. Fitzgerald.

We are reminded in this report that the poor-land areas since 1932 have "become pockets of unemployment where the city worker is stranded, unable to wrest an adequate livelihood from the soil and, at present, unable to move back to the city" (Vreeland and Fitzgerald, p. 59). As for the youth at home:

> The problems of the delayed migrants are similar. These persons comprise a large block in our unemployed population, representing innumerable youths who might have gone to the cities had industrial conditions permitted, but who, with the depression contraction of industrial opportunity, were forced to remain on the land. The effect of this has naturally been to intensify the pressure conditions prevalent there.

The pressure conditions resulting from the "piling-up" of youth on the farm are primarily evidenced in a sharpening of competition, a cheapening of labor, and a lowering of the rural standard of living.

The evolution of farming methods tends to go forward in spite of the overabundance of farm labor. This applies to the trend toward mechanization on the farm. Efficient farmers find it economical to use tractors, trucks, and other labor-saving equipment, which in turn renders still more farm labor unnecessary.

Coyle says,

> In the past, whenever hard times fell upon the comparatively crowded sections of the East, a wave of young emigrants swept into the West. With many casualties and losses, they settled and built up the country. Over the short time of their migration, perhaps they ended up poorer than they were when they left home, but in the long run their movement was the great historic readjustment that has given form to our Nation. (p. 7)

In those days of pioneering, youth could without loss linger longer on the farm. In previous depressions the farm was a retreat and snug harbor for many a person who needed temporary economic haven. Now the dam is filling to a danger point.

At this point we can do no better than quote from *Seven Lean Years*, a brief but excellent review of this problem by T. J. Woofter, Jr., and Ellen Winston.

> Coming of age on the farm during the depression of the nineteen thirties involved unprecedented dilemmas. It has been pointed out that the entry into agriculture has been growing more difficult, that the depression made entry into industry almost impossible, and that during the period of contracting agriculture and stagnant industry there was an increase of more than 200,000 in the farm males of working age. On the threshold of productive life, at the age of readiest adaptation to work and to family and community life, youth of this generation faced an economy which, at least temporarily, did not need them. (p. 45)

In that situation is found the perfect setting for frustration and broken morale. Some are calling this a perfect background for a great mass movement for demagogues who would use the means of democracy for ends that are anything but democratic.

13

Migrancy and the Labor Market

Seasonal and Casual Labor

At this point consideration will be given to the work that the migrant does. It is recognized that the migrant who looks for employment in a community of destination will not get the pick of available jobs. If jobs are few, preference will ordinarily be given to residents. We have heard of employers giving preference to strangers, but this is usually motivated by some ulterior purpose, perhaps to cheapen labor rates locally. Normally, the migrant, being a marginal person, must content himself with marginal jobs, unskilled jobs which rarely last long. Of such there are two types: (1) seasonal jobs in agriculture or industry and (2) casual jobs.

Seasonal jobs are of many kinds and vary in duration from a few days to several weeks or months. They have this quality in common, that they open with regularity in a given season of each year. Lumbering in the northern border states was once a seasonal occupation. The logs were cut in the winter when snow and ice made hauling easier. Another seasonal phase of lumbering was the floating of the logs to the mill, an operation which began with the break of spring. Summer was layoff time in the lumber woods. Before the advent of ice-freezing machinery, the ice harvest was a winter occupation. Construction, especially dirt moving, once was more of a seasonal industry than at present. Fishing remains a seasonal occupation; salmon, for example, can be caught only when they "run" the streams in season.

Agriculture is extremely seasonal. Once the planting was done as dictated by the phases of the moon. While those folk rules carry less conviction today, the usual operations from the planting to the harvest are dominated by the growing and maturing of the crop. Fruit must be picked "in the season thereof," or it will waste. Vegetables must be gathered when they are ready for the market. Frost, rain, and sunshine,

From *Men on the Move* (Chicago: University of Chicago Press, 1940): 269–300. © 1940 by the University of Chicago.

Pea pickers in a field near Calipatria, California. (Photo: Farm Security Administration, by Lange.)

like the tides, do not bide the convenience of man. When the various jobs in agriculture are ready, a labor supply must be available. When the work is finished, the labor supply is of no more use until the seasonal demand returns. As in agriculture, so in the pastoral arts the seasonal labor requirements are present. Sheep must be sheared when the wool is ready.

For industry the seasonal demands are less arbitrary, but here, too, there are seasonal fluctuations in labor demand. A conspicuous example is the clothing industry. Even in the machinery and automobile industries there are changing demands for labor according to seasonal consumption.

Casual labor is not substantially different from seasonal labor. While employment opportunities in casual labor do not come and go with the changes of weather from spring to winter, such jobs resemble seasonal jobs in their brevity of duration. According to Webb: "The term 'casual employment' is generally used to describe unskilled jobs for which the principal qualifications are bodily vigor and the presence of the worker at the time of hiring" (*Migratory-Casual Worker*, p. 2).

Agricultural workers in a carrot field near Meloland, Imperial Valley, California. These workers pull, clean, tie, and crate carrots for eleven cents per crate of forty-eight bunches. A good worker can earn about one dollar per day. (Photo: Farm Security Administration, by Lange.)

Not all casual labor is unskilled. In the construction industry, for example, skilled work may be more casual than unskilled. Bricklayers, plumbers, carpenters, plasterers, painters—each craft is hired by the hour as needed. The old-style, dirt-moving construction jobs were in part seasonal, but frequently they were also casual, depending on the length of the contract. The men who followed such work, so long as there was regularity in the seasonality of the pattern of work, went from one type of job to another. Some migrated to the North or the South with the changing season, doing the same kind of work. Winter closed up dirt-moving jobs in the North, but other jobs would open for the winter in the South.

Some workers moved from one seasonal occupation to another: perhaps on construction jobs in summer, or they worked in the lumber woods in winter. If they worked in the lumber woods in winter, perhaps they followed agricultural jobs in summer. If they worked at seasonal agriculture in summer, perhaps they worked at casual labor in some city during the winter. Most of the old cycles have been broken by the advent of technological devices, but technology has not entirely abolished the seasonality of some types of work. Nor has technology eliminated the casual jobs. On the contrary, casual jobs tend to increase with technological change.

A basic objective of management is to operate an industry with the least amount of labor, to use more machinery and less labor, to use less high-priced labor and more unskilled or semiskilled labor, and to hire only as much labor as is needed. A diminishing percentage of workers are provided with relative security in their jobs, but the great majority of the workers are hired and fired in accordance with the day-to-day needs of the plant. The element of casualty permeates the employment practices to a rising degree with each nether level of the occupational pyramid. The workers at the bottom have least job security. They must wait around without knowing when they will be called back to work or for how long. Many meet this dilemma by drifting from one hiring line to another, even from one town or city to another.

"What," asks Sir William Beveridge (p. 76), "will be the economic and social effects of a system of employment in which rapid and irregular fluctuations of work at a number of different centres are met by the engagement for short periods of irregular hands, who in part at least are taken on by chance as they present themselves?" He posed this question as the introduction to a discussion of the wastefulness of casual labor.

The casual-labor market is an economic luxury because of the trial-and-error principle upon which it operates. Workers go here and there in a chance search for jobs. Such a hit-and-miss search occupies the attention of many more workers than are needed. Many are busy in the search, but few are busy at work. All workers in the casual-labor market, consequently, are underemployed. Because so many workers are generally available in this market, all tend to be underpaid.

To a large extent the modern migrancy problem is an extended job hunt in the casual-labor market. This would be more true of the migrations from town to town or between industrial centers. This migration is often in response to shifts in labor-market demand. For example, while this is being written, rumors are flying to all parts of the United

States that there will be an employment pickup in the automobile manufacturing cities or in other industrial centers likely to manufacture airplanes and war equipment. Tool and diemakers are already on the move. Many who hope to be skilled workers in these industries are moving. Still others who would be satisfied with casual jobs are en route to Detroit, Akron, Chicago, Wichita, and other places.

Why Depression Migrants Are Different

Frank Bibb Smith migrated with his wife and three children from Alabama to Cincinnati. He had been employed in the rubber industry in his home state, but the job he had was minor, and the work irregular. Somebody told him that the rubber industry in the North offered greater opportunity. He wanted to get away from irregular employment. He wanted to settle in a good neighborhood, work steadily, and send his children to good schools.

The pertinent facts regarding Smith are that he loaded his family and effects in an automobile and set out with money enough for a week if he did not spend too much for gas and car upkeep. His funds ran out in Cincinnati. He applied for relief and obtained some emergency help. The relief agency was willing to send him back to Alabama but not on to Akron. Smith would not agree. Being a handy man and energetic, he set out to find work. He got a few odd jobs by asking from door to door. He heard they were hiring in a factory. He got in somehow through the crowd of applicants and was hired. The job closed in a month. Imposing on himself the utmost frugality, he was able to save enough to continue his journey to Akron.

The arrival of Smith in Akron turned out to be as disillusioning as the arrival of the Joad family in California. He found odd jobs, occasional jobs. Always he found many more applicants than jobs. He may be in Akron still, and he may eventually find something better than casual work, but the fate of Migrant Smith is the fate of most migrants entering a crowded labor market. He had to start at the very bottom doing the most menial work. He had better jobs in Alabama but he would not consider returning to Alabama; he was too sure that he would get something better in Akron at that time.

It may be safely said that most modern migrants do not set out to become casual or seasonal workers. They accept such employment as a means to an end. Often as casual or seasonal workers they submit to indignities which they would not tolerate otherwise. They bear up under conditions of employment as debasing as penal servitude, and the fact that they submit is the best evidence that in another year they expect to be settled on regular jobs. They accept or ignore the hostility

A sharecropper in town during the tobacco auction at Douglas, Georgia. Many of these sharecroppers have lately turned migratory and seek seasonal work in the fruit and vegetable crops. (Photo: Farm Security Administration, by Lange.)

of resident people toward them, mainly because they have their minds set on a destination where things will be different.

Employers generally assume an opportunistic attitude toward casual labor. They may feel a responsibility for their regular employees, but they feel very little for the part-time or occasional workers. Employers of seasonal labor, especially in agriculture, have frequently evidenced a ready willingness to break faith. Employing farmers through their organizations have been known to invite migrant workers to the community in excess of local needs. They been known to employ workers at one rate and pay them off at a lesser rate or to reduce the rates of pay after the workers got on the job. Having no civil rights in

Mexican agricultural migrants in a beet field near East Grand Forks, Minnesota. (Photo: Farm Security Administration, by Lee.)

the communities where they seek jobs, the migrants are also without the pale of local public sympathy. They must accept the lot of casual workers and either take what is offered or move on. If they protest, they face the prospect of being adjudged vagrants by the local organized community and forced to move.

We have no information about the volume of seasonal and casual labor employed each year in the United States, nor do we know what proportion of all labor is of intermittent character. Information is also lacking on the volume of seasonal and casual labor there is available to migrants. We know that picking cherries in the Traverse City area of Michigan is a type of seasonal work on which many migrants can be used for possibly two weeks. Much of this work, however, is done by local persons who are not migrants, persons who leave other jobs temporarily. Many migrants who go into that area are not migrants in the true sense; they may be city workers on vacation.

The beet-sugar industry, centering mainly in Colorado, Wyoming, Nebraska, Montana, and Idaho, employs in the fields many seasonal workers, but not all are migratory. Some take leave from other work

TABLE 1

	Number of Workers Hired		Percentage Peak-Month Requirement	Percentage Nonresidents among Total
Month	All Workers	Nonresidents		
January	46,448	13,004	23	28
February	48,973	16,829	25	34
March	61,316	13,319	31	22
April	79,982	19,407	40	34
May	126,160	38,513	64	31
June	125,717	30,634	63	24
July	140,461	36,366	71	25
August	158,530	41,053	80	26
September	198,349	41,258	100	21
October	182,531	49,551	92	27
November	85,624	17,744	43	21
December	46,833	7,620	24	16

for the season. Yet it is necessary to ship in thousands of workers. Not all who are shipped in return later to their places of origin. Often their earnings are so meager that they cannot afford to return. They remain and try to get on relief. It has been found that a considerable number of families working one year in the beet fields of Colorado or Wyoming will appear the next year in the beet fields of Idaho. They are en route west. They may be found the third year in Washington or Oregon, later, perhaps, in California. They started as refugees but are settlers in purpose.

Table 1 is adapted from a *Survey of Agricultural Labor Requirements in California in 1935* by the California State Relief Administration. It shows the estimated total number of such workers needed by months during the year in the 33 counties using such labor, the number of migrant workers, and the percentage of migrants to all workers.

An examination of the distinction between resident and nonresident workers employed in California crops would reveal little difference. The residents are no less migratory than the nonresidents. Most of the seasonal labor is migratory in response to a market demand that ranges from 100 percent in September to 23 percent in January. It is met to a great extent today by family groups, but in earlier days it was the special province of the hobo workers described by Carlton Parker about 1915 in his well-known essay, "The Casual Laborer."

California is a state of summer employment. The seasonal activities of the canneries, the state's principal industry, illustrate this fully. In August 1909, California's canneries employed 16,047; in February but 2,781. Of the 150,000 migratory workers employed in the summer, a mass of direct and indirect information indicates that fully 100,000 face sustained winter unemployment. Driven out of the lumber and power construction camps and mines in the Sierras by the snow, out of the highway camps by the regular winter shutdown, and out of agriculture by its closed winter seasons, with a winter's stake estimated to be on the average $30, these tens of thousands "lie up" for from five to six months in the cities of the coast. A San Francisco count of ten- and fifteen-cent lodging houses and cheap hotels of the foreign quarter, made in December 1913, showed that over 40,000 were "lying up" in that city. A Los Angeles estimate gave 25,000, Sacramento showed approximately 3,000; and important additions came from Stockton, Fresno and Bakersfield.

But not all work done by migrants in California is agricultural. Much is associated with industry and commerce. Much is part-time labor, but in the main it is labor which does not offer steady employment, and the wages are low. For these workers the available jobs are the most insecure kind. Most of the work in the migratory market is unskilled, for which reason it is next to meaningless to speak of migrants' having occupations. However, it is pertinent here to consider some of the available information about the occupations of migrants.

Occupations of Migrant Workers

An occupational classification of the migratory casual workers who performed so much of the seasonal work of the country during predepression years would have revealed an array of callings but little mentioned today. Some of those men were itinerant construction workers. They were mule skinners, rock workers, stations men, harvest hands, lumberjacks, or railroad maintenance men ("gandy dancers"). It was not always the craft a man learned that rated as his usual occupation. Of the 500 migratory-casual workers studied by Webb in the federal transient bureaus (*Migratory-Casual Worker*, pp. 5–7) the following were the principal fields of employment:

> Wheat harvest in the middle-border states
> Fruit picking and packing, mostly on the Pacific Coast
> Vegetable farming along Atlantic Seaboard and Pacific Coast
> Sugar beets in the Mountain states and California
> Cotton in both the Old South and the new western fields
> Railroad right-of-way maintenance and construction
> Construction of levees, roads, tunnels, and power and pipe lines
> Oil-well drilling and oil-field work, including gas
> Logging, mostly in the Northwest but some in the South

In his effort to classify the 500 casual migrants according to occupation Webb was forced to confine them to three broad classes. He rated some as agricultural workers, others as industrial workers, and still others were "combination" agricultural and industrial workers.

For the depression migrants, the unattached transients, Webb found that 92 percent of these workers were employable and less than 5 percent reported no work experience. A greater number, possibly 10 percent, reported no usual occupation (Webb, *Transient Unemployed*, pp. 45 ff.). About 65 percent of the unattached persons reported usual occupations within the semiskilled or unskilled categories. The percentage of semiskilled and unskilled in the general population for 1930 was 37.7 percent. In the main, these were occupations at which they had worked before migrancy and hoped to work at again after migrancy. They were not necessarily occupations in which they could expect employment while migrating.

About 17 percent of the unattached persons were rated as skilled in occupations which were mainly in the construction field. A review of the various occupations reported by the skilled migrants showed a disproportionate number claiming to be painters or carpenters. It is the claim of construction craftsmen that pretenders are most likely to invade the skilled classifications through the painters' or the carpenters' trades, for in those trades pretending is easier on simple types of work.

The conclusions regarding the occupational status of the unattached migrants were based upon scattered samples which would give a fair cross-section of the 200,000 transients served. At the same time the federal transient bureaus rendered service to some 200,000 migrant families. Information was secured regarding the occupational status of the heads of these families. The two groups—unattached transients and heads of families—differed in certain significant respects (Webb and Brown, pp. 107 ff.).

Heads of migrant families were more earnestly determined to find work. They were more ready to accept any work, regardless of their previous occupational experience. Family heads were only a little less employable, 90 percent as compared with 92 percent. Since family heads were of an older median age than the unattached migrants, they quite naturally showed fewer persons who had had no work experience or usual occupation. Most of the family heads who could report no work experience were mothers traveling alone with children. They had never been anything but housewives and for that reason were usually classed as unemployable.

While the occupational classifications of migrant family heads were higher than the heads of relief families, they were not higher than that for gainful workers reported in the Census of 1930. This study of migrant families comprised a selected sample numbering 5,489 cases of

TABLE 2

Laborers of all classes	995
Agricultural laborers	349
Industrial laborers	357
General laborers	289
Skilled workers and foremen, construction	664
Skilled workers and foremen, manufacturing	441
Foremen and farm operators, tenants, etc.	382
Truck, tractor, and power-equipment operators	327
House, hotel, and personal-service workers	324
Semiskilled factory machine operators	298
Salesmen, canvassers, solicitors, etc.	282
Profession and technical workers	203
Proprietors, managers, officials (except agricultural)	203
Semiskilled construction workers	125

TABLE 3

Manufacturing and mechanical industries	1,664
Agriculture	753
Transportation and communication	613
Trade and commerce	553
Household, hotel, and personal service	345
Professional service	233
Extractive industries (mining, gas, oil)	203
Public service	61
Fishing and forestry	41
Persons without work experience	9

the families sheltered at the federal transient bureaus during September, 1935. A review of the statistical data on the occupations of these family heads (Webb and Brown, p. 159) reveals a distribution of occupations not unlike any other cross-section of the working population. Table 2 gives a list of the principal groups of occupations for the 4,475 male family heads.

Such was found to be the occupational classification for the heads of migrant families on the road in search of employment and settlement. These are not the usual occupations of people who do migratory labor with regularity; the proportions are not the same; and this fact should be kept in mind in view of so much current discussion about migratory labor. Not all are agricultural workers, either by experience or by preference. In table 3 the occupations of the 4,475 male family heads are classified according to industry.

That the migrant as a worker belongs as much to industry and other fields of enterprise holds for the unattached as for the heads of migrant

TABLE 4

Usual Occupation	Unattached Persons		Heads of Migrant Families	
	Male	Female	Male	Female
Unattached persons	16,906	309	1,855	157
Percentage distribution	100.0	100.0	100.0	100.0
Professional and technical	2.3	5.8	3.6	7.0
Semiprofessional, recreational	0.4	1.3	0.9	. . .
Proprietors, managers, etc.	3.5	1.9	15.2	6.4
Clerical and office workers	4.9	8.1	3.5	7.0
Salespersons, canvassers, etc.	6.2	9.1	8.3	7.0
Telephone and telegraph operators	0.2	1.3	0.2	2.6
Skilled	17.5	1.0	20.8	. . .
Semiskilled	23.2	24.3	19.1	28.0
Unskilled	31.2	2.6	22.5	7.6
Domestic and allied service	10.6	44.6	5.9	34.4

families, is shown in table 4 by Webb's comparison of the two groups (*Transient Unemployed*, p. 110). This table is based on a sample for male and female migrants sheltered by the Federal Transient Service during January 1935. It should be noted that while the number of women in each group is small, it is of sufficient size to show how the occupations of the females on the road differ from those of the males.

Insofar as the migrants had skills, these were mainly found among the workers 25 years of age and over. Between 60 and 70 percent of the younger workers were found to be without skills.

While the job opportunities for the unskilled laborer may be found in any of several industrial fields in a locality, the job opportunities for workers with special occupations may be widely scattered and subject to seasonal and cyclical fluctuations. Accordingly, depending on times and conditions, occupations differ in their requirements; and, whether general labor demand be lively or depressed, special demands for special types of labor may be lively or depressed in an opposite relation to the general condition of the labor market. Thus, even a year of prosperity for most workers may be depression and moving time for special occupations. However, if employment in related fields is good, the workers of a temporarily depressed occupation do have available to them other job choices which may be less desired but which may serve in the emergency. For such temporarily disadvantaged workers, seasonal or casual employment may serve a need.

Thus, to discuss the occupations of migrants is to discuss not what the migrant does to earn a living but what he once did to earn a living or what he hopes some day to do again. For the most part, the occupations that migrants claim are the occupations of resident people, and herein is their chief incentive to become again resident people.

As between occupations in the pattern of industry, the relationships are constantly in transition, necessitating the adjustment of the worker either to develop new skills in relation to his occupation or to find a new occupation if his old one was abolished by technical change or other influences. This changing in the occupational field may or may not involve migration. Often migration cannot be avoided, as, for example, in agriculture. The percentage of gainfully employed agricultural workers in the United States declined from 53 per cent of all gainful workers in 1870 to 21 per cent of all gainful workers in 1930. It is probably much lower now, or would be if the surplus labor on farms could migrate to other employment as it freely did before 1929 and must eventually do again.

Earnings of Migrant Labor

Sheepshearing is highly paid labor. Workers who migrate from the Canadian border to Mexico from one shearing location to another until the season ends are not only paid well on the piecework basis for their labor, but if they know well how to time their schedules from job to job they can even earn a goodly amount during the year. Although some of the migratory sheepshearers earn much, others earn little; it depends on the wideness of their acquaintance. It depends also on the deftness of their fingers and the strength of their wrists. We lack information about the annual earnings of sheepshearers, but we do know that they rank among the aristocrats of migratory workers.

The migrants who have special skills—sheepshearers, building craftsmen, industrial mechanics, oil-field workers—do their traveling without much attention. Their existence may not be noticed unless in addition to their migrancy they become dependent. When faced with unemployment in their own crafts, skilled workers have the advantage of being able to apply for jobs in lesser occupations. A carpenter can take a job as a helper or laborer. An industrial machinist can apply to advantage for a job as garage mechanic. When skilled migrants drop back into semiskilled or unskilled jobs, they crowd others out. These better-trained workers are in a position to secure more days of employment per year in the course of their wanderings, and their total earnings are likely to be greater. Unskilled workers, being less essential in an overloaded labor market, are likely to be both underemployed and underpaid.

TABLE 5

Year	Migrant Families Reported	Average Earnings	
		Mean	Median
1930	578	$381	$343
1931	614	361	326
1932	648	326	308
1933	680	330	299
1934	722	314	287
1935	753	289	261

TABLE 6

	Average Weekly Income
Oklahoma	$ 9.00
Arizona	10.14
New Mexico	10.25
California	11.80
Texas	13.00

Referring again to the study of agricultural migrants made by the State Relief Administration for California in 1936 (M. H. Lewis, *Migratory Labor in California,* pp. 121–24), we find the figures for family earnings shown in table 5.

Between 1930 and 1935 the number of migratory agricultural families in California increased. The effect of that increase is shown in the decline of average annual earnings per family from $381 in 1930 to $289 in 1935. Here is the explanation of the tension among migrant workers in that state—an annual family wage of less than $300.

A study of cotton pickers in Arizona, published in 1939 by Malcolm Brown and Orrin Cassmore, reveals a condition not unlike California. In this survey 518 families and unattached persons were interviewed with reference to their earnings for 1937 (Brown and Cassmore, p. 13). The average annual earnings per case were $393. Counting incidental benefits received while employed, the average earnings were $459, and this average included payments received from WPA and CCC. According to the same report, the average weekly earnings of migrant cotton pickers varied widely but were low throughout the Southwest. This refers to long-fiber cotton (table 6).

If steady employment were available in the cotton fields at the rates shown above, these migrants would fare about as well as WPA workers in the same states. But they work no more than a third of the time, and few of them could get WPA assignments during the off months. They are strangers and not eligible for public relief locally. Being ineligible

TABLE 7

Total reporting on their earnings	185
No earnings	15
Less than $25	12
$25–$49	19
$50–$74	24
$75–$100	47
Between $100 and $200	27
Between $200 and $300	13
Between $300 and $400	12
$400 and over	16

for relief, they cannot be assigned to WPA. In a few states there is some emergency relief for indigent migrants, but in most states there is none, except from private agencies.

The Welfare Council of New York City in an unpublished study made of resident homeless in 1931 and 1932 attempted to secure information about the earnings of these itinerants. It was found that most men cannot recall the amounts of money earned. A total of 185 men were interviewed regarding their earnings. The average was somewhere between $100 and $200, and this range of estimate could not be narrowed even with close questioning. The men interviewed included a small number of transients. The earnings reported were doubtless much lower than normal, because 1931 was a year of low employment (table 7).

Sutherland and Locke in their Chicago study, *Twenty Thousand Homeless Men,* attempted to secure information about earnings on 400 selected cases for the year 1934. Odd jobs and casual jobs were not included. The average weekly wage of these itinerants had been about $25, with $23 being paid for unskilled work, $27 for semiskilled work, and for skilled labor, $51. The average duration of the last steady job had been 4.4 years (Sutherland and Locke, pp. 39–40). The authors added the reservation: "It is probable that the wages and the duration of the jobs were exaggerated." Their comment on method raises doubts about the value of the findings: "The 'duration of the last' job was defined primarily with reference to the type of work. If a man worked as a track laborer each of the last ten years and the season lasted six months, it would be classified here as a job of five years' duration." This device of arithmetic would give the worker five years with double his usual earnings and five years with no earnings at all. It would make the actual earning average of the workers not $25 but considerably less. It would be a liberal estimate to place the average earnings of homeless men in Chicago for the several years preceding 1934 at $10 per week. A considerable portion of the unattached workers who migrate about in cities and between cities would be living in relative luxury if they had a steady income of $7 per week.

It is a well-known fact that the earnings of migratory workers in agriculture are notoriously low, and low because employers can get plenty of labor, however much they may depress wages, so keen is competition for jobs in this field. Concerning agriculture, however, it is possible to secure fairly accurate reports on earnings. The Children's Bureau of the Department of Labor published a study in 1939, *Welfare of Families of Sugar-Beet Laborers,* and among other items regarding beet workers in Colorado, Michigan, Minnesota, Montana, Nebraska, and Wyoming, the report indicates that the "average [median] earnings . . . for the entire season were $340 per family for 374 families interviewed . . . for work on the 1935 beet crop." Information was secured regarding other income received by 343 of the 374 families. It was found that the average income for the year for these families, after including all earnings, was $430. In addition, 63 percent of the families received public relief, which was not included as part of their income.

The social implications of low wages need not call for discussion here. The situation is one that involves not only low wages but intermittent employment with periods of uncertainty between jobs. It is said of the California agricultural workers that competition among them for available jobs sometimes leads to ruthless undercutting. This is said to be less true in localities where the migrant families have formed camp communities and have resided together long enough to develop social bonds. It is said to be much less true of the families that have been exposed to the socializing advantages of the camps established by the Farm Security Administration (FSA).

In the FSA migrant camps these stranded families have an opportunity to rest and get acquainted. The camps become "cities of refuge." The migrant families can talk about their problems. There tends to develop among them, instead of suspicion and discouragement, a sense of solidarity. This may explain the rise of unionism among the migrants in California. It may explain also the strong opposition among the landed interests of California to these camps.

What is happening in California among the migrants, mainly because of low earnings and the lack of job security, may happen in other sections where migrants "pile up" in areas of destination. If they cannot secure the employment or settlement opportunities they expected, they may be driven together into organizations.

Labor Organization among the Migrants

In 1905 a number of seasonal workers met in Chicago to form a union—the revolutionary, direct-action Industrial Workers of the

Workers' alliance organizer speaking at a meeting of the unemployed at Muskogee, Oklahoma. (Photo: Farm Security Administration, by Lee.)

World. Among the founders of the IWW there was some difference of opinion, and the conservative or right-wing section broke away to form the Workers' International Industrial Union. Thus, in 1908 there were two unions of migratory workers which differed only on the issue of political action. The IWW argued: "We are migratory workers. We have no vote, nor can we get the vote, so that weapon is not available. We must fight with other weapons."

The Workers' International Industrial Union reached its peak in 1912, having then 11,000 members. The Industrial Workers of the World, fighting its battle "at the point of production," prior to the World War attained about 100,000 members. Definite information about the IWW membership is not available. There was so much joining and dropping out. It has been estimated that the seasonal joiners numbered 60,000.

In addition to the revolutionary unions already mentioned there were several attempts to form unions of the hobos. In 1905 James Eads How organized the International Brotherhood Welfare Association (IBWA), the official organ of which was the *Hobo News*. The organiza-

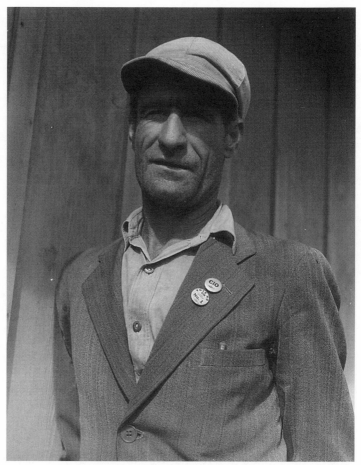

Former farmer from Oklahoma who migrated to California to work in agriculture. He joined the union and became a leader in the strike of cotton pickers. The union demanded an increase from seventy-five cents to a dollar per hundred pounds. (Photo: Farm Security Administration, by Lange.)

tion, revolving as it did about How, who paid the bills, did not attain much size. John X. Kelly and other former associates of How tried to form the Migratory Workers' Union (MWU).

Certain observations can be made about the efforts of the past generation to organize the migratory workers.

1. The organizations were fluid and without discipline. The members multiplied in summer but often dropped out in the winter.
2. The membership was almost entirely drawn from the hobo workers, who were most migratory in the spring, summer, and autumn. They tried to dignify migratory work as an occupation. They took

such work for granted and tried to regulate and improve the employment conditions of migratory work.

3. These organizations passed out of existence during the period between the World War and the 1929 depression. They receded from the scene with the passing of the hobo worker.

4. The migrants who comprised the membership of such organizations or unions were almost entirely unattached men. There were many more unattached men among the modern migrants, yet they displayed little interest in forming unions. If they have any allegiance to labor organizations, it is to unions with which they were associated in their communities of origin and with which they hope to be associated in their communities of destination.

Among the unattached modern migrants there is no evidence of such unions as the IWW, the MWU, or the IBWA. This would indicate that these depression migrants have acquired no proprietary interest in the jobs available to them. This generalization appears not to hold for the migrating families. Several attempts have been made, for example, to organize the sharecroppers into unions. The sharecroppers are migrants in a limited sense, milling around within a county or within an area comprising several counties of a state. Out of this group some families pick up and move perhaps to neighboring states or to towns and cities, then back to some other rural section.

Concerning the migration of workers who would be settlers, Paul S. Taylor has written:

Mobile agricultural labor has grown in importance in the West with the demands of expanding irrigation. Although it has declined in the wheat belt because of the combined harvester, it has increased in the cotton belt as cotton has moved on to the plains of Texas and Oklahoma. In a modified form the pattern of mobile labor is now expanding in the richest delta land of the South. It has grown, too, in the Southeast along the Atlantic Seaboard, and in the berry and fruit crops of the Mississippi Valley. As industrial opportunity continues to lag, and agricultural depression is prolonged, evidences of the growing class character of agricultural labor, whether mobile or not, become plainer and more widespread. And they make agricultural employers uneasy, as the early trade unions made industrial employers uneasy. ("The Place of Agricultural Labor in Society," paper read before the 12th meeting of the Western Farm Economics Association, June 15, 1939.)

Large-scale farms, operated more like industrial establishments, are on the increase with the introduction of power equipment and other types of labor-saving machinery. Gradually but surely these farms have expelled a good share of the regular year-round workers. They need seasonal labor and will continue to depend on such labor only occasionally during the production, harvesting, and marketing of crops. Concerning this new type of labor situation, a representative of the agricultural department of the Los Angeles Chamber of Commerce said in 1926: "The old-fashioned hired man is a thing of the past. . . . There is no place for him, and the farmer who does not wake up to the realization that there is a caste of labor on the farm, is sharing too much of his dollar with labor. We are not husbandmen. We are not farmers. We are producing to sell."

Paul S. Taylor, who quoted the above statement in a paper read before a meeting of the Western Farm Economics Association in June 1939, added the information that the changed order of agricultural labor is becoming more prevalent. The conclusion is reached by Taylor that among the roving farm families there is a growing restiveness. Perhaps this restiveness is brought on in part by the organization of the employer farmers, especially in California where upwards of 200,000 workers, most of them members of itinerant families, try to live by doing occasional jobs for industrialized agriculture.

California agricultural employers were on the alert about the organization of agricultural labor as early as 1907. The following is quoted from the proceedings of the Fruit Growers of California Convention for that year:

> The Japanese farm laborers, although unorganized, as pointed out before, had among them a sort of spontaneous organization that made them not quite as tractable as the Chinese. The concensus of opinion of growers on the subject is almost unanimous in the early years of the Century. It was customary at that time to engage them from camps maintained by contractors who were paid upon the completion of the work for such work as the men under their control did. Often, when conditions did not satisfy the Japanese, he would walk off the job. The longing for the good old days of the Chinese grew more and more prevalent in those days among the growers.

The speaker quoted above related a complaint from a grower who compared the Japanese, then being employed, with the Chinese employed in earlier years: "The Chinese, when they were here, were ideal. They were patient, plodding and uncomplaining in the performance of the most menial service. They submitted to anything, never violating a contract. The Exclusion Acts drove them out. The Japanese now coming in are a tricky and cunning lot."

After reading the above sentiment, there should be no mistaking what California industrial farmers expect of the workers they hire. Later, these farmers could no longer get Japanese labor, so they turned to other sources. In 1927 there was discussion about the choice between temporarily importing Mexicans or encouraging the migration of Puerto Ricans. In the convention of 1927 of the Fruit Growers of California one of the officials expressed this opinion:

> Again, if we do bring in these two types we cannot handle them like Mexicans. A Porto Rican has as much right to stay as we have. He cannot be exported as can a Mexican who becomes indigent. As you know, the Mexican likes the sunshine against the adobe wall with a few tortillas and in the off-time he drifts across the border where he may have these things. No one can deny that the Mexican in the State of California is a liability to a certain extent. We must admit that the social service people in the state and the welfare organizations in Los Angeles have a tremendous problem in handling the Mexican laborer and his family. But that is not at all out of reason because, as Dr. Clements of Los Angeles has well said, if charity spends one dollar on the Mexican in California, the state profits two dollars by having him here. The Mexicans can be deported if they become county charges, but the others are here to stay and they are less efficient.

The above policy of economic statesmancraft was proffered about three years before California was confronted with the deluge of agricultural exiles from the cotton country of the South, described by Carey McWilliams, author of *Factories in the Fields*, as "an army that marches from crop to crop. Its equipment is negligible, a few pots and pans . . . and its quarters unenviable. It is supported by a vast herd of camp followers, mostly pregnant women, diseased children and flea-bitten dogs." This army in California is having the idea driven home that, however much its labor is needed on occasion, California is hostile territory.

If the great fruit growers were worried by the Japanese and irritated by the IWW during the World War and before, they have been frustrated even more by the "Grapes of Wrath" people; the refugees from the Dust Bowl, the sons of the "Sooners" of Oklahoma, the disinherited sharecroppers, and other varieties of economic exiles—all of good American stock looking for a stake in the land.

Agricultural employers of California in 1933 joined for defense, because these new immigrants do not behave like the Filipinos, the Mexicans, the Japanese, the Chinese, and the usual quota of unattached migrant seasonal workers. This move was taken by the California Farm Bureau Federation and the State Chamber of Commerce. From this union was born Associated Farmers. Employers of seasonal labor in agriculture "pledged to help one another in case of emergency. They agreed to co-operate to harvest crops in case of strikes and to offer their services to the local sheriff immediately as special deputies in the

A migratory cotton picker on strike for a 25 percent wage increase. This young man lives in the Farm Security Administration migrant camp at Shafter, California. (Photo: Farm Security Administration, by Lange.)

event of disorders arising out of picketing and sabotage." Associated Farmers then proceeded to establish a unit in each county for the sole purpose of keeping agricultural workers from organizing.

Said Carey McWilliams:

> An efficient espionage system is maintained by Associated Farmers. In 1935, I inspected the "confidential" files of the organization in San Francisco. At that time they had a card index file of "dangerous radicals" containing approximately one thousand names, alphabetically arranged, with front- and side-view photographs of each individual including notations of arrests, strike activities, affiliations and so forth. (*Factories in the Field*, p. 233)

Whether or not the migrants are themselves susceptible to labor organization, there is plenty of evidence that they may be used by employers for the purpose of defeating labor unions. It is an old practice of agriculture or industry to meet a strike situation by bringing in a new supply of labor. New workers are encouraged to migrate from other places. The following example was sent to the writer by Gerald A. Elliott of Grand Rapids, Michigan—an example followed since by the auto industry.

> It came off like clockwork. The great Railroad Strike of 1922, that is. It was 10 o'clock of the morning of the First of July. With the precision of the pistons that drove the great engines they worked on, the men of the Pere Marquette and Pennsylvania Railroad (it was the Grand Rapids and Indiana line, then) shops picked up their coats and lunch buckets and walked out of the shops. The railroads had announced a general wage cut. Mechanics had been getting 77 cents per hour; helpers, 62 cents; laborers, 50 cents per hour.
>
> While the union prepared their strike technique, established picket lines and held meetings in the union halls the railroads were busy. Representatives of the various lines were busy in Chicago—in Missouri—in Alabama. Negroes, unskilled, inexperienced in railroad shop work were hired to replace the strikers. Before the strike was many days old, passenger trains loaded to the platform with colored strikebreakers were rolling into the Grand Rapids Yards.
>
> The roads weren't taking any chances. They housed them in the shops. They fed them, distributed tobacco. But they couldn't make mechanics of them. Many a train pulled out with an inadequately sealed valve during those six weeks. By the middle of August an injunction was secured against the pickets. The strike began to wane. Strikers trickled back to the shops. Many of them went to work in the shops that they had not hithertofore worked in. All of them lost their security rights. Their pass rights. But their wages weren't cut. A few years later they secured a wage increase.
>
> But what about the Negroes who had been lured to Grand Rapids by the promise of good jobs? Well, some of them couldn't stand the severity of the weather. Others just didn't like it. And so they wandered away. But many of them remained. They nourished hopes of securing jobs in the community; a community made up almost exclusively of craftsmen employed in the furniture industry. What was left for them? Well, a few got jobs in the summertime on the asphalt gangs; for the rest, relief. They still live there; down among the railroad tracks and the gas plants, Grand Rapids' only slum district; looking forward to possible WPA employment.

The rest of the story is that few of the Negroes who were brought in to break a union are themselves now unionized. They are casual workers now. Seasonal and casual labor, especially mobile labor, is not easily unionized. That seems to be the problem of migrants in both agriculture and industry. They cannot be unionized if they are dissociated from the supporting influences of community life. They may strike, but, the strike over, the organization disbands. That was the history of the IWW. They conducted many strikes, but they were too migrant to maintain organization solidarity.

Migrant workers may be strongly union conscious. A wandering mechanic may "carry a card" in an international union, but he rarely uses the card en route. The mobile existence of migrancy seems not to be congenial to labor organization.

14

A Family in the Hobomania Era

I

The national archives in Washington is a treasure house. One time when I went there in search of some documents on western history I chanced upon a handwritten letter signed and sent by the president of the United States to some key member of Congress. It was dated in the early 1880s and I faintly remember it was signed by Chester A. Arthur. Since it was not related to what I was looking for, I took no notes from it.

In this one-page letter of perhaps a hundred words the president related an appeal he had received from a group of ranchers in New Mexico who were being harrassed by cattle thieves, known today as "rustlers," and they asked the government to take some action against them. What I do remember vividly is this short sentence regarding the rustlers: "They are called cowboys."

Such was the original image of the cowboy. What the story writers and Hollywood have done to change that image is remarkable. The cowboy was indeed a frontier type, but so was the hobo, the itinerant jack-of-all-work on the frontier. He has been fair game, not for story tellers and Hollywood alone but for historians and journalists. To-gether, they have made of him an irretrievable never sweat, often a clown character as well.

It is not my concern to wage resistance to that ongoing trend; it would avail little. It is my task to present the hobo as he figured in frontier development, for he was, in fact, of the frontier work system. I knew him as early as 1905 and I knew many old timers who dated back twenty years or more earlier.

Above all, the hobo was a worker, one who moved from one kind of work to another when and as needed and who went his way when not needed. He displayed a way of appearing when and where new work

From *The American Hobo: An Autobiography* (Leiden: E. J. Brill, 1975): 1–15. Reprinted by permission.

was about to begin. He was an independent fellow who would leave any job if he felt conditions were unfair. Again, he would work six months or longer, then go with his stake to some city to "hole up for the winter," or to "rub off," or merely to "blow his pile." His next job might be in any direction or at any distance. Money gone, he did not shrink from "panhandling" (begging on the street) or from knocking on back doors for handouts. He was no walker from place to place, if freight trains were running.

To repeat, however, the hobo spent his money on gambling, women, hard liquor, or steak dinners. Work figured heavily in his conversation, whether on the job or "doing the town." In terms of the kinds of work he could do or had done he respected himself and on that basis he judged the worth of his fellows. Much that expressed his prejudices or his pride often stemmed from his attitudes toward work.

Typically, the hobo was native-born American, at least most of the seasoned old timers were. The few alien hobos were most likely to be Irish ("chaws") or English ("limeys"), although one occasionally met a German, a Swede, or other. The hobo was no perennial who thought of his go-about existence as going on and on; one day he would settle down. I have known men who had been hobo workers. Perhaps many can still be found. There was that minority who never could settle. For such there was only one course, to go down as they aged. We will meet a number of these in the pages ahead.

Fifty years to the month have passed since the University of Chicago Press published a book by me, *The Hobo*, written when I was a graduate in sociology at that university. More about that in its proper place later. Nothing about me or my personal acquaintance with hobos and their life appeared in that volume. I wrote an introduction making up for that lack for the paperback edition which appeared in 1964. The reason for keeping my past anonymous is understandable. I could not talk to fellow students about my background. I could anticipate too well their reactions, like trying to describe a foreign civilization. I let them believe that all the material in *The Hobo* had been assembled in Chicago's Hobohemia, the chief "main stem" for migratory workers in the Middle West.

Among those who knew better it was a credit item to have had acquaintance with hobos and their way of life. But most people above the working-class level reacted otherwise to these men who came from God knows where. If, as often happened, after *The Hobo* appeared, someone asked me about my own background I found ways to evade the question. Today I am otherwise known and the old attitudes have had a generation to recede. For years, however, the book, which is still being read, in various ways put the "Indian sign" on me, and not always to my liking. This account is not an answer to all that; indeed, an answer is no longer needed, the hobo has moved into history.

Although this story must be in part personal, my wish is to make it seem not overly autobiographical. Rather, as I am able, I prefer to describe the scenes as they pass, observing the characters who come and go. The story should be theirs. As far as my knowledge goes their story in these terms has not been told.

Necessarily, I must bring in my father and the Anderson family. And I dare to say that we represented one type of American family quite prevalent before 1900; one American-born parent and one foreign-born. My father was a Swedish immigrant, an 1882 arrival, aged about thirty and, although illiterate, he was both a qualified bricklayer and, what was then equally important, an equally qualified mixer of mortar, which most bricklayers were not. My mother was born in St. Louis of Scottish immigrant parents. She had about four or five years of schooling and was an unskilled factory worker when she and my father met.

My father was born in a Swedish peasant village and was orphaned in early childhood by a cholera plague. At about age fourteen he migrated with a kinsman to Germany where he remained for about eighteen years. He arrived in America able to speak, at the workingman's level, two languages, and within three or four years had achieved the common man's working knowledge of English. Those first few years when he wandered here and there learning America remained the most treasured of his life. When visitors were present he never failed to relate some happenings he liked to recall. He had been a hobo.

Settling down, which my parents intended to do in Chicago, was something Father was not able to do. He was not wishy-washy; he had a goal from which he never turned. Actually he came to America with two goals; the first, to marry an American woman and bring up a large American family. In the course of fourteen years the Andersons settled, broke their home and migrated to settle again ten times. During that period ten of my mother's twelve children were born. We were a hobo family, always in poverty, or near it, but only once did poverty get us down. We didn't know that word, although we did use the word "paupers" in referring to certain other families.

Father's second goal was to own a large farm, to be surrounded in time by a cluster of farms owned by his children. It was this second goal which kept him on the move. He pushed the ideal too hard; none of his children became farmers, but in his old age he did have a good farm. It may have been his stubborn life goal plus an equally firm peasant conviction that it was his duty to make major decisions for his children that sent his boys on the road in different directions.

II

In Chicago Father teamed up with a Tim somebody, an Irish immigrant, a plasterer, and the sort of man he trusted. This was important since Tim could write and keep records. Father, of course, could do brick work and mix mortar. The pair became "job contractors" taking little contracts, making much better than wages. My father never ceased remembering Tim with respect. Every three weeks or so Tim would fail to appear. His wife would come running in panic, and Father would have to make the rounds of the barrelhouses to find his partner and sober him up.

That partnership which provided better than average security suddenly came to a close one evening when Father listened to my mother reading the news and came to a story about a great fire in Spokane, Washington, in which most of the town had burned down. He imagined a big city in ashes. There would be much rebuilding, he concluded, and wages would be high. Mother knew that Spokane was somewhere out West but she had never learned where or how far, but she liked the idea of going.

My father had heard much about "out West," but he never imagined opportunity would come in this fashion. By morning that goal of becoming a contractor lost its worth. Tim agreed to buy his share of the business and father related often how they bargained: "He offered me $400. I said $200. So we settled for $300." He had to be off to find his Spokane job and a place to live. Mother had the burden of managing her own takeoff, with the help of Tim. The furniture they bought in a secondhand store nearly three years earlier she sold back to the same dealer. Mother never whined or complained, but she never forgot how she managed that takeoff with two babies to care for, Bill a little more than a year old and me a babe in arms. I heard her tell it to other women, the packing and all and the five days and nights in an immigrant chair car.

Father, self-sufficient himself, expected self-sufficiency of his family. He worried about our arrival but took for granted that Mother would manage, as he knew such a strong woman could. But his image of a woman was that of peasant women who worked in the fields when needed. His one remembrance of our journey concerned the odors we brought with us. On the train Mother could not wash my diapers, nor would she throw them out the window. They accumulated in a bag which did not contain the odors. People sniffed and stared, and I was the cause of it.

My father had a job at good wages and he had rented a shack in a shantytown area called "The Flats." I think the evidence does not exist, but it is a safe assumption that every American city in its beginning had its "flats," its "shack town," or some place called "the bottoms," which may have their place sometimes in local city history but as an aspect of frontier development. On these Spokane flats the come-and-go people, families going about in covered wagons, would stop for weeks or months if work was to be had. Some would move on, others remained to become permanent. My father was among those who had no wish to be an old settler. Nor would he wander about as did many families in covered wagons, going from job to job, living a kind of family hobo life.

His yearning for good farming land was my father's real reason for moving to the West, a wish my mother shared to a degree, although she knew nothing about farming, had never milked a cow or tended chickens. She reasoned: "It is not so different from other work, once you learn it." His work, laying brick or mixing mortar, was a way to get money to get a farm. He bought a horse and western saddle, prideful possessions for a man who could never have owned such in the Old Country. Each Sunday he went riding in one direction or other asking about land for sale. Any place he liked was beyond his prospect to pay.

In the course of one such horseback tour Father learned of a timber claim twenty miles from Spokane held by a man who would sell his equity in it. On the claim was a house of a kind, a well, and outbuildings. The facts I never heard, nor are they important here. My father somehow got possession of a piece of land which could be made into a farm, once the tall timber had been cleared away. Some land could be tilled, but first my father would have to accumulate the means to set himself up as a farmer. Whatever the plan, it was quite to my mother's liking. She would have a cow, a couple of pigs to fatten for meat, chickens, and a garden. She would stay with the children on the claim while he worked in the city, riding home weekends on his horse, Charley. To have more time for work at home, he did his riding at night. My mother was well able to manage her end of the partnership. For her, the loneliness of the spot was an accepted fact of life. In one direction was the nearest neighbor, about two miles distant. Behind our place was the forest where the wolves howled at night. What concerned her only was that they might get her chickens. The rifle she had for protection she would fire into the air. That was warning enough. The howling stopped.

Slowly Father came to the conclusion that one man's lifetime would not be enough to convert the timber claim to a viable farm. But for Mother the situation was quite satisfactory. They might have disagreed had he suggested moving away. The decision to move was based on another sad occurrence. Her third baby was born soon after settling on the claim. Within months the baby, Dorothy, died despite the drug store remedies Father brought from the city. I was sick much of the time, a "blue baby" Mother thought. Within another year Celia was born. When it seemed I might be improving, at least, not getting worse, Celia began to show the same symptoms. Father was able to sell the farm at a profit. Much later Mother concluded that the illness was due to the well water, but it had not affected her or my brother Bill.

What would have seemed strange, if not impossible two years earlier, they now accepted as the proper thing to do. They had learned how families moved about in the West. Father bought another horse, a wagon and harness, a tent, and other things needed for the road. Mother's sewing machine, the cook stove, bedding, clothing, and kitchen things were loaded. Furniture which Father made of pine lumber remained behind. The Andersons in their covered wagon, like many others they had seen, set out looking for land.

What my parents were learning during their stay, first in the flats by Spokane and then on the timber claim, was the fluidity of life. One rarely met an adult who was born there. Few of the children in the families on the flats had been born there. Mother mentioned often how the flats were "just a campground." Many of the families she met had already moved several times and would move again. There were lone men among the flats population, sometimes two or three "batching it" in one of the rented shacks. Hobos all, moving about was a way of life.

Now the Andersons, all their possessions in their wagon, had joined that meandering stream. Neither Father nor Mother had ever slept in a tent and neither knew how to pitch one, nor had they learned the art of cooking over a camp fire. Neither knew the art of managing without getting overly wet if the rains came. Moreover, as was true of other moving families they met, Father was looking for land but he had no idea where to find it. He soon learned it was the right thing to stop to exchange information with each covered wagon outfit coming alone. More than likely, each would have bad news about the people and conditions experienced.

Not all of those migrating people were land seekers. Some were looking for work and some of those, so Mother remembered, "made a business of it." Here they would go to the wheat harvest, there to pick apples, or they worked on construction projects or in the lumber woods, making the rounds with the seasons. The land hunters, as Father remembered them, had been farmers, but were moving to find better land or more land. About all my father learned from them was that the good land in Idaho, Oregon, and Washington had already been taken.

Somewhere near the Idaho-Washington border Father talked with one of those land hunters who had seen much of Idaho. He had passed through the Nez Percé Indian Reservation where he saw much good land owned by the Indians who had not yet learned to be farmers. He told of one Indian who had considerable crop land and the equipment to farm it. The Indian asked him to remain to help him work the land for half of the crop. This he could not accept because he was averse to the idea of a white man working in partnership with an Indian. He was amused that Father was interested, but he told him in some detail how to find the place.

III

Father knew very little about Indians but that little was enough to plant in his mind a firm positive feeling for them; they had been robbed and badly treated by the white men. Perhaps there was some fellow feeling in his attitude. Alien that he was and not yet a citizen, he was continually on the defensive when dealing with the native-born. That sense of being an outsider never left him even after he became a tax-paying citizen. But Father refused to do what is often common among immigrant groups; he would not settle in an all-Swedish community or an all-German community. He would have his children "grow up American." Not unlikely, that awareness of being an outsider helped to mellow his meeting with an Indian who had land to share.

That Indian and his family were to enter our experience. He had taken the name of Joe Bronjo. He was an elderly man, but hearty and able, father of two married sons who had refused to join him in learning the white man's way of farming. They preferred to work with white men in the lumber woods or in the mines, leaving their wives and children with Old Joe in the farm. It is pertinent to mention here that Old Joe had been a leader in his tribe. As the story came, mostly to Mother, he was one of the older leaders who concluded that the Indians could not hope to win against the whites. All would be killed; even women and children would not be spared. Better, they argued, to accept defeat and find a new life on their reservation. This course was taken but it was not to the liking of the younger Indians who would have fought on. They were averse to becoming tillers of the soil, a view which was held by the sons of Old Joe. None of the story came to us from the old Indian, who talked some English, enough, plus sign language, for him and Father to get on with their work, but knowing the story increased my father's regard for him.

Old Joe's habitat included four stout cabins; two occupied by the wives and children of his sons, the third by Old Joe and his equally elderly wife. Some may say I should use "squaw," the Indian word for wife or woman, but I never liked that term. The fourth cabin was taken by the Andersons. There were stables for the livestock and sheds for the farm equipment. Less than a hundred feet from the row of cabins was a tree-lined creek, large enough for wading and watching the tiny trout. Except when the weather was bad, the Indians preferred cooking on an outdoor fire to the stoves in their cabins. Mother did likewise, but for baking she used her stove and from her the two younger women learned to bake her kind of bread. She sat with them on the ground and conversed with sign language.

It was on the Reservation where my first memories began. Bill, who claimed that he could remember many bits about the timber claim and all about traveling in the covered wagon, was that much ahead of me on the Reservation. He played mainly with the Indian boys and was able by one ruse or other to leave me behind. It was my task much of the time to look after Celia who was beginning to wander a little. It was Old Joe who made me his playmate. When he was not with Father in the fields he braided rawhide lariat ropes which were sold to cattle-men. I was fascinated watching his hands at braiding. With short strips of rawhide he could not use, I tried braiding. He said nothing, but would move his hands carefully and slowly when I stood watching. Within days, after endless errors, I too could braid but my four-year-old fingers were not strong enough to press the overlappings down firm. He was the perfect teacher and my first hero. After we moved to Lewiston he came to visit. I was then seven or eight, and he gave me little notice. I had changed from child to boy.

Father was highly pleased with the first year's crop, and satisfied with the market for oats, wheat, and potatoes. Especially he was satisfied with his Indian partner. They decided it would pay better if they bought young brood sows and raised fifteen to twenty pigs, fattening them with their own wheat. The pork would bring good prices in the mining camps and lumber camps. They put more land under cultivation, bought the sows and the sows brought their litters. Then they were floored by the unpredicted; the bottom dropped out of the produce markets.

The "Cleveland Panic" was on. Father went to Lewiston to look things over. He returned with the news that Wall Street caused the panic, Wall Street and the Republicans. They would punish the people for electing Cleveland, an explanation often heard in the years ahead. I also heard later how when the panic started thousands of hobos from all parts of the nation undertook a march to Washington to demand that the government start a national road building program. But they were not called hobos by many then, rather, many papers, if they did not speak of "vagrants" or "tramps" used the term "industrials."

The partnership faded out. Father and Old Joe agreed to store their grain. Old Joe would go on fattening the pigs, selling them later as he could. The Andersons moved to Lewiston, there to occupy an old house on the street where a dike had been built (Lewiston was at the junction of the Snake and Clearwater rivers.) It was a good house, built before the dike, standing on posts three feet above the ground assuring safety when the floods came down the Clearwater. There was a stable for the cow mother brought from the Reservation, and for our horses. Old Joe came with his wagon loaded with bags of oats for the horses, wheat for the chickens Mother planned to get, and potatoes for the family. That move was made early in 1894, and I have one good reason for remembering it. One day a neighbor woman asked me to do an errand to the store on the next street. She wrote on a grocer's order pad the things wanted and signed her name. On top of the pad was a line for the day and month, which she wrote. I have forgotten that, but then came in print 189– to which she added 4. I was then in my fifth year.

IV

At this point an explanation is in order answering whosoever may wonder what the pertinence of all this is to the story of the hobo. I think of it as part of my own education and I hope this will be evident as we move along. To this I must add that the first ten years of the family odyssey has already appeared in print,[1] and I am trying to note bits which may contribute something to my own preparation, as I believe our stay in Lewiston did.

For some reason, and I have not tried to get an explanation for it, my father found steady work either as a bricklayer or mortar mixer, or doing both. Building went on in Lewiston. My father did not lose as much at farming as he sometimes claimed. Little by little Old Joe sold bags of wheat or oats and he was able to dispose of the pigs when they were ready for slaughter. Old Joe brought Father's share of the spoils to Lewiston. Whenever he came, usually bringing his whole family along, he would sit with Father exchanging thoughts mainly through sign language, while Mother did the same with the Indian women in the kitchen, laughing over coffee and coffee cake.

Especially for me, Lewiston was an important experience, all one could wish for in a Western town far from the railroad, a town that served ranchers, miners, and woodsmen. Two kinds of people were served: the respectable who did their shopping on the main street and

1. Nels Anderson, "The Private and Last Frontier," *The Sewanee Review* 77, no. 1, (January–March 1969): pp. 25–90.

others who went to what the respectable called "the saloon street." The main street contained the kind and number of stores and services one would expect in a town of about 2,000.

The Salvation Army arrived while we were in Lewiston, and settled on the saloon street. It goes where the need is greatest, among saloons and gambling houses. This was a man's street with its women to serve them. Here the mobile men who shifted from job to job came to spend when they had money. Lewiston, like other towns, had its "off limits" quarter, or "bad land." Most of the boys I played with were forbidden by their mothers to go there. For my mother no place was off limits. "They got to learn to take care of *themselves*" was her credo. The saloon street had its wooden sidewalk as good as the one on the business block of the main street. Once when peeking through the cracks between the sidewalk planks, hoping to find nickels or dimes dropped by drunken men, I found a half-dollar.

Mother did the washing for "Old Jim," a gambler of that district, the best-dressed man in town. He came to her because it was hard to find a woman who could properly starch collars and cuffs. From him we learned that whiskey flasks could be sold in any saloon for five cents each. Bill and I hunted and found some. He lost interest but I went on finding the likely spots where the drinking men would throw flasks away. Ordinarily I would find four a day but more on weekends. I chanced to get acquainted with the women who lived in houses behind the saloons. Mother called them "chippies" but to Father they were "dirty things," yet she had no bias against them. These women saved flasks for me and often asked me to run errands to the stores. I was paid nickels for that. I was giving Mother about $2.00 a week from my business.

As with all good things, my lucrative activities ended. Someone who worked with Father told him he had seen "that boy of yours" going into a saloon. His shame abated somewhat when Mother told him what I was earning. He worried about what neighbors would think, but stood by his stop order. One of the women in those houses told me when I met her accidently, "Your father is right. When you have bottles bring them to me. I'll get the money for you." Mother thought that arrangement not so bad, so secretly I was in business again, this time with a partner. Mother was glad to get the money, which went into the same earthen crock in which she put money for eggs sold and money earned washing for Old Jim, the gambler. A week later, perhaps longer, she thought better of her decision, "Papa would get hopping mad."

The sort of men I would see on the saloon street were the kind I was to know later when I sold papers on Madison Street in Chicago, the same types I would work with much later. Many times I would pass the campgrounds where mobile families lived in tents pitched next to their covered wagon. They, too, were of the moving population of the West. On jobs where Father worked, men from the campgrounds would also be working. From his talk at home I would hear that some of these men were not good workers, others he spoke well of. Mothers on our street would tell their boys not to hang around the campgrounds. Bill and I were as free to go there as on the saloon street.

Settled people in Lewiston held the campground people, called immigrants, in low esteem, as Father also thought. Once when he expressed such an opinion Mother answered, "Everybody in Lewiston came here in a covered wagon." The settled people would say that when they came the covered-wagon immigrants were different.

Years had to pass before I realized how much Lewiston reflected the way of life of the West of the 1890s. It was market town for Indians from the Reservation. Each time Old Joe and his family came to shop they would pitch their tent next to our house. Mother would go with the women to the stores, mostly to look after their money, listing things they wanted most and least. Tricksters were there to sell them whiskey, which was illegal. Indians who got drunk were usually also robbed, and sometimes arrested. Herds of cattle would be driven along the river bottoms beyond the dike behind our house. I would run with the other boys to the dike to watch men on horses driving the herds. We followed as the herd was driven to a point below the Clearwater ferry. Those in front would not slide down the bank into the river. They were pushed in by the crowding behind, egged on by the men on horseback. Those in the water would swim toward the opposite bank. The rest followed and we got the thrill of seeing the whole herd swimming, only their noses and horns above the water. We didn't know that those men on horses were "cowboys" and not "ranch hands." To us they were important men. There were other such crossings, but I remember following only one.

Father gained his citizenship in Lewiston and he voted there the first time. He could now talk politics with other men but he held fast to his view that the Republicans had caused the Cleveland Panic. He got the notion that our weather beaten old house could be made attractive. He had a hired man who used our horses and wagon to work on construction, hauling materials, scooping out basements. That was extra income. If there was good earth to haul away it was brought to our lot, making a soil base for a lawn and trees in front, and a garden at the rear. Evenings and Sundays for three years he worked on the house, which no longer stood on posts but on a brick foundation. He covered the outer walls with clapboard siding and reshingled the roof. When it was painted, the house was the bright spot on the dike street.

As I much later recognized, he had a secret purpose in mind; the old house which he bought cheap would later sell at a high price. During our fourth year in Lewiston he began talking about moving and having a good farm. Working for wages, he would say is "not safe. I might get sick or get hurt and we would be soon poor." His second argument was more immediate; Bill and I, in his thinking, were running wild, nothing to do but play when we could be learning to work. "Boys without work grow up lazy." Also there was Lester, born soon after we reached Lewiston. Next came Leslie who died in infancy. Mother knew later that it was due to an infected breast which caused much trouble and which later atrophied. Her next six babies nursed from one breast only. Before we left Lewiston Belle was born. Father was thinking of three boys who would be his helpers if he had a farm.

V

Bill and I were hearing that talk about moving from Lewiston but it made only a surface impression. It became reality one evening when a possible buyer came to look at our house. Mother told us later the man didn't have enough cash. But the step was taken. Bill was elated. We would see new places. Until we were on our way weeks later, the idea of moving depressed me. Against moving at first, mother began warming up to the idea. From families moving from Lewiston she had acquired various pieces of furniture of which she was proud. The only parlor the Andersons ever had was there, nice furniture, carpet on the floor, lace curtains on the window. It was the forbidden room unless visitors came. Women came to look, and bit by bit the parlor became an empty room. She found buyers for her chickens and her cow.

Old Joe and his family came and heard the bad news. I should mention that soon after we came to Lewiston Father found that our horses were too light for the heavy work and he bought a big team of blacks. He asked Old Joe to take Jim, the bay, and Charley, the gray horse. He was not so concerned about Jim, but Charley had been his saddle horse when we lived on the timber claim. Charley had carried him in the night scores of times between the claim and Spokane. A day or so before we left Old Joe came with his wagon driving Charley and Jim, so father could say good bye to his "Charley horse." He went away with the wagon loaded with things Mother wanted his family to have. Father remembered him not as "a good Indian," but whenever he recalled Old Joe he was an "honest friend."

The house was sold sooner than Father expected. Mother was firm about not having the neighbors see us drive away "like wagon immigrants." The wagon was loaded after dark, the bows put in place and the wagon cover stretched over. We slept on the floor and were away well before daylight.

At dawn we were first in line to cross the Snake River on the ferry to Clarkston in the state of Washington. Clarkston was yet only a village. (Lewiston and Clarkston were named for Lewis and Clark, the explorers.) That was a fearful crossing for me. I had always kept away from that river, a giant compared with the Clearwater, always muddy, always swirling. It was a relief when Father drove off the old ferry and up the slope to stop, make a fire, and have breakfast. That was an event for Bill and me. Our bare feet and legs were cold. We ran about gathering bits of wood for the fire, stopping often to look across the Snake at Lewiston, pointing to buildings we knew. Mother was doing the same. Father was pointing out the red brick normal school, so new it had not yet been used. We didn't know what a normal school was for. "What difference does it make?" Mother said. She began pouring the coffee. There was no milk and we never used sugar. She passed around the sandwiches made the day before and a hunk of spare ribs for each person. It was like a picnic. We made fun throwing the bones over our shoulders. The sun was now up and the cold was leaving my legs.

Our parents were secretive about money matters. Bill and I never knew how much Father paid for our Lewiston house or what he got when he sold. We never asked. We knew the money was kept, gold pieces, in Father's buckskin bag, hidden somewhere in the loaded wagon. We were never curious about where. Nor did we know until half an hour after breakfast why we camped on that spot, not until we saw a man coming out of the Clarkston village leading two gray horses. Father had traded our big blacks for that smaller pair of grays. There was the usual horse-trader talk, Mother taking part, the rest of us listening. The man counted out to Father some money "to boot," they shook hands, and the man led the blacks away.

One of the new team, Ben, the larger of the two, the man described as real gentle. The other, Brigham, he said, was a little spunky. He would bite maybe, but never real hard. That settled, Father said it was up to Bill and me to look after the horses. When Bill said he would take Ben, I was glad of his choice. I could not have reached up to put the harness or collar on the larger horse. In about three months from our departure I was nine years old, Bill was ten years and six months.

When harnessing horses, height and weight favored Bill. As the weeks went by I had other reasons for liking the spunky Brigham more than the big, phlegmatic Ben. I imagined that he accepted me from the start. If I went near he might put his ears back and even nip me, but never to hurt. If he nipped Bill, as he did a few times, it was never gently.

Father was more sure of himself than when he and Mother left the timber claim six years earlier. He was now a citizen, and he knew much more about getting on with people in the American way. He had not failed in Lewiston. Taking once more to the road, he was fairly certain that now luck would be ours within three or four weeks. We were more than three months traveling. He did no searching in Washington. Mother had no wish for it, "We had only bad luck in Washington."

Our going about looking for land was an adventure for Bill and me. We went daily except for about every other Sunday when Mother had to do the washing, and there were half-day stops when Father would go about talking to people or to look at farms for sale. His conclusions never varied; good farms were beyond his purse, but he would not go in debt to bankers. In the course we would learn life on the road as a "prairie schooner" family, the outfits I had seen frequently at the campground in Lewiston. We were to see other campgrounds and to meet each day as many as a dozen such outfits. These were the taken-for-granted facts of life, and there were many thousands of such all over the Northwest.

We were meeting the understandable aftermath of the mass covered-wagon migration to the last frontier. Some were latecomers, arriving after most of the choice land had been occupied, others had settled but were looking for a better location. Most of them, as my parents would say, were migratory working families going from one kind of job to another, the familial counterpart of the hobo, who moved unencumbered except for the bed roll on his back; sometimes miner, sometimes lumberjack, sometimes harvest hand or construction worker.

We were meeting them on the road but I do not recall meeting them in frontier history or in sociological studies. Twenty years later, meeting such an outfit on the roads we traveled would have been an oddity.

Father was a believer in system, as careful about using time or energy to advantage as he was of saving money. Our daily routine had to be organized. Each time we stopped Bill and I had to unhitch the horses, take off the harness, and put each in place. After leading the horses to the nearest and best grass we would hurry back and take the grub box off the wagon so Mother could get busy. It was for us to gather wood for the fire and after that to put up the tent. Father showed us how, remembering how he had learned the trick before my memory, when we traveled after leaving the timber claim. We were impressed when, despite some fumbling, he did it in less than a half hour. Before two weeks or so Bill and I had our own system. Usually with some argument, we learned to do the job in about fifteen minutes. Celia's job was to look after Belle, the baby, and Lester, a bothersome little boy. Father had to be free to go around talking to people.

Our route took us into Oregon. From outfits we met we learned that there was a building and land boom in Baker City, Oregon, later known as Baker. It turned out that two to three hundred other families had received the same information. The one main street was filled with covered wagons. They were camped along the road in different directions. Father found no encouraging information and he accepted Mother's decision that "We better get back to Idaho where we belong." For the next several weeks our course zig-zagged north or south as we moved east across Idaho, now in hilly country, now in dry desert.

The main course of travel was along the old Oregon Trail route. There was no paved road anywhere, except in towns where roads were graveled, and not always were there bridges over streams or irrigation ditches. After a rain wagons would be seen bogged in the mud. "Rules of the road," seldom breached, required every traveler to help another. Going up steep hills Bill and I would have to carry stones to block the rear wheels when Father stopped to let Ben and Brigham get their wind. Going down steep hills he would chain a rear wheel so it would drag, relieving the horses of the push of the load.

Every opportunity he had, Father talked to the settled people about land. He became more and more aware of the dislike they had for the wagon immigrants (not immigrants in the sense of being foreign-born but because they moved about; rarely were they foreigners). They sensed that we were real land hunters. He would hear how the immigrants would steal horses, take fat ones and leave their bony ones behind, or how they wouldn't take jobs. We heard the immigrants declare how the settled people paid only starvation wages. Immigrant families differed from those with good wagons to those with wobbly wheels braced with boards and baling wire, from those with hearty, able horses to those whose horses were bone thin, harness-scarred, and footsore, from those who were reasonably clean and well-kept to the rag-tag lot lapsing into various levels of gypsyhood. Mother would say, "That's how we would be if we would be a year or two on the road." Collectively such people repelled her but individually if they came to "borrow" some sugar, salt, a cup of flour to make gravy, some fat for frying, a bit of coffee or tea, she would give it and then get into conversation.

Some outfits had extra horses following behind, stopping now and then if they saw tempting bits of grass, then trotting to catch up. Almost all had dogs, sometimes two or three. Father was against having a dog; meat was expensive. At one point a sheep dog, black with brown markings, began following. Father told Bill and me to chase him back, but he would not go, despite stones we threw at him. He kept out of reach and followed again. Celia, always riding and tending Lester and Belle, complained. Mother agreed and so Shep came into the family. He turned out to be a perfect watchdog as if trained for that occupation. He became the third partner to Bill and me. We rarely rode the wagon but ran ahead or behind, using Shep in efforts to catch jackrabbits, prairie dogs or those little brown owls that lived in prairie dog holes. We never caught one.

Whenever in camp, if there was visiting with other immigrants, almost without fail conversation would turn to the Mormons. Father would hear how most of the settled people along the way were Mormons. He found in talking with farmers that seldom as many as half along that route were Mormons. He heard what fine farms they had in Utah. Mother knew there were such people but Father had never heard of Mormons. They decided we might have better luck in Utah where some immigrants feared to go, believing it was dangerous country.

Cache Valley, just over the line in Utah, was an impressive contrast to all farming areas we had seen. To Father it was farming in all its glory; rich fields of alfalfa and other crops, snug houses, clean yards, often flowers and shade trees in front of the house, and well-kept fruit orchards. Father stopped before one of those farms where a man with a gray beard stood near his house.

Father climbed down from the wagon and the two exchanged greetings. The old man's attention was more on our horses. He lifted the collars and saw no shoulder sores, talking all the while. He turned to Father, "Any time I want to know what kind of a man a man is, I look at his horses." That was praise for Bill and me too but we got no notice. We stood respectfully apart listening.

We heard how as a follower of Brigham Young he had settled there more than forty years earlier and we heard the advice he was giving Father. "Don't stop in Utah. The good land is taken. Go north, far north to the Teton Basin. Not many immigrants go there." He told of families who had settled in the "Basin." He told Father how to get to "new country."

Father would not return over the same hot desert road. He took the "Mormon Trail" from Ogden through the mountains, continuing to Wyoming, then back to Idaho and up to Pocatello, a railroad town. A "boom" was on. Buildings were going up. Scores of immigrant outfits were camped around. Father went about talking to workers and came back with a plan. If we found no land in the Teton Basin we would come back and settle for a while in Pocatello where he would find plenty of work.

Bill and I were curious about the railroad. We had seen trains pass but only at a distance. Father took us there and we got a close look at a locomotive and passenger cars. He took us to see flatcars, gondolas, and boxcars. We had heard him tell about "beating it," so he showed us boxcars, the kind he once rode in, "But that was before I knew Mama."

Three days after Pocatello we were in the Teton Basin. We met few traveling outfits, none on the third day. We were getting higher up, where pine trees were and there was good grass for the horses. We stopped at the first place in the Basin, an old log house with a clay covered roof occupied by widower Goe and his two preteen boys, Ben and George, who impressed Bill and me with their saddles and horses. We impressed them with talk about where we had been and the speed with which we could pitch our tent. Goe took our horses into his stalls, the first time Brigham and Ben had been in a stable since they came to us. The boys brought meat and we had juicy steaks for supper. Here was not a breath of that hostility toward immigrants we knew along the main line of travel.

Goe told about land some two miles distant, school land which could not be homesteaded, the main reason it had not been occupied. It could be occupied until improved, when the occupant would pay rent. The prospect appealed to Father. And Mother liked it too. "When we get money we can buy land." Next morning Father got his saddle out of the wagon and on a borrowed horse went with Goe to see the place, and there was no "if" in his talk when he left, not in Mother's thinking. Bill and I loaded things and were ready to move when he returned.

We ran with Shep along the trace of a road until we came to a small creek, flowing there out of its own canyon. A full half mile over gently sloping land covered with tough sage brush, the wagon came bumping along where wheels never rolled before. Bill and I unharnessed the horses and they turned to the rich grass along the creek. Father kicked the earth loose to show Mother how good the soil was, but her attention was first on the mountains across the valley, the three sawtooth Teton peaks, sharp and snow covered, a tall one between two shorter ones. These were the first real mountains we had seen.

The first few hours were given to unloading the wagon and, in case of rain, we put the wagon cover over things not needed. We set up the stove and now could have home-baked bread. At last we were settled.

15

The Sort of Jobs the Hobo Brought

I

While employed at the Home for Incurables there was little time to be a student and no time for contacting BYU friends in Chicago universities. The building in which my classes met was adjoined on one side with the Law School where LeRoy Cox met his classes. After several weeks LeRoy came looking for me, thinking I was avoiding him for reasons of anger. Arthur Beeley, getting his doctorate at the School for Public Welfare Administration and teaching classes, was in another adjoining building. We met by accident and he chided me for not attending the Mormon church and for avoiding my friends. Obviously, he did not accept my explanation, which LeRoy could understand. Cox, too, was avoiding the social life. Deep in study, he would not risk failing his first year and perhaps lose his government support. Beeley, for whatever reason, was active keeping former BYU students together.

When I had more free time later I did attend the Mormon church and went to an occasional social gathering there. But I was making other friends in Chicago, mainly in the social welfare agencies. It bothered me that word had passed around that I was making a study of hobos. Mormon missionaries in the Chicago region came to see me and to warn me against the company they heard I was mixing with. My long explanation of what I was doing seemed not convincing.

On several occasions, friends from Utah visiting the city would get in touch with me, especially if they had read *The Hobo*, wanting to make a tour of the Madison area. Some went away with lurid images about the area, the habitués, as also about me, which were talked around when they returned home.

My concern after the book was published was getting the next job. It turned out that Burgess had also been on the lookout. He told me that the Juvenile Protective Association (JPA) had been asked by its

From *The American Hobo: An Autobiography* (Leiden: E. J. Brill, 1975): 171–83. Reprinted by permission.

board to move ahead with its investigation of homosexuality in Hobo-hemia. The idea had been widely spread that runaway boys were drift-ing into the Madison area and were being "snared by the wolves." I knew, as did Reitman, that Hobohemia had its homos. When I sold papers on Madison Street I knew and had a great fear of "friendly men." They were the reason Steve who was my friend wanted me as a partner. His mother would let him sell papers if he would work the street with someone. I had reported some evidence of homosexuality in the pages of *The Hobo*, but it was not a major interest of the study.

Reitman, who could have written the report out of his own case files (some homosexuals may also contract venereal disease), thought I should do the study but not try to be an authority on the subject, "Unlike other social problems, this the University would not dare touch." That I knew, as I also knew better than to talk about it among fellow students. What I did learn, which I had not mentioned in *The Hobo*, boys were much more exposed to homosexual contact in down-town movies and along the lakefront park than in Hobohemia. In the midtown area was a homosexual community. Their loafing and meet-ing area was on the benches along Grant Park. Most of these homos were young men, most of them better dressed and most of them cher-ished a professional image of themselves. From some I was able to secure enough information to write them up as cases. My daily reports and the cases were left with the JPA and may be among other papers collected by the University of Illinois, the Chicago branch.

The JPA, one of Chicago's respected agencies, grew out of a commit-tee of leading citizens which about twenty years earlier was occupied with investigating the moral and other hazards of children in the city. As a result of its efforts, the first juvenile court in America was estab-lished in Chicago. The committee then formed itself into the Juvenile Protective Association as a friend of the new type of court, an idea for which the legal professional had little sympathy. It was a professional agency in the best sense of the term.

Some months earlier the JPA had imported from New York a profes-sional vice investigator. In a short time, without difficulty he visited about a hundred Chicago brothels securing the standard types of evi-dence on each: address, time of visit, number of customers, clients (called "johns" in the trade), number of girls, giving names and de-scriptions of some, selling of liquor, presence of guards or "bouncers," price asked for service, identity of the "Madame," and so on. He in-cluded the various types of places from "notch houses" patronized by the common men to the luxury houses at which the patron had to be introduced, "good-name houses."

City officials and, to some extent, the papers poked fun at the JPA report. Incensed, the JPA board would repeat the investigation, going about it quietly. A young social worker, Blinstrob, on the JPA staff was assigned to that review and I was asked to assist him. We two would visit various addresses on the previous list, except the luxury places. We were to get other addresses and to include the hotels which accepted the "street trade" but not apartments occupied by two or three girls as independent operators. We were gathering the same types of information that were reported by the expert before us. We were given the addresses only.

As a newsboy in that same area more than twenty years earlier I had entered many of those houses. Not only did those girls buy my papers, they often had me run errands to bring something from the grocer or beer from saloons. But those houses were open, perhaps illegal, yet permitted in certain areas. In the meanwhile they had come to be outlawed but, with their own guards, continued to operate. Police surveillance was at the see-nothing, hear-nothing level. Occasional raids were reported in the papers but usually the word came ahead of the police who would find a few men sitting at tables drinking "near-beer" and the "madame" in charge of a private "club;" no girls in *moulin rouge* costumes.

This was another kind of house from what I remembered. With few exceptions, on the second floor, a former residential flat, the front room a type of lobby where customers sat on benches fixed to the walls, sometimes a table and four or five chairs, a bar in one corner, the rest of the flat divided into several tiny cubicle rooms, each with a chair, bare bed, and a wash stand; the elemental properties were few and could be moved to another location in an hour or two. At the rear was the escape exit. A guard, usually outside the bottom door would question approaching customers. If admitted, he would press a buzzer and the guard at the head of the stairs would press a button releasing the lock. But at the head of the stairs was a second firm door, similarly opened from within. The top guard through a small window would observe customers as they ascended the stairs. These doors would delay the police in the event of a raid.

Since typically hobos with money to spend when in town, and not averse to it, would visit such places, I thought it necessary when on the hobo study to know a number of them. The owners, "syndicates," operating these houses employed physicians who periodically inspected these girls for venereal disease. This was what Dr. Reitman did about three forenoons each week. I went with him on two such rounds, being introduced each time by him as Dr. Anderson, a friend. These visits were not especially pertinent and were not reported in *The*

Hobo. They did serve to make me less a stranger to the "notch houses" when I joined Blinstrob on the JPA investigation.

Gathering the information needed was not difficult. Nor was getting in and out a problem if several customers were present drinking beer and kidding the girls. We would buy beers and beer for one of the girls, engaging her in conversation the while (selling beer was also a source of income), getting needed information, giving her a tip and leaving. A few times, only a few, it seemed best for one to act drunk and seem about to vomit on the floor; the other would be told to take him out. Most of the places catering to the crowd were in the Madison area, the area to which the ordinary workers in the city would come to drink or see women, both being cheaper there. A house with eight to ten girls, starting around six in the afternoon was able to serve in eight to ten hours around a hundred "johns." Hobos with money were among them, to be sure, but they were a minority.

II

Reitman, who would tell how he had given me my start in Chicago, was averse to my working on the vice investigation. "Your sociology friends will not be proud of acquaintance with one who is an expert in vice problems. It is safer to be an expert on poverty, if you don't get too close to the poor." Reitman was a religious man, but his own kind of Christian. One day when I sat in his waiting room among several of his patients, he opened his door and a young woman walked out. He nodded to me, "Come in, doctor." That woman, he said, was of a rich family. She had a venereal ailment and dared not tell her name. She could not visit the family physician. "I put her in my 'X file' as Mary X." Weeks later I asked about the woman. "She's well, sent me a letter of thanks with the money in cash, signed Mary X."

Reitman called prostitution the world's oldest profession. "Whatever the reformers do, it goes on and on," yet he favored the curbing activity against it. It was he who suggested that we visit some of the low-cost hotels on the Near North Side where one took a room and gave the desk clerk some hint. The girl would come knocking on his door. The same room would then be rented to another customer. Some of the lower-cost downtown hotels catered to the same business by another method; the girl would meet her customer on the street and take him to the hotel where he rented the room. These were independent operators much as those who as a pair would rent an apartment. They had to exert more initiative and resourcefulness than was needed for girls working in the "notch houses." But they were in greater danger of being picked up by plainclothes police. When the houses were not being raided at all, the police would occasionally make a show of rounding up a few "streetwalkers," girls not protected by the "notch house syndicate."

Getting information about the assignation hotels was not difficult. It was merely a matter of being in the streets where one was likely to be accosted. While the JPA wanted this information, its main objective was getting facts about the brothels operated by the "vice ring." On the list of addresses given Blinstrob and me was an occasional address which had been vacated, but we had no difficulty finding other addresses. We then helped in putting all the data in a form which could be used by the JPA board. They used different tactics in feeding the facts to the newspapers. The high-society lady who was president of the board could now repeat with conviction her earlier charge that "Chicago is more vice-ridden than Paris." Partly as a result of this exposure, Chicago about a year later elected a reform government.

The JPA did not again launch another such showmanship study but, in the interest of protecting juveniles, for example, Blinstrob or I would be sent to investigate complaints about men molesting children or parents being cruel to children. One complaint concerned a candy store in a Polish neighborhood. Blinstrob and I found prostitution in the back rooms, also gambling. He, being a deputized officer, arrested a woman and four men and held them until the police arrived. We had to appear next day in court as witnesses.

One continuing activity of the JPA was investigating nightclubs and the many drink-dance places in the city, being on the lookout for men bringing in teenage girls. A man and woman team was needed for this. My partner was a seasoned social worker, expert in spotting deviant conduct on the part of drinking patrons, prostitutes seeking customers and the spender with teenage girls. The nightclub was strange for me and, except being her escort and eater of expensive sandwiches with her, I was of little use for some days to my companion. She would point out her observations which I would witness next day when she wrote her report. Within days, I was able to spot delinquencies on my own.

This personable, efficient widow was the mother of two young girls who knew what her work was. She could not have told them had she been assigned to some other phase of spotting prostitutes. This work had another status. It was an adventure to boast about if one got caught in a nightclub raid and taken to the police station to be questioned. This work I could talk about among fellow students. Some envied me my job which lasted from three hours before midnight to three hours after. It was near enough to vice to be naughty but not taboo, as knowing the hobo was.

III

The reports on observations in nightclubs would be sent by JPA, in abbreviated form, to the office of the district attorney. Whether true or not, it was widely believed that he had a tender regard for nightclub owners, as for the vice ring. Once, and only once while I was nightclub inspecting, a tip came from the office of the district attorney that a certain nightclub would be raided about midnight. We investigators went there, not the lady and I but Blinstrob and I. Jesse Binford, JPA director, thought there might be roughhouse.

Some twenty minutes before midnight several women, obviously there soliciting, left quietly by the rear exit. After that a waiter passed our table with the message; if we had liquor in our pockets put it on the floor under the table. Those who had bottles of liquor, for prohibition reasons, were expected to place the bottles under the table, anyhow. There would be a raid in a few minutes; no reason for excitement, everyone keep his seat. If the police find the bottles, "Say you didn't know it was there. You don't claim it." All other waiters were doing the same.

The police with whistles blowing came rushing in. Everyone was ordered to keep his seat. Police ran from table to table collecting a number of ownerless bottles. The only ones arrested were four or five drunken men and the women with them. Then service continued, the orchestra struck up music, dancers returned to the floor, and the women who had made the rear exit returned.

Shortly after that raid Burgess was able to tell me that the money expected for research scholarships had arrived and he had reserved one for me. For the first time I could be a total academic student, able to read certain books I had until then no time for. The great amount of catching-up I had to do had become a major concern. There was time, too, for working on the ecological maps of Chicago. The "Chicago Group" was then confronted with much criticism among other sociologists for the new ventures in which they were engaged, especially ecological studies. Indeed, *The Hobo* was that kind of study. I was able to join the several students who were developing ecological maps and ways of putting data on maps.

That enjoyable escape from JPA investigations lasted less than four months. The city election brought into power a reform administration. A veteran social worker, Mary McDowell, head of the Stockyards District Settlement House, became Commissioner of Public Welfare. This was probably as good a choice as any, since most of the welfare work in the city was done by private agencies. The committee on the problems of the homeless man had been holding discussions on a plan to reopen the old Municipal Lodging House. This long-dormant establishment would be revitalized to become a rehabilitation center. The plan was accepted and the Commissioner named a committee, including me, to write and conduct an examination to select a director for the center; each had to read all the examination papers.

Thomas Allison was selected, an elderly man and definitely the most competent of the list. Allison was indirectly a World War I casualty. His only son, reared in the ideal atmosphere of the social settlement, refused to go to war. He went to prison instead. The father, after some twenty-five years as head of the settlement house, who, while not in agreement with his son, refused to denounce him. He was discharged by the zealous board of the settlement. There was objection from veterans to his appointment.

The advantage Allison had was his long acquaintance with the social agencies in Chicago. His name had been for years respected among them. They were as one in believing that he had been unfairly treated. It turned out that he was no stranger to the problem of the homeless man and he was well aware of the role of the migratory hobo in the changing work system. He was a professional, no starry-eyed sentimentalist.

However it was initiated, perhaps by Burgess, all along my unobtrusive manager as well as my professor-father, I was asked to become Allison's assistant. Burgess thought it was an opportunity to make some observations about the hobo, as well as other types of homeless men; I could be at the same time an employee at the Municipal Lodging House and a student doing research, my research scholarship would continue the next few months to its termination. He thought it a good idea to have one or two graduate students assigned to our Rehabilitation Center to make case studies. An idea which Allison accepted, but Burgess was able to get only one willing to touch that kind of fieldwork, Guy Brown, of rural background in North Dakota who had some acquaintance with hobo harvest workers.

The Lodging House was the traditional service for the homeless, much like the one of long standing in New York, except that only men were served. As I came to learn, the New York Lodging House had one floor for women. Our limit was lodging for three nights followed by breakfast. For the chronic case it meant three nights "on the city," then disappear for a few days and return for another three nights. The nightly load ranged from twenty or so under two hundred to twenty or so above two hundred. This meant much routine work each day, watching the costs and keeping the records which fell naturally to me. Each day brought its list of individual problems which called for contacting other agencies; helping men find jobs, getting a runaway boy back home, arranging medical care for some other, called referrals. This and meeting with other agencies took much of Allison's time. I could not engage in systematic fact-finding, but, talking informally to many men, I was learning that most of our clients, if not natives of Chicago, were long-time residents, persons who had seeped down to this special urban slum.

Hobos, as they were in the early 1920s and before, whether going about or on the job, if in Chicago and penniless, would have been averse to asking for bed and breakfast at the Municipal Lodging House. Perhaps the typical hobo had spent his money on drink and women, perhaps lost some gambling, perhaps had been robbed, perhaps had spent a day or so in self-recovery; he would turn to panhandling or to begging back doors rather than go to the Lodging House for bed and breakfast. He would soon be out of town. He took pride in getting over the road and finding work. It was not demeaning to do his kind of begging. There were exceptions. Allison and I did meet such hobo workers at the registration desk. But we met more older men who would even brag a little about how once they were able to get over the road, but had become odd-job hunters in the city, where odd jobs existed but were not easily found. They could not compete if they wanted steady jobs.

IV

There were intellectuals among the hobos. The Industrial Workers of the World (IWW) was on West Madison Street, its headquarters from about 1905 on. It was at first active from Chicago westward, to organize the hobo workers. It would use these mobile men as messengers to spread the idea of "One Big Union." IWW activities from Chicago eastward were carried on later in the factories. The movement died but not before getting the idea going among industrial workers that craft unions, dividing workers as they did among several crafts, were a hindrance to industrial unionism which would put all occupations into a single union, according to industries; mining, rubber, steel, automobiles, machinery, and so on. That came into force after 1935.

Westward, the IWW continued working with the "bummery." Strong locals, for example, were formed in the western lumber industry. Each summer the organizers were in the harvest fields. Some who were not official representatives at all would go about signing up members and keeping the initiation fees. Many of these hobo organizers were serious believers in the one-big-union ideal when the workers of the world would become a mighty force and would put down grafting employers. It was a song-promoting movement, giving out its little red songbook "to fan the flames of discontent." The story of the movement is but marginally important here except as it pertains to the occasional intellectual hobo. While he went out to jobs, he spent more time than most hobos in the cities, not drinking, but talking. I came to know most of these in Chicago's Hobohemia. Mostly, they were soapboxers.

Reitman a year or two before I knew him took the initiative in establishing what he euphemistically called the Hobo College which operated in rented space for an audience of about a hundred. It was not a membership organization, but a point at which hobos of serious bent would gather, including the soapboxers. Most of the men were migratory workers. The college operated only in the autumn and winter months. Reitman was the hands-off director. Like the "Bug Club" on the North Side, the Hobo College was an attraction for the curious. Reitman, as money finder, was able to bring distinguished persons, writers, actors, physicians, professors, engineers, to speak at the college, or to debate with hobo intellectuals. Always a collection was taken to help defray expenses. One year, before my acquaintance with the college, so Reitman told me, Mary Garden, a Chicago opera singer, paid the cost.

I made an effort to become personally acquainted with about a dozen of the men who gathered at the Hobo College, men who had moved about working in the typical hobo occupations. Not one could be called an educated man, but all were serious readers. Dragstead of Swedish origin liked to tell privately that a kinsman of his was a science professor at the University of Chicago. He had moved and worked much, thought of himself as a poet, knew that everything in society was wrong, and had identified with different movements turning from each. And, while no speaker, he would try asking provoking questions at meetings.

John X. Kelly was an old hobo who had settled down and was a long acquaintance of James Eads How, sometimes called the "Millionaire Hobo." He was a nephew of James Buchanan Eads, famous bridge-building engineer. How maintained a hobo organization in Cincinnati. He would organize the hobos into a brotherhood. He supported a paper, the *Hobo News*, which hobos sold on the streets in different cities. Kelly tried but failed to convince How that the brotherhood would not work. Within the limits of one having little education, "John X" was a thinker, wise enough to settle in a steady job ahead of old age. He was a trusted nightwatchman, but he liked to visit the Hobo College to get into the argument.

One young man who came to the meetings told me he was from the iron mines of Minnesota. His parents were Finnish. He had worked in the mines, in the lumber woods, and in the harvests. In conversation he liked to tell his skill in getting over the road. He called himself a Socialist and he believed the ideal society would come, but he was no activist or speech maker. At the meetings he would ask sharp questions.

Like certain others, he would preface the question with a few minutes of argument. He told me that he would see more of the hobo life, "Then I'll write novels." Well he may have done that; he was an observer with a mellow sense of humor. Most of the hobo speakers were men with fixed ideas whose speeches varied little.

One hobo intellectual I came to know, a man of middle age who once had worked and wandered, had finally become a "home guard" in Chicago. He was living as a street peddlar, once selling a patent can opener, another time an unbreakable comb, again a mixture to take stains out of clothes. He was appropriately known as "Gabby" among those who called his occupation "mushfaking." He called himself a writer and "correspondent" for the *Hobo News,* and he carried clippings of articles he had written to prove it. Gabby also dabbled in poetry. Once he appeared at the Hobo College when Reitman was present. While he never engaged in the economic debates, he responded when Reitman asked him to sing "The Cook County Jail," which was Gabby's own. He had experienced life in that jail for his illegal peddling activity. I had him write it down for me. Now I recall two lines about the bedbugs:

> They were crawling on the ceiling, on the sidewalls and the floor;
> They were falling in the toilet singing "Pull, boys, for the shore."

That song, among better reasons, prompted me later to spend two weeks in the same jail. I shared a cell with two drug addicts, but found no bedbugs then.

V

As might have been known, the rehabilitation objectives of the Municipal Lodging House were difficult and often impossible to realize. Few of those men were "employer's choice," some could find odd jobs on their own more readily than jobs could be found for them by the public employment agency which was seldom used by most employers. The requirement that jobless men register at the employment office and present themselves there daily was hard to enforce. It was a waste of time for many who could do as well hunting on their own. Many, for one or another obvious reason, were only partially employable; they were near the bottom or at the bottom of the labor pool.

A Mrs. Cross, a seasoned and efficient social worker, who was ac-knowledged as a professional, was our case expert. As any profes-sional, she saw herself as both a servant of society and sustainer of the public conscience. Her job was to "save the brands from the burning," to select likely cases for rehabilitation. That meant a random sampling, say, one out of each twenty or thirty entering the Lodging House. It meant not one interview but several, perhaps some letter writing. Guy Brown worked with her on several cases and he devoted many days on a single case, a man who had spent a total of more than fifteen years in several different prisons from New York to New Mexico, each time for the same check-writing trick. Now old and in poor health, a man of middle-class family whose brothers were in business, the prob-lem was to get them to take him back. He was willing but they were not, although they finally did. The case illustrated the difficulty in set-tling an extreme type. An occasional younger man was persuaded to return to his family, perhaps to remain, perhaps not.

Now and then a job was found for a man who was not a seasoned go-about. The basic idea of the Rehabilitation Service was to make steady citizens of the footloose, often begging employers to give them a chance. The mobility of the hobo or tramp, whether worker or not, was his pathology; he should be persuaded to belong somewhere and be near his kin. Much as the self-sufficient hobo was rarely seen at the Lodging House, so a full-employment labor market would doubtless have taken most of the employable men who did use the lodging house. A public pension system would probably have removed many of the elderly.

I was permitted by Allison to be absent one afternoon a week to teach a sociology class in Elkhart, Indiana, an appointment arranged by Burgess who wanted me to have some teaching experience. I would need some experience if a teaching job came.

One did come quite unexpectedly. R. D. McKenzie, professor at the University of Washington, a colleague of Park in the study of ecology, was going on leave. He accepted the suggestion of Park and Burgess that I should replace him for the winter. In a hurry they gave me my master's examination, using *The Hobo*, two years published, for my dis-sertation. My leaving the Lodging House was just as sudden. I had time to finish my teaching at Elkhart and to be in Seattle in time for the autumn term, six months of that, two quarters. That prospect was more frightening, teaching juniors and seniors, than entering the Uni-versity of Chicago.

While I didn't fail as a novice professor, I was far from satisfied with myself. What was rewarding in some respects was the opportunity to be part of a faculty, sitting on the other side of the desk. It was capital investment when I would be looking for a university job later.

This was my opportunity to break away from Chicago and my hobo identity. I went to New York. I had written to William I. Thomas, a former Chicago professor of sociology, then in New York. He knew me and, on his recommendation, I was given a class at the New School for Social Research, which brought a little money and some opportunity for acquaintance. Through various referrals I came to be employed on a study of the YMCA in New York. During the next four years, like many others I met in that city, I worked on one research project after another, taught extension classes, and was trying myself out as a free-lance writer. I took classes at the New York University and went about it, as I found time, doing my doctoral dissertation (history of the slum on Manhattan). In 1930 I got my degree at age forty.

The Great Depression was impressively present. Peddlers were at every corner, especially those selling apples. In every city there were parades of the jobless. Private welfare agencies were staging drives, not getting a fraction of what they needed. Local public welfare was severely limited and only a few state governments were appropriating funds for relief, claiming that was a responsibility of local government. Neighbors were being asked to help neighbors. There were give-a-job drives: "Find a few days of work a jobless man can do." Social welfare associations were demanding that the federal government launch work relief programs. Employer associations, fearing socialism, opposed the idea of work relief, the labor market had to remain their monopoly.

VI

The depression of 1893–1894 was remembered most vividly by many because of the march on Washington of thousands of jobless men, most of them from the Middle West and "out West." They came riding freight trains. In the West they were called "industrialists." Towns along the routes forced the railroads to take them on their way eastward. Most of those men were hobos who worked on isolated jobs in areas which were only sparsely settled. They knew how to get about on freight trains. They were remembered as "Coxey's Army," after Jacob S. Coxey, an Ohio businessman who initiated the idea. He would have the central government put his army to work building roads, a widely approved idea a generation later, but not then. I came to know Coxey who came often to Chicago. Each time he would visit Dr. Reitman.

The Great Depression brought a new army of train riders, most of them young men who, having no work in their communities, ventured forth to find work elsewhere. Again towns along the routes would force the railroads to take them away. Associations of war veterans in 1931 were demanding not jobs, but war bonus payments. They came in thousands to Washington on freight trains from the far states, by automobile, usually with their families, from nearby states. Some from near came in groups on freight trains or in their cars. They had their organized camps in and about the city.

President Hoover refused to meet the delegations. He called on the governors of states to have their veterans return home. The responses were various, but Franklin D. Roosevelt, governor of New York, announced his willingness to cooperate with the president. He asked Harry Hopkins, head of the newly established state relief administrations to take on that job, and Hopkins passed that mission to me. Hopkins knew well (and doubtless Roosevelt did too) it would not work. I didn't need to be told to be available if news reporters came for interviews. I interviewed the leaders of New York groups; if men had to return home for emergency reasons I could arrange for their transportation, which I did for not more than a dozen. A month or so later the president ordered the army to drive the veterans out.

The city of Buffalo was overwhelmed by increasing numbers of familyless men, a majority of them being seamen who worked on freight vessels plying the Great Lakes, a special type of mobile worker, one who continued the same type of work but worked now for one shipping company, now for another. An appeal was sent to the New York Emergency Relief Administration and Hopkins sent me to Buffalo. New York City was having the same problem but that city had a Municipal Lodging House. I was then working on that study of the homeless in New York sponsored by the private agencies serving homeless men, each agency wanting to read good words about its work when the report came out. Not one could do a good job; the task was too great and the funds too limited. I was beginning to be silently cynical about all their efforts. I was happy to go some weeks to Buffalo. The leaders there did not assume they could make steady citizens out of jobless mobile workers. They would have a program for the duration of the emergency.

In Buffalo my experience in reviving the Chicago Municipal Lodging house as well as my work experience with migratory men served well in getting a center started. Whatever the report made to Hopkins, it may have had some influence later. When Roosevelt became president and he named Hopkins to head the Federal Emergency Relief Administration, I was asked to be the labor relations officer. It was also true that nobody seemed anxious to take the job, or use pressure to get it.

That was in 1934 in the spring. I had been teaching some five years at the Seth Low Junior College, a branch of Columbia University located in Brooklyn. While teaching there it was possible occasionally to be active part-time in doing research for the New York Social Welfare

Council, also trying my hand at freelance writing. The full-time job in Washington I took with some hesitancy; the search continued for that position in a university. Being over forty was one drawback and working for the relief administration was another. Never was there a more maligned public administration in America, and never one that rendered better service. That job took me away from the old hobo identity and gave me a labor relations identity.

I shared the view of most, including many in universities, that one who became a functionary in government was taking the easy way out. That could be said of many in the public service, but it did not hold for the relief administration. We were emergency workers who would be out when prosperity came "around the corner," as industrial and business leaders were predicting.

My office was there to handle complaints and demands. Trade unions complained that jobs were for "reliefers," too few for the union members. Industrialists complained continually, holding that work relief was preventing recovery, standing in the way of private enterprise. All work projects, they argued, took business from the private sector. Minority groups in hundreds of communities claimed they were discriminated against in getting work relief jobs. Often they were.

Most demands came from unions of the unemployed, mainly in cities. Understandably, they wanted higher payments, or they wanted higher classifications. The allowances were too low and the number of jobs available, around three million, was far too few. Funds provided by the Congress were never ample. We had to meet the delegations, and in our office as in the state offices there were sit-in strikes.

VII

Prosperity did not arrive. The relief program dragged on until rendered unnecessary by World War II. I moved to the War Shipping Administration, another emergency job. The merchant fleet grew by hundreds of new ships and more hundreds. Qualified seamen and officers were in low supply, although thousands did leave landside jobs to sail again. A rapid training program was established and our branch also had to establish centers for American seamen in many ports around the world. We could not find anyone to accept the "hardship" post in the Persian Gulf area, called isolated, hot, and disease ridden. I did not believe that, and volunteered for the job, the feeling I had during World War I, to be in the action. It meant two months on a ship sailing alone through the Panama Canal and around Australia.

About fifty ships a month arrived in the Persian Gulf ports bringing food and material for the Russians. It was a job of seaman care and labor relations, dealing with the "hobos of the sea," for which my work background served well. We worked with the army, used its facilities and were subject to its discipline, which held also for the civilian merchant seamen. Sick men taken from ships were put into the hospital. Seamen getting into trouble on shore or aboard ship were handled by the military police. If ships were about to sail short-handed, replacements would be taken from arriving ships. Men released from the hospital or incarceration were lodged at the seaman's center until they could be placed on ships leaving. Many, who aboard ships were well-disciplined seamen, became problems on shore. I had met their types at the Municipal Lodging House in New York two years earlier. There they were docile. In Khorramshar or other Iranian ports they were in the money, getting two hundred or more dollars a month, as much as an army captain, they were often in trouble. Their jobs were highly hazardous, more so than that of soldiers in Iran, yet to many soldiers they were draft dodgers.

During my two years there, including brief missions to ports in Egypt and India, no official arrived to inspect the work, whereas many went to "inspect" the work in Britain. At the close of the war I had the assignment of helping close the work in ports from Iran to London.

Through the help of army engineers with whom I had worked on the relief program, a job came with the labor relations unit of the U.S. military government in Germany, later changed to the High Commission, where I remained until 1953 when the American Embassy was reestablished in Germany. I was then due for retirement. I did not qualify for employment with the state department.

Fortunately, since I had been active in promoting research in Germany, a job came my way in the newly established Unesco Institute for Social Sciences in Cologne of which I was director until the institute closed in 1962–1963, when unexpected and unsought, an offer came to teach sociology at Memorial University, Newfoundland, at the rating of full professor. Two years later I went to the University of New Brunswick. The goal of my dreams forty years earlier was not reached until ten years after entering active retirement. I cannot recall ever having dull jobs, or ever having a more satisfying one than in this professor's chair, which truly is a little large.

Urban Context: Work and Leisure

16
Some Dimensions of Time

How one uses one's days and one's years is perhaps for no people more of a concern than for Western man. His main preoccupation has been to use his time to his advantage for material gain, for advancing himself in one way or other. At least his material civilization is witness to the effectiveness of his efforts. Some have reasoned that these achievements are due to the fact that Western man lives in a stimulating climate; that if he had not worked he would have frozen or starved in winter. Whatever the explanation, Western man has not only worked, he has evolved a cult of work, and he has become the most time-conscious of humans. He invented clocks and watches so he could work more effectively.

Because he has worked to advantage in the accumulation of material goods, Western man has won free time when he can turn from his work. How this has come about is one of the themes of this chapter. We will also consider how man in his striving for progress has surrounded himself with a civilization in which time acquires new meanings for him, which change during the cycle of his life.

The Time-Investment Cult

Vontobel, in her study of German Protestantism, was impressed with the importance placed on time, of which man had a limited measure and his salvation depended on the good use he made of it. In the later life, time may be without end, but in this life, according to Protestantism, the shortage of time made the wasting of it a sin. The little given to man for his life cycle was like money on loan, a loan he could repay only with work and good works.[1]

Max Weber, speaking of Protestantism, observed, "Not leisure and pleasure but only deeds serve the unequivocal revealed will of God for the increase of his glory. Time wasting is the first and heaviest of

From *Work and Leisure* (London: Routledge & Kegan Paul, 1961), 50–73. Reprinted by permission.
1. Klara Vontobel, *Das Arbeitsethos des Deutschen Protestantismus*, 1946, p. 71.

all sins. The time span of life is infinitely short and precious when one may perform his work. Time loss through socializing and lazy gossip is a luxury."[2] It was Weber's well-known thesis that the ethic of Protestantism formed at least a good share of the ideological basis of modern capitalism. Its advocacy of serious and continuous work and its intolerance of idleness was matched by Puritanism in England. But Puritanism in its later development was not entirely a religious ideology. As noted by Lewis and Maude, it stood for thrift, diligence in work, frugality in spending time and money, and sobriety in living habits, especially for the working classes. Too, it was a cult of work.[3]

Puritanism began before the industrial revolution as a religious and moral reform movement, but even then it had its practical aspects; time was for work and good works, but the money values of work were not overlooked. This may be seen in John Wesley's sermon on money. The first rule of money, he said, was to "get all you can," but he added that one must get money honestly and with a clear conscience. However the keeping of the conscience was an individual matter.

John Wesley's second rule of money was "save all you can," and he advocated frugality in living in order to save the more. By saving, one would not be in want if ill fortune befell him.

Wesley's third rule of money was to "give all you can," which contradicted somewhat his second rule. In saving one was avoiding the temptation to "gratify the desire of the flesh, the desire of the eye or the pride of life."[4] In giving one satisfied the soul. Again, it was left to the individual conscience to determine how much such satisfaction one needed for his soul.

These three rules of money, in Wesley's thinking, rested on a more basic rule that one must work continuously and wisely, being severely diligent in the use of his time. This was the basis of the time-investment cult that evolved with industrial enterprise. This fundamental doctrine of work and time was carried from England to New England where it flourished. John Wesley himself took it to Georgia, but his ideas of work and life were so strenuous and he was so unpopular that he was glad to return to his more sedate England.

The work-centered time-consciousness of both Englishmen and New Englanders was doubtless stimulated from about 1800 by other forces as well as by the ideology of Puritanism. In England where industry was then getting under way and where towns and cities were beginning to grow; also where much work had to be done, such a

2. Max Weber, "Die protestantische Ethic und der Geist des Kapitalismus," in *Gesammelte Aufsatze zur Religionssozelogie*, 1947, p. 17.

3. Roy Lewis and Angus Maude, *The English Middle Classes*, 1950, pp. 37–40.

4. John Wesley, *Sermons on Several Occasions*, 1746, p. 583.

doctrine was highly useful. Two centuries after Wesley the time-investment cult had become more of a business than a religious ethic. It was less related to preparation for heaven than to personal advancement and security. The greatest apostle of the time-investment cult for nearly half a century in England was that untiring purveyor of inspiration for success, Samuel Smiles.

We mention Smiles because his writings on work and success were widely read in the United States, especially his *Self Help*, which was translated into several languages between 1860 and 1900. It preached the gospel of success through individual effort, every man for himself. He said of time:

> An hour wasted on trifles or in indolence would, if devoted to self-improvement, make an ignorant man wise in a few years, and employed in good works would make his life fruitful, and death a harvest of worthy deeds. Fifteen minutes a day devoted to self-improvement will be felt at the end of a year. Good thoughts and carefully gathered experience take up no room, and may be carried about as our companions everywhere, without cost of encumbrance. An economical use of time is the true mode of securing leisure; it enables us to get through business and carry it forward, instead of being driven by it. On the other hand, the miscalculation of time involves us in perpetual hurry, confusion and difficulties; and life becomes a mere shuffle of expedients, usually followed by disaster.[5]

To Jean Calvin, Martin Luther, and John Wesley time and work were seen in fairly general terms. Theirs was the easily understood, although strict proposition, that man must work and do good works, that being the way to serve God. All three were preindustrial and for them most work was on the land or in the handwork shops under guild supervision. The factory with its division of labor was yet to come. Workers had not yet become mere sellers of time. The system under which time is sold in units measured by the clock, when selling and buying units of time became a transaction in terms of units of money, had not yet taken form. When that system arrived it brought with it different time values for different kinds of work, which meant that those who bought or sold time had to think precisely about it.

The New Time Awareness

Gradually, without plans to that end, industry developed means and goals within itself, and time acquired meanings quite removed from the transcendental meanings of earlier periods. It was oriented to in-

5. Samuel Smiles, *Self Help*, 1859, p. 236.

dustrial work, and industry, as an earthly institution, became the core element in a new way of life.

From the outset, the industrial revolution was little more than a variety of independent efforts by private enterprisers to find new ways of organizing the work of others and of making goods with their labor. They had to make goods faster, hence cheaper than could be done with hand labor. But each effort to operate a factory was an experiment. Capital was scarce and risks were great. Experience was lacking, and was only gained through trial and error. This fumbling beginning of enterprises is often overlooked by the chroniclers.

On the one hand, the emerging factory system was a venture in technology, one of making machines and using the machines to multiply the effectiveness of labor, for then the cost of labor was the chief outlay in making goods, or generally so. On the other hand, the factory system was a venture into using labor *en masse*, so the product of one worker would be equal in quality and amount to that of another. Effectiveness required that the tasks of all workers be linked into a single production process, something new in the history of work. Work time paid for had to be used so the employer would gain. Ways had to be found to measure work effectiveness, even though labor then was cheap.

Labor was often exploited to the extreme of human endurance. Often to earn a bare subsistence, both father and mother, sometimes even the children, had to sell their labor to the factory. The work day was perhaps not longer than sometimes under the old guild system, but the guild system of security was lacking. For most workers economic security was about down to zero.[6]

But the factory, as it gained in the efficiency of its equipment and its organization, brought about a division of labor that was hardly possible in the beginning. Now there were different types of work calling for different degrees of skill. Some work called for high degrees of speed or deftness, some for strength and endurance. Some work called for more initiative than others. Thus developed scales of pay according to the nature of the work, and with this increasing refinement in the division of labor, more precise methods of measuring work effectiveness were developed. The workers found themselves in a labor market where different types of labor are bought and sold in units of time for units of money, but for different amounts of money.

It is not pertinent here to do more than mention that, paralleling the evolution of industry, there was a corresponding social evolution.

6. For the story in England where industrialism began, see Sidney Webb and Beatrice Webb, *History of Trade Unionism,* 1920; also J. L. and Barbara Hammond, *The Town Laborer,* 1917.

Industrial working conditions were improved. The work day and the work week have been shortened from the extreme of fourteen hours to eight and from seven days in many cases to five or five and a half. It is hardly necessary to add that this and other changes for the better did not result without continuous struggle on the part of the workers. In the process of advancement, in addition to the shortening of work hours, wages have increased and levels of living have risen. It turns out to be necessary that workers enjoy higher levels of living so they can buy the products which industry turns out in greater quantity using less labor than ever before.

The result of this evolution which is pertinent to our present chapter is that all work, or almost all, has come to be visualized in terms of the time dimension, and the time dimension is concretized in money terms. These two common denominators cut across all the activities and interests of modern industrial urban man. Each of these denominators time and money tends to be the yardstick for measuring the other. Judgments boil down to such questions as: Is it worth the time? Is it worth the cost? The worker, and his employer, count the hours and minutes when he works, the minutes and even seconds needed for performing a specific task. The worker usually knows in terms of minutes the time needed to go from his work to his home. Often the time-consciousness which marks his pace in his work follows him when he turns from his work to leisure or to various nonwork activities.

Whether the modern Western man any longer behaves as a Puritan towards his work is doubtful, but he has become more strict than a Puritan about the use of time. Whether at work or away from the job he is continually thinking of time in precise terms. Even when he takes a vacation he continues to wear his wrist watch, as he must, for all others do the same.

The Coming of Clocks

It is pertinent here to digress briefly to consider the role of the clock in the evolution of industry and the urban way of living. The clock, by which our day is dominated, is relatively new in the history of cities. Although cities got along for centuries without the clock, today it would be a calamity if suddenly all the clocks should stop. Many of our mechanisms, especially systems of communication and transportation, could hardly operate, and the coordination of mechanisms would be difficult.

In order to afford some regularity in the comings and goings of people, many of the medieval cities made use of sun dials. The church found need for correctly marking time and, quoting Mumford, it had the "collective Christian desire to provide for the welfare of souls in eternity by regular prayers and devotions," and it took the initiative in the promotion of "time-keeping and the habits of temporal order" in the minds of men.[7] The need for temporal order in religious affairs was matched by an increasing temporal precision in secular matters, especially with the increase of commerce.

Those first clocks were mechanical devices that marked the time when church bells would be rung, and they appeared during the tenth century. By the fourteenth century tower clocks with systems of wheels appeared and these were later supplemented with faces and hands. By now clocks had become a recognized necessity and the smaller models were being made, but it was not until about 1500 that a clock small enough to put in the pocket was made. In 1590 clocks measuring the seconds were achieved and this, as Sombart observed, was highly important to the development of industry. He also mentioned that the clock became increasingly essential to the measurement of money values.[8] Mumford wrote this on the technically strategic position of this mechanism:

> The clock, not the steam engine, is the key machine of the industrial age. For every phase of its development the clock is both the outstanding fact and the typical symbol of the machine: even today no other machine is so ubiquitous. Here at the very beginning of modern technics, appeared prophetically the accurate automatic machine which, only after centuries of further effort, was only to prove the final consummation of this technic in every department of industrial activity.[9]

More than the essential device for measuring the work of machines and the appointments of man, the clock freed man from the clumsy limitations of natural time. It enabled him to conceive time as an abstraction by which meaning was added to man's understanding of other abstractions, for example, space, distance, and speed. He can thus better measure other quantifiable values. To a degree, this has always been done with natural time, but the precision provided by time-measuring mechanisms was hardly necessary. To mark time into periods and to give meanings to the particular days, weeks, months or years facilitates social living, and affords order in sequences or durations of time, which also involves abstraction. Durkheim wrote about man and time with these social implications in mind, and he understood how peoples develop time rationalizations.

7. Lewis Mumford, *Technics and Civilization* (New York: Harcourt, Brace, 1934), p. 14.

8. Werner Sombart, *Der Bourgeois,* Munich and Leipzig, 1923, p. 421.

9. Mumford, p. 14.

It is an abstract and impersonal frame which surrounds, not only our individual existence, but that of all humanity. It is like an endless chart, where all duration is spread out before the mind and upon which all possible events can be located in relation to fixed and determined guidelines. It is not *my time* that is thus arranged; it is time in general, such as it is objectively thought of by everybody in a single civilization. That alone is enough to give us a hint that such an arrangement ought to be collective. And in reality observation proves that these indispensable guide lines, in relation to which all things are temporally located, are taken from social life.[10]

Preindustrial man with his natural time did not have to be concerned with exactness as when the pulse is counted or when marking the revolutions of a wheel or the speed of a machine.[11] Modern industry could not cope with some of its problems if it did not have the stopwatch to measure fractions of a second. And now the stopwatch has become the necessary device in leisure, for timing races, etc. The clock becomes a universal instrument because, as Walker observed, it enables man in all activities to dissociate time from human events. Moreover, it helps to "create a belief in an independent world of mathematically measured sequences."[12]

Once man achieved these precise temporal measurements, he was able to measure work in meaningful units; his own work and that of his machines, and to project these measurements into the future. The builder of an apartment house or a factory can estimate with impressive accuracy the amounts and costs of the many types of labor needed. The experienced operator of a movie theatre, once informed about the coming and going of people at different periods of the day, can estimate approximately the number of patrons to expect at different hours between opening and closing time. One can communicate by mail, telegraph, or telephone with anyone anywhere on the globe with time precision, and just as precisely keep appointments, knowing that others are equally clock regimented.

This means that over all in this man-made environment people are pacing themselves in work and leisure to the ticking of clocks, and

10. Émile Durkheim, *The Elementary Forms of the Religious Life,* 1915 (trans. from the French by Joseph Ward Swain), p. 10. For analysis of time in the modern world, see Alfred North Whitehead, *Science and the Modern World,* 1925, esp. p. 184.

11. Jean Daric, in a discussion of "*Milieu technique et milieu naturel*" (see Georges Friedman, ed., *Villes et Campagnes,* 1953, pp. 416–18) described machine time as "pure," and he observed that work under pure time results in nervous as well as muscular fatigue, but work under natural time in muscular fatigue only. He held that nervous fatigue is less easily relieved than is muscular fatigue, hence there are more nervous illnesses under industrial urbanism.

12. Patrick G. Walker, *Restatement of Liberty,* 1951, p. 61.

they are severely inconvenienced if they do not. If industrial urban man wishes to go to work an hour earlier in summer, he cannot unless all others in his general region do the same. Hence a law must be passed requiring that all the clocks must be moved an hour forward or backward. Thus urban man gets daylight saving time. But the farmer, who is said to be regimented by natural time, must also set his clock even though he may be opposed to the idea, regarding it as another evidence of urban inadequacy. Thus even the farmer must adapt to the urban clocks.

Time, Work, and Tempo

There is an uncompromising relentlessness about mechanical time which is very different from that of natural time. The mechanics of transportation and communication may slow down with the coming of night, but they do not stop. The factory must operate whatever the time as marked by the presence or absence of the sun. It is too costly to close down the plant and start again, so work continues around the clock. This relentlessness of the clock has so impressed Fearing that he wove the thought into one of his stories. He saw the Big Clock as more powerful than the calendar, something to which every man adjusts his entire life, a great impersonal machine.

> The machine cannot be challenged. It both creates and blots out, doing each with glacial impersonality. It measures people in the same way it measures money, and the growth of trees, the life span of the mosquitoes and morals, the advance of time. And when the hour strikes on the Big Clock, that is indeed the hour, the day, the correct time. When it says a man is right he is right, and when it finds him wrong he is through, with no appeal. It is deaf as it is blind.[13]

And the clock is always near; there on the tower, on the mantel or on the wrist. While he is dominated by it, man enjoys the illusion of being in control because he winds it himself. As Blum noted, there is nothing transcendental about mechanical time, that element has "disappeared slowly under the blows of the rising industrial system." Man's attention is fixed on the immediate world and what he is about as he strives to get somewhere or to get something done. He is relieved of the need to contemplate for "the emphasis on the immediate result minimized contemplation and channeled human energy toward activity, toward work."[14]

His energies so channeled and paced, industrial man is so preoccupied with immediate goals that mansions in heaven lose importance.

13. Kenneth Fearing, *The Big Clock*, 1948, p. 146.
14. Fred H. Blum, *Toward a Democratic Work Process*, New York, 1953, pp. 193–94.

He is driven to activity by the dread of empty time, which unfortunately for many is what leisure often turns out to be. One can be so perfectly regimented in his work activities that when he turns to play with the same tempo consciousness the result is often boredom. In leisure activity one must find his own interests and take command of himself. Leisure calls for a degree of casualness, which is foreign to the tempo of work. With leisure comes a restlessness which is not satisfied with driving to far places on a holiday or going to ball games. Leisure becomes what MacIver calls "the great emptiness," a gift many are not prepared to use. "Time is theirs, but they cannot redeem it." They seem to have no choice but to escape the great emptiness. There are different escape routes but none a cure for the great emptiness. MacIver mentions, for example, the plight of the go-getters.

> When they are efficient or unscrupulous or both, they rise in the world. They amass things. They make some money. They win some place and power. Not for anything, not to do anything with it. Their values are relative, which means they have no values at all. They make money to make more money. They win some power that enables them to seek more power. They are practical men.[15]

The great emptiness is a social malady which would not matter in the stereotyped preindustrial society, but in the modern society where one must be somewhat of an individual, being an individual is more of a challenge than many can meet in leisure, but they can meet it in the regimentation of work. Again quoting MacIver, "They have never learned to climb the paths leading to the pleasures that wait in the realm of ideas, in the growing revelation of the nature of things, in the treasuries of the arts, and the rich lore of the libraries." They keep the pace and tempo in work but cannot in leisure, as one must at times do, set their own pace and tempo; but more important still is that above work and leisure there is a lack of life goals and interests.

This proclivity of Western man for work activity was remarked by Sombart in the 1920s and he wrote about "tempo" and feverish effort. People hurry from appointment to appointment feeling that they must. One hurries even when he wishes to pause, but to pause would be to feel guilty. "He will do more economic activity every minute of his life." Sombart thought this lust for activity is so great that the Westerner seems without balance and the values of literature, art, and nature vanish into nothing. "He has no time."[16]

Sombart was very right when he added that this life of hurry is not

15. Robert M. MacIver, *The Pursuit of Happiness,* New York, 1955; see chap. 6, "The Great Emptiness."
16. Sombart, p. 454.

something which can be blamed on the industrialists. Employer and worker alike are in the same treadmill. He apparently considered the situation one in which everyone is stimulated by everyone else, and there is no curb except the physical and nervous capacity of the individual. Sombart ended his thought with "Tempo! Tempo! That is the watchword of our time."[17]

Much has happened since Sombart wrote about tempo; in fact, the tempo of his day, compared with today, would seem tame. Wages have increased and relatively more workers have moved out of the unskilled into the skilled categories. More people have moved into the higher levels of living. Veblin today would say that there is even less incentive for the "instinct of workmanship," but he would find that the "instinct" has not vanished, only it is found, as Arensberg noted, not always on the job but often in one's nonwork activities.

> The instinct of workmanship flourishes now, we are told, in leisure. It flowers in the endless do-it-yourself work, the care of cars and hobbies and mechanical toys, the inventive puttering of life after work. Inventiveness, once a part of every artisan's work, has become instead the career job of the technician and the research man. The loss for work democracy, and even work interest is clear, and no one denies it.[18]

This trend, taking interest and personality out of the job for many workers, has also gained momentum since Sombart, perhaps a necessary accompaniment of the increasing tempo. In the meanwhile the individual finds his deep interests in leisure and nonwork activity. It does not mean that work has become dull and without interest, instead, other interests have gained importance. But the time consciousness and the tempo are not limited to work activities, they are seen in leisure and nonwork activities as well. They belong to the industrial urban way of life, as the clock by which they are paced.

The tempo problem, if we may call it that, evidences the inherent cosmopolitanism of modern life in which man is behaving much of the time, at work or play, in relation to his own creations in the mechanized environment. It is a curious relationship in which he seems impelled ever to be in motion and he is ever short of time.[19] Even if he hurries

17. Ibid., pp. 228–29.

18. Arensberg, "Work and the Changing American Scene," see Conrad M. Arensberg, *Research in Industrial Human Relations*, New York, 1957, p. 63.

19. This thought is expressed in the following verse from *Der Arbeitsman*, by Richard Dehmel (*Gessammelte Werke*, Berlin, 1915, Band II, p. 170).

Wir haven ein Bett, Wir haben ein Kind,
mein Weib.
Wir haben auch Arbeit, und gar zu zweit,

all his walking hours, keeping the tempo, still he does not have time enough.[20]

Money Values and Time

Sumner was of the view that the modern civilization can be sustained only if man works wisely, but he must also accumulate if he would live well. "This can only be true, however, when labour is crowned with achievement, and that is when it is productive of wealth. Labour for the sake of labour is sport. . . . Labour in the struggle for existence is irksome and painful, and is never happy or reasonably attractive except when it produces results. To glorify labour and decry wealth is to multiply absurdities."[21] But Sumner also saw absurdity in the American passion for labor merely to gain wealth. This thought has been expressed in different ways by many others; one should work as much as he needs to that he may live well, and it is a senseless thing for one to force more work on himself merely for the sake of gain.

Sumner did not recognize that most men who work are really selling their time and few could accumulate wealth through that means alone, although most of the work he knew was marketed much as it is now. This is one of the unique characteristics of industrial work, that man sells or invests his time. He invests his time when he studies or submits to training in order to be advanced in his work, as the apprentice who gives three or four years of his time at a miserably low pay in order later to come into the state of the artisan with reasonable job security and good pay. For years American colleges have notoriously been proclaiming how "higher education pays off," and the professor can prove it with pencil and paper. But the best evidence of this investment concept of education is the popularity of "practical" compared with "cultural" courses in American colleges. Engineering students feel apol-

---

und haben die Sonne und Regen und Wind,
und uns fehlt nur eine Kleinigkeit,
um so frei zu sein wie die Vogel sind;
Nur Zeit.

(We have a bed, we have a child, my wife. We also have work, we both, and we have the sun and rain and wind, and yet we lack just one small thing if we would be free as the birds are, only time.)

20. Hawley indicates what time, rhythm, and tempo mean in relation to the ecological processes in nature, tempo being the number of events per unit of time and rhythm the periodicity with which events occur. "Rhythm, tempo and timing, therefore, represent three different aspects in which the temporal factor may be analysed, especially as it bears on the collective life of organisms." Amos H. Hawley, *Human Ecology*, New York, 1950, p. 289.

21. William Graham Sumner, *Folkways*, Boston, 1906, p. 162.

ogetic if required to take advanced courses in English. But the investment of time takes other forms, in one's savings, for example, and in his life insurance.

There are still those to whom the idea of selling time seems a little vulgar. They like to think of work as being a source of joy, and they remind us of the artist or the inventor and the sacrifices they sometimes make in order to carry on their creative activity. All work can be so if we will it.[22] But even the artist blesses the day that he sells his first painting or his first piece of music. Most ordinary folks are satisfied to stand in line at the hiring office and they are pleased if later they can line up at the pay office to receive their "time." Time to ordinary workers means the pay they receive for the service hours they have sold. The ordinary worker tries to find in the labor market the job that will pay the most for the bits of his life that he surrenders. What he wishes, quoting Soule, is "less *work* and more time of their own, time not for sale."[23]

Employers, customers, clients, patients, or spectators at a ball game are the buyers of this time. It comes in goods or services. They try to get as much value as possible for the least cost. The major part of all consumer expenditures for food, housing, clothing, transport, entertainment, and so on moves through the channels of trade to pay for work. The pay is also for the skill invested in the work as manifest in the quality of the goods produced or the excellence of the service rendered. It matters not whether the time finally paid for is that of the manager or mechanic, the doctor or nurse, the shopkeeper or errand boy, the baseball player or radio entertainer.

Time, Money, and Leisure

Working and earning money is time-passing activity, and most forms of consuming or spending money are also time passing. When one buys a ticket to a concert or a movie he pays to be entertained for about two hours. It is no mere coincidence that concerts, movies and ball games usually last two hours or so; apparently that has come about through long experience with audience behavior. It is not that people could not endure longer, but they usually have other things to do. The two hours of entertainment fits into the average daily time schedule.

22. On this thought Jacks wrote, "A master in the art of living draws no sharp distinction between his work and his play, his labour and his leisure, his mind and his body, his education and his recreation. He hardly knows which is which. He simply pursues his vision of excellence through whatever he is doing and leaves others to determine whether he is working or playing. To himself he always seems to be doing both." Lawrence P. Jacks, *Education through Recreation*, 1932, pp. 1–2.

23. George Soule, *Time for Living*, New York, 1955, p. 94.

Remember also, entertainment is business. For the ballplayer, a two-hour game with all the before and after work that has to be done comprises a fair day's work. For the owner of the movie theatre the two-hour show permits the same program to be repeated four to six times in a day.

Time and cost considerations are especially present in radio and television programs. In countries where these are private enterprises, air time has high value. A program of fifteen, thirty, or sixty minutes might end a few seconds short, but it must not extend longer to encroach on the next program. When this time must be divided between entertainment and commercial announcements there is competition for time between the sponsor who wants to sell soap, cigarettes, dog food or what not, and entertainer who must get as much "show" as possible into the few minutes allowed.

Under such circumstances, the entertainer is forced to pack as much as possible of humor, sentiment, thought, and whatever else into his time. Thus we get songs including the melody, one verse and the chorus a couple of times. Jokes have to be to the point and quickly over with. Conversation must move fast, touching only the high points. Discussions and speeches must be stripped of all except the bare essentials. The leisurely manner has no place except to stimulate wit. These observations would be less pertinent if the programs were merely heard or seen and then dismissed from mind. On the contrary, radio and television tempo enter into daily communication. In contrast to richness and mellowness, humor must be sharp and quick. Conversation becomes sketchy and the story is glossed over. It perhaps contributes to the glossing-over tendency in our reading. Other factors are certainly involved, but the influence just mentioned doubtless contributes to making so much of modern leisure a pursuit, a pursuit not related to anything in particular. This charge must be made with the reservation that it applies to only some of us much of the time, but it does apply to most of us some of the time.

It is often said that leisure time and spending are excessively set apart from work and the confirming evidence is that workers put the job out of mind as soon as they leave the work place. They hardly mention their work when they are about their nonwork activity. Blum found that to be true of workers in a packing plant, "work has no meaning for their life off the job." But they talk about their leisure and nonwork interests when they are at work. And if a worker is forced to stay away from the job a few days because of illness he is not only restless to get back to work, but he talks about the job.[24] Otherwise,

---

24. Blum, pp. 95–97.

work holds a neutral position so long as there is no worry about losing one's job. Since one does not plan the work or guide it, it would be an idle waste of time to talk about it. This is the pertinent point; the worker does not need to worry about wasting time on the job. That is left to management. But he does concern himself about the waste of time in his nonwork activities. That is, if he worries at all about time, this is the time that gives him concern, and he rarely has time enough for all he would do.

Mills observed that a man's attitude toward his work may be determined by his leisure values. He may also be an effective worker and not mix his leisure values at all with those of his work, although if he is ambitious he may learn to use nonwork time for advancing himself in work, while keeping nonwork time in a realm apart. Most people acquire some capability for keeping work and leisure interests from intruding upon each other, even those who seem at times disorganized in their use of nonwork time or leisure.[25]

Work and Leisure in Lockstep

Time for hire has one value for the seller and another for the buyer, who must use it to gain some economic worth. Time not for hire, meaning leisure, also has economic worth and for industry this time is a resource of emerging importance. The importance emerges from the increasing amount of leisure that people have and the increasing amount of money available for leisure spending.

We have already noted how leisure made possible many productive enterprises; the entertainment industries, tourism, professional sport, the mode industries in dress and cosmetics, and many special industries. Other industries may be less directly involved, including automobiles, boatbuilding, house furnishings, liquors, fancy foods, transportation, and communication. All depend on leisure spending.

With the rising prevalence of vacations with pay, each industry becomes a major contributer to leisure spending from which others benefit. But each enterprise must find ways to carry on work with no additional money cost or loss in output while members of the work force take vacations. This very important concession to leisure by the world

25. "While men seek all values that matter to them outside of work, they must be serious during work: they must not laugh or sing or even talk, they must follow the rules and not violate the fetish of "the enterprise." In short, they must be serious and steady about something that does not mean anything to them, and moreover during the best hours of their day, the best hours of their life. Leisure time thus comes to mean an unserious freedom from the authoritarian seriousness of the job." C. Wright Mills, *White Collar: The American Middle Classes*, 1951, p. 236.

of work is but one among many; the many concern the new markets opened by leisure upon which industry generally must depend.

We know how modern industry, American industry in particular, takes pride in its technical achievements and high productivity. Largely this advancement has been forced upon industry by competitive necessity. Not the least of the complicating elements in this continuous competition has been the changing position of labor. The industries that point with pride to their rapid evolution and mention the high living standards of American workers are the same that resisted every step of the way all efforts by labor to diminish hours of work and to increase wages. While insisting that the concessions could not be made, industry was able to find some new adjustment. Each adjustment has meant a more efficient use of labor and greater productivity.

One day, to be sure, the limit of this spiral will be reached and both labor and management will be faced with diminishing returns or some form of dead level, but that point is still not in sight. In the meanwhile, more workers have been winning more leisure time and more money for leisure spending. The worker has become infinitely more important as a market than in the era of the 14-hour work day; in fact, he has become a variety of new markets to which industry must cater. The new markets in many respects are the more colorful. They take up more space in newspapers and periodicals and of radio time than all other markets combined.

These new markets may be more fickle and less predictable than, for example, such markets as oil, rubber, steel, or machinery, but they are not less profitable. We can estimate how many workers in a given country will have vacations with pay next year and how much money they are likely to spend. We can be sure that perhaps a fifth of all consumer money will go into some form of leisure spending, but there is so much opportunity for individual choice and, since choices change radically from year to year, we can hardly predict the where and how of spending.

What is pertinent here is that, while industry is watching and cultivating the leisure markets, it is also forced by increasing leisure time to be equally diligent in the use of the diminishing amounts of work time. As total work time becomes less plentiful and more precious, it must be utilized with greater skill. In the plant or office the work of each must "gear in" more precisely with the work of others. The work of related departments and plants must be coordinated, so also the work of related industries, so the inflow of raw materials and the outflow of goods and services.

While industry must do this to survive, moving in the direction of automation, the trend is often seen as dehumanizing or regimenting, but if modern man wants more leisure and a higher standard of living, he has no alternative. Industry is accepting leisure and adjusting to it. Forced to use less work time, it is also forced to use that time more effectively. Unwittingly industry, in adapting itself, contributes to a new conception of time use, an example of what Blakelock calls an interdependence of a concept of time and regular collective activity.[26]

Habitual Time-Use Patterns

We mentioned above that it was necessary to pass a law in order to realize the idea of daylight-saving time. Clocks must be moved forward or back in unison, enabling us to start or leave work an hour later or earlier. This illustrates how all people are linked in our civilization. Whether in work or leisure, the coming and going of the individual depends on the coming and going of others. Work time is said to be *liquid* in that it can be exchanged for money which, in turn, can be used for many things. But Blakelock reminds us that time may have the qualities of *flexibility* and *rigidity* in that certain units of time may be put to any of several uses, or rigidly assigned to a specific use.

> It can be seen that not only the length of time an activity takes but also its flexibility is important in determining the demand it makes upon one's supply of time. The least flexible activities, perforce, structure one's other activities, which must be fitted around them. If the least flexible activities take up an individual's time of greatest liquidity, he may be relatively poor in time. The night worker gives an example of this.[27]

The night worker is exchanging time for money during some of the hours when most other workers are exchanging their leisure time money for fun, but during the day when he has free time most of his friends are at work. Unless he has a very individual pattern of time use, he is likely to feel that much of his free time is lost; he cannot use it as he would normally wish.

Time uses tend to be structured into collective patterns. Whether working, shopping, going about his leisure, or some other activity, the individual tends to behave in concert with many others doing much the same thing at the same time. What he does in the forenoon, after-

26. Edwin Blakelock, "A New Look at the New Leisure," *Administrative Science Quarterly* 4, no. 4 (March 1960): 451. Without recognizing industry's own adjustment, managers worry about the lack of worker interest, but workers also make their adjustment, being indifferent to the job without diminishing their work efficiency. The worker has, says Dubin, "a well-developed attachment to his work and workplace without a corresponding sense of total attachment to it." Robert Dubin, "Industrial Workers' Worlds," *Social Problems* 3, no. 3 (January 1955): 131–42.

27. Ibid., p. 452.

noon, or evening is largely influenced by what others do, which itself may be a source of satisfaction. Here we can point to an experiment undertaken by an industrial establishment in California where a new work-leisure time schedule was adopted with the approval of the labor force.

Briefly stated, the plan was this: for the first and second weekends of each month the workers would be free on Saturday and Sunday, the usual schedule. At the third weekend workers would be free on Saturday, Sunday, and Monday, deemed to be an opportunity for a three-day trip to the mountains or some other family activity. On the fourth weekend the workers would be free on Sunday only, working Saturday to "pay back" for the previous Monday.

The experiment proved to be unsatisfactory for all concerned. On the free Monday management personnel had to be at work because other firms were working. Goods and messages had to be sent and received. Few took advantage of the three-day weekend. For most of those who looked forward to the extra free day few were able to use the time, especially on Monday which is washday for most housewives. Workers were free on Monday when all others were working and they worked on a Saturday when the neighbors were having a free day. Family schedules could not be adjusted.

It might have been otherwise had all the workers been neighbours, but almost all owned their automobiles and they lived scattered over a 20-mile area. Few lived near enough together to take advantage of the new schedule. Surprisingly, none of the difficulties had been anticipated. After some months the scheme was rejected by the workers almost as unanimously as they had approved the idea when it was initially proposed.[28]

Tradition and Time-Use Patterns

If any place could be called traditionless, it would be California, yet people there behave *en masse* even though the behavior is ever changing. The compelling force is the mode, not tradition. If the time- and tempo-conscious and novelty accepting Californians had been more tradition-directed (Riesman's term), they probably would not have accepted the new work-leisure experiment described above. Tradition-consciousness finds expression in fears that new ways may disturb the old ones. This is illustrated in a report by Vito describing resistance to change in communities on the Island of Sardinia. Here were old

28. Rolf Meyersohn, "Some Consequences of Changing Work and Leisure Routines." Paper presented at the World Congress of Sociology, Stresa, Italy, September 1959.

communities of small peasants and shepherds settled in their genera-
tions-old way of life, and now they face change.

In their long isolation these Sardinian communities had achieved a
total adaptation to the situation and they needed little from the outside. The old nature-oriented time-use patterns there came to be chal-
lenged by different influences from the outside; new work, new goods
and services, and new forms of leisure activity. These were resisted by
those of the old order.[29]

The shepherd's garb, Vito observed, is one of the symbols of the traditional way of life, as the overalls are the uniform for the new town
worker and his ways of life.

> The young man dressed in overalls working in a carpentry firm,
> watching television, criticising or approving such or such a singer or
> programme, thinks in political or trade union terms, while the young
> man in the shepherd's uniform represents the proud outlaw who re-
> fuses the State, its laws and instruments of mass media, free of all
> constraint, authoritative and autonomous in a classless society. In this
> same area economic development impoverishes, in fact and espe-
> cially relatively, the traditional forms of wealth and prestige.[30]

This economic development coming to Sardinia means more than
economic change; it also means quickening the tempo of one's daily
round. The young man in overalls must carry a watch, something the
shepherd never needed. Whether he likes it or not, the shepherd's
tempo must also quicken. In his traditional way of life he could foresee
his work for tomorrow, next month or next year, and the pace of his
work had become habitual as the work itself; one was geared, as Vito
noted, to "subjective time." Not so for the man in overalls; his work
may change from day to day and his way of life can hardly be predicted
in long-term perspective. These elements of uncertainty are now entering the way of life of the Sardinian shepherd.

According to the traditional way of life the work of the parents, their
songs and dances would be repeated by their children. The time-use
pattern of the parents for the days and seasons would not be changed
by the children. But the man in overalls can pass little of traditional
ways on to his children. In the changing situation they will have their
own time-use patterns.

The situation of the Sardinian shepherds is unique, but it is not basically different from that of other isolated peoples who have had to

29. Francesco Vito, "A Sociological Survey of the Cultural Factors of Economic and
Social Development." Paper presented before the International Social Science Council,
Paris, 19–25 March 1959, p. 5.

30. Ibid., p. 8.

adapt to change influences from without. They offer various degrees of resistance and display degrees of what Dumazedier calls "inadaptation,"[31] but little by little the old time-use patterns are changed for new ones.

Of Man's Total Time

Seen in religious terms, man's life cycle is given to him that he may work and perform good works and thus gain salvation in the life to come. The life cycle is a prelude to eternity, a period of preparation and continuous effort. The first concern of the good Christian, according to the plan of life and salvation, is to live his days in this life so he will store up treasure for enjoyment in the next life. The key to this plan is work, and the worth of a man is that he works his entire life span and performs good works.

Without doubt, Western man has been influenced by one religious ideology or another in becoming the worker that he is, the saver of money and the investor of his time, although not always for next-life goals. Thus, too, he may have been stimulated to viewing his life in long-term perspective. Other influences have contributed as well to this way of thinking, perhaps the fact that the very existence of industrial urban society depends on long-term thinking and planning has been a factor. However much he may still be motivated by transcendental considerations, Western man is seriously preoccupied much of his time with the life-span implications of his earthly existence.

Perhaps in no other civilization has so much emphasis been placed on private insurance, on schemes of public insurance or on saving for old age. And perhaps in no other civilization has so much emphasis been placed on the life investment importance of education. Even more essential than for cultural reasons, education is seen as a way to economic advancement and final security. Perhaps, too, no other people have equalled Westerners in working to gain more leisure, only to insist that leisure must not be wasted but should be used for self-improvement. Even participation in play and sport is often justified with arguments that it develops useful skills and traits of personality which one can use to advantage in his work.

It is Western man who developed the clock and found hundreds of ways to use it in the perfection of his work. The benefits of these achievements he tries now to pass on to other peoples who are less clock-conscious. In his striving for precision in the use of time he has surrounded himself with a clock-dominated environment to which he

31. Joffre Dumazedier with G. Friedmann and E. Morin, "Les loisirs dans la vie quotidienne," *Encyclopedie Française*, T. 14, 54.9.

tends to be subordinated whether working or at leisure. In these efforts he is finding new and still newer ways of using his time and his work to greater advantage, that is greater productiveness, only to become the more encased by the time and tempo demands of his mechanized environment. That same time-consciousness he devotes to his work is carried over to his uses of leisure.

This urge to Western man to keep occupied and use his time to advantage is no mere day to day interest, it extends across the years ahead, of which he is reminded again and again from childhood on. His code of life through the years has imposed on him the responsibility for his own life-span security, although in most industrial countries public insurance programs are coming to the rescue. Yet most of the responsibility for getting educated and trained, for advancement in his work, and for accumulating material reserves still rests with the individual himself.

This individual responsibility for security during one's own life span is something new in human history. It hardly exists among truly rural people and it was not a problem of older societies. The security of the individual was a group responsibility, but even the group did not plan for the future, storing away material things. The pattern of living was so established that the young had only to follow day by day into the steps of the old. Perhaps the individual carried charms to safeguard himself against unseen evils that might assail him today or tomorrow, but he took no personal precautions for his own life-span security.[32]

The life span for modern Western man is a procession of starting or terminal dates, with full measures of activity packed between. It is certainly a full measure for the child to learn all that is expected between kindergarten and his graduation from the primary school. In the next phase of his education he is again loaded until his exit from high school. There may be many starting and terminal dates in his work life as he moves from job to job or from one promotion to another. So he moves through the cycle of his private nonwork life. Slowly he comes to the point when he dreads the approach of the terminal dates; he is entering the short end of his life span. All along, as he lives through one phase of his life cycle to enter another his way of living must change accordingly. His problem of total time is ever before him.

We can do no better in our examination of the phenomena of work

32. See Clellan S. Ford, *Smoke from Their Fires*, New Haven, 1941. An Indian chief tells his story to Ford. Especially pertinent are the chapters in this narrative about the childhood of the old chief, the magic performed in his infancy to protect him against evil. Much of his preparation for his work life was gained through play. No thought was given to his future economic security.

and leisure than to consider these types of activity and interest in relation to man's life cycle.

Summary

Perhaps never in human existence has it been so necessary for man to be so time-conscious as Westerners are today. Man marked the seasons as they came and went and he counted the years, but he had no need of a watch for dividing time into tiny fractions. Western man not only counts time in tiny fractions but he measures the hours and minutes against money much as he measures goods and services against money.

Through the different religious ideologies, Western man has learned well the injunction that life is a period of probation, that life is short and one must invest his time in work and good works, thus to gain salvation. The minimum of work for a livelihood is not enough, he must do effective work and create surpluses. Under the pressure of such motivations, modern industry emerged and flourished, creating in turn a new time awareness coordinated to the on-going demands of coordinated mechanisms and to the equally insistent demands of a coordinated division of labour.

It was no accident that the clock came on the scene in the urban milieu. Rural man could not have invented the clock, which he did not need, any more than he could have invented centuries later the gang plow, the reaper and the cream separator, which he did need. It was both coincidental and providential, however, that the clock came on the scene ahead of the factory and mechanical power. It was the clock that made possible the coordination of mechanisms on the one side, and the coordinated division of labor on the other, a combination that placed man in a new and more precise relationship with time.

This new relationship with time, if we may over-simplify it, manifests itself in two overlapping activity spheres: the individual as seller of his work exchanges time for money, and the individual as buyer in his leisure exchanges money for time; time already invested through work in goods and services. In both spheres the relationship with time is competitive, having taken to itself the success and progress motivations of the religious ideologies which originally stimulated the work-dedicated way of life. Success and progress mean getting more product out of work and more value out of time. The tempo of this efficiency mindedness carries over to the use of leisure.

Efficiency mindedness in the workplace, while creating leisure, also not illogically excludes leisure from the work sphere. Sellers of time are, however, left to their own devices in using their own time. The minority who work are responsible for efficiency and the tempo of production. Those of the majority, while performing their work well, share no responsibility for it, or very little. They turn elsewhere for their interests in living and social intimacy.

The mechanisms of industry have not destroyed the workers, as many feared a generation ago. Without planning or guidance, those of the majority are learning to meet in full the demands of work while centering their life interests in a sphere apart, submitting to management's time control at the workplace but in command of their own time outside. It may be true, as many claim, that they have yet to learn to use their own time, but the learning process goes on. In the meanwhile they are still tempo-dominated in their leisure.

While learning how to use his own time from day to day, modern man from childhood to old age must also be concerned about the total time of his life span. The individual in earlier civilizations merely followed the footsteps of the generations; he was not confronted with major choices along the way. For modern man time has a different meaning with each phase of his life span. Decade by decade his style of life changes and through his own efforts his fortunes may change. Depending on the converging of influences, changes take place in the roles of this living worker, spouse, parent, neighbor, citizen and so on. He must be continually conscious of short-time and long-time goals and make decisions accordingly. The span of his years, which science has been able to extend somewhat, is a continuous challenge to his time-using ability.

17

The Trend of Urban Sociology

Introduction

What we label urban sociology in this chapter is little more than an impending departure from sociology in its more general aspects. It is the beginning of an attempt to put special emphasis on social origins, social interaction and the culture patterns of urban life. Urban sociology is focused on that segment of society dwelling in the city, and on other segments as they relate to the city. As a science, it is only approaching an identity, though in the process of becoming, its evolution has paralleled the development of the other social sciences. If we may call all those early attempts to understand the city and deal with its problems the antecedents of urban sociology, then we are able to distinguish at least three stages in its development: the reformatory, the descriptive and the scientific. These three stages represent so many methods of study or approaches to an understanding of the phenomena of the city.

The reformatory approach is essentially idealistic and rarely fails to reveal some inclination to manipulate the city or mold some phase of its life according to preconceived values. It may be either positive or negative, or both. The positive reformatory approach turns to exhortation and propaganda, or to movements for playgrounds, building codes, city planning, and other humane legislation. Negative reform spends itself seeking out and denouncing evils, or in passing prohibitive legislation. In either case, the reformatory approach is emotional. Most early analyses of the city or of social problems in the city proceeded from the reform motive.

While it is not dead, the reformatory approach has been giving ground to a descriptive method. It might be called the method of personal contact—of seeing a problem and teaching it so that one might have sympathy. Description would include anything from empirical

From *Trends in American Sociology* (New York: Harper & Brothers, 1929): 261–96. Reprinted by permission of Addison-Wesley Educational Publishers, Inc.

sightseeing to block tabulations and census enumerations. Adherents of this method put to themselves the task of observing the city and of examining and describing its details. Much of this finds its way to the printed page in the form of narrative or "atmosphere" articles. Many of the early attempts at urban sociology resorted to this method of "knowing the city" or of learning "how the other half lives." In its morbid aspects this approach degenerates into forms of slumming.

What we call the scientific approach is not altogether divorced from the two that preceded it. While they are partial, it approximates completion. It involves description, but it goes after the meanings behind the observable. It seeks norms, ratios, and generalizations. In the analytic or scientific method, description is not so much an end as a means to an end. In its antecedent stages, urban sociology has been reformatory; it has been descriptive and, finally, it is becoming scientific. In this development there are no evidences of any straight-line evolution. A complete story of its growth would include an examination of the part played in this development by religion, philosophy and other influences.[1]

The term urban sociology, even when used with reservations, does carry the implication that the science is already abroad. Not only would it be difficult, but meaningless, to defend such a position. In a number of universities courses are given that bear the name;[2] but in no sense could we say that there is any uniformity in the method or content of these courses. At the present stage of its development, it would be difficult for the partisan in the field to point to any accumulation of tested material sufficiently unique, or a realm of investigation sufficiently integrated, to merit the name of urban sociology. A mass of literature is emerging from the whole range of science, as well as the arts; but even that is nebulous, and the process of coördinating it is hesitant.

---

1. Viewed from another angle, we may say that the emergence of urban sociology paralleling the growth of the social sciences in this country falls into four periods: (1) The philosophic period in the university which ended in the seventies. (2) The evangelistic period in the missions where the universities as arms of the churches found themselves involved. This period ended in the late eighties. (3) The philanthropic period beginning in the late eighties with the rise of settlements sponsored by the universities. (4) From 1910 on, we have the scientific period, which we may identify with the increase of laboratories and clinics.

2. DeGraff collected data by a questionnaire from 32 colleges giving courses in urban sociology or related subjects. He found they had little in common, not even a textbook ("Urban Sociology in the Colleges," *Social Forces* [December 1926]). In 1925, R. E. Park and E. W. Burgess published *The City,* a collection of articles and papers on urban sociology with a detailed classified bibliography by Louis Wirth. In 1927, S. E. W. Bedford published his *Readings in Urban Sociology.* The first textbook on urban sociology, by Nels Anderson and E. C. Lindeman, appeared in 1928.

In view of the present state of urban sociology, it would be without point to discuss the subject in terms of trends. The data are too dispersed and the ends too scattered for any comprehensive tying together. Any attempt to present a bird's-eye view of the field would be so presumptuous and foolhardy that the present reviewer passes the task by. Instead of trying to take cognizance of and relating trends, he will content himself with calling attention to some of the subject matter that obviously falls within the scope of urban sociology.

The Development of Social Science

American sociology, according to Small,[3] dates back about half a century. Its beginning was so generally vague and amorphous and so involved with the development of social science in general that it would profit little to seek the relationships. Moreover, during those initial decades all the sciences were in difficulty. With no traditions of science in the universities to curb the theory groups, there sprang up a number of cults, each trying to encompass in its scheme of things the whole universe of knowledge and to subjugate all the other cults. Most of the theory was a rehash of European thought, rather than a product of experience and the situation here.[4]

It has been the situation here that finally brought sociology down from the realm of philosophy to a plane of objective application to social problems. It would be difficult to think of that transition apart from the growth of the American city. But the American city itself has been a symphony in transitions, or transformations. Some of these may be listed briefly:

1. The scholastic awakening of the university during the seventies and eighties, due to the invasion of a group of scholars trained abroad.
2. Under their influence the university changed slowly from a center of theological and moral science and, as such, an auxiliary of the church, to a center of research.
3. Following the Civil War, there was a rapid swing of the country to industrialism. Towns rooted in a Puritan homestead culture suddenly became cities of heterogeneous hordes gathered in from every culture and every country.
4. With the sudden shift from a rural to an urban base, the newly acquired fortunes began to concentrate in the cities, forming a moneyed aristocracy without aristocratic tradition.

3. A. W. Small, "Fifty Years of American Sociology," *American Journal of Sociology* 21 (1916); *Origins of Sociology* (1924); E. S. Bogardus, *History of Social Thought* (1922).

4. H. E. Barnes, *History and Prospects of the Social Sciences* (1925); J. P. Lichtenberger, *Development of Social Theory* (1923); F. Thomas, *Environmental Basis of Society* (1925); A. J. Todd, *Theories of Social Progress* (1918).

5. During the four decades preceding 1910, most of the railways were built, ushering in an era of unprecedented and undisciplined mobility. This, in turn, was followed by wasteful raids upon our natural resources and by a wholesale migration to western land.

6. From 1890 to 1910, the automobile and other forms of rapid transit came into use to increase mobility within the city and to project its life into the suburb.

7. This outward spread of the city was supplemented by an increased use of vertical space (both up and down) when, through the aid of steel frames, elevators, electric light and scientific ventilation, the skyscraper came into vogue.

8. Along with all these transformations are to be considered such phenomena as large-scale production and distribution, the increase of advertising, the standardization of commodities, and the social implications of such factors as the increased use of the printed page, telephone, radio, movies, etc.

That these developments influenced one another, or that singly and severally they have conditioned American culture, is not a matter of speculation. Taken together, they constitute the ingredients of a fluxing environment, making the last four or five decades of American city building a period of riotous change. Everywhere the industrial revolution was a spur to city building; but here, with no guiding traditions and no past to hinder, cities grew in a manner that was both rapid and incoherent. How much and in what manner all this tearing down and building up had to do with the growth of social science is problematic. At least this is certain; the contrasts of wealth and poverty, comfort and misery, as well as the increase of crime, vice and sickness, was a challenge that could not be ignored by social science. Nor was it ignored.[5] A cursory review of the literature reveals that even the most theoretical of sociologists who worked during this incubation period were cognizant of specific social problems and were proffering solutions.[6]

Out of contact with the social problems there was developing a group of sociologists who could not in any sense be called theorists. As they were short on theory, they were long on action. Shunning the study and the armchair for the field, they devoted themselves to details and specific maladjustments without attempting to relate details to the larger situation. By the methods of science, as they understood them, they sought "the ethical basis of charity, the ideals of philanthropy, and

5. H. N. Shenton, *The Practical Application of Sociology* (1928). A brief review of attempts to make sociology apply to problems.

6. F. H. Giddings, *Inductive Sociology* (1901); W. G. Summer, *What Social Classes Owe to Each Other* (1920, new ed.); A. W. Small, *Between Eras: From Capitalism to Democracy* (1913); L. F. Ward, *Applied Sociology* (1906).

the social mechanism for attaining . . . what ought to be."[7] The "ought to be" was an a priori objective determined largely by what had been. The "ought to be" did not always grow out of research but was generally included in the premises of research.[8]

One significant fact of this struggle of sociology to become a science needs emphasis here, and that is the popular assumption that the name of sociology was synonymous with service and reform. More than political economy and as much as political science, sociology became the haven of any and all who wanted to do good. As a result, while sociology drew its share of outstanding scholars, it also attracted this fringe of well-meaning people and panacea promoters with their "common-sense" solutions for social problems. It was a refuge for numerous thoughtful clergymen who were no longer comfortable in the church. Sociology offered them an opportunity to bring together the tools of science and the idealism of religion. This last-named group constituted the Christian branch of the applied sociologists. In the main they were militant. They saw the problems of the city; but more than most students of urban social maladjustment, they saw the city itself as a social problem.[9] Most of them, through personal contacts with poor people in urban churches, came to feel that evangelism was not enough. They set out to supplement evangelism with charity, neighborhood work and social legislation.[10] Among their number are many who still see the city as a venture in sin, and all social problems in terms of good and evil.

Any attempt to relate these early interests in the city and its problems, or to reconcile them one with another, would be both profitless and confusing. There were many and varied approaches. Often they were contradictory, but they had at least one thing in common, and that was their point of attack, the slum, which we now proceed to consider.

7. See C. R. Henderson, *Dependents, Defectives and Delinquents,* preface, (1901); also E. T. Devine, *Misery and Its Causes* (1913); R. Mayo-Smith, *Statistics and Sociology* (1895); A. G. Warner, *American Charities* (1896); C. D. Wright, *Outline of Practical Sociology* (1899).

8. H. Paul Douglass, who was kind enough to read this chapter in manuscript, suggests that while sociology has progressed much since the time when it was dominated by rescue motives, the spirit of the "ought to be" goes marching on. The pioneer reform sociologists were diligent in setting up agencies and organizations of welfare and guidance. Out of their energy there grew up numerous departments of public welfare in states and cities. As these have taken on institutional form, they have defined their programs and policies according to the philosophy of reform social science.

9. L. Abbott, *Christianity and Social Problems* (1897); W. Gladden, *Social Facts and Forces* (1897) and *Social Salvation* (1901); E. G. Peabody, *Jesus Christ and the Social Question* (1900); W. Rauschenbusch, *Christianity and the Social Crisis* (1910); C. Stelzle, *The Workingman and Social Problems* (1903); J. Strong, *The Challenge of the City* (1907).

10. H. P. Douglass, *The Church in the Changing City* (1927); C. H. Sears, *Baptist City Planning* (1926).

The Drive on the Slum

However doubtful the parentage of urban sociology may be, we do know that its cradle and the scene of its early nurture was the slum. As most economic Utopias and evangelistic drives were inspired by the concentration of misery in the slum, so the slum inspired welfare movements in social work and welfare interests in social science. With the sudden growth of cities, it was the great sore spot; and for all types of social students, social critics and social reformers, it was the avenue of approach to most ills of the city. It has not always been such a problem. We have had slums as long as we have been city builders. It was the modern industrial city, reorganizing urban life generally, that forced them on our attention.

The steam-power factory and the crowding together of cheap labor around the factory contributed most to the creation of congested poor areas. Thus, in the reconstruction of the city and the reorganization of its life, the slum emerged, a sort of unexpected but baffling anomaly. Upon this, attention was first fixed emotionally and we had rescue moves such as those of the Salvation Army, or the protests of the artist, such as we find in the writings of Dickens. Slowly attention became more objective, and we had the beginning of painstaking study, such as the work of Charles Booth in London.[11] In American cities it was the humanitarian evangelist like Brace, or the humanitarian journalist like Riis,[12] who sounded the warning that our cities were also chaotic at the core. They had, as contemporaries and followers, a school of humanitarian statisticians, the pioneers among whom were Henderson, Mayo-Smith, Warner, and Wright. Yet their work, perhaps because it was too involved with appraisals and hasty conclusions, lacked the intensive qualities of the studies made by Booth.

Once social science turned from the university to the slum, it found no base for operations except, perhaps, the mission. There was need of a non-evangelistic point from which to work. Whether this need gave rise to the university settlement movement we cannot say; but once the settlement appeared, the university contributed much to its rapid rise. The movement started with Toynbee Hall in East London in 1875, a settlement initiated by students from Cambridge and Oxford. It was brought to New York in 1887 by Stanton Coit, a former resident at Toynbee. Hull House in Chicago was opened by Jane Addams two

11. C. Booth, *Life and Labour of the People of London*, 16 vols. (1890). Also P. G. Frédéric Le Play (monographic studies of family budgets in various industries) *Les ouvriers euro-péens* (1855); *L'organization de la famille* (1871).

12. C. L. Brace, *Dangerous Classes in New York* (1880); J. Riis, *How the Other Half Lives* (1890).

years later. During the next two decades dozens of such centers, many of them sponsored by the universities, were started in the slums of American cities. They bear witness to the fervent social idealism then pervading the university. As social laboratories or, better still, observation posts, they were surpassed by no other institution at the time.[13]

Settlements set out to become the leaven that leavens the socially chaotic slum. They hoped through social programs to inspire slum classes to higher things and by coöperation to convert slums into neighborhoods. While settlements have rescued individuals like brands from the burning, their success in neighborhood reorganization has been meager.[14] But they did accomplish other things, at least three of which should be noted: (1) In so far as there has grown up any community organization in cities, the social settlement has been active in bringing it about.[15] In spite of the optimism in some quarters, community organization in our cities has never become more than an ideal. (2) The settlement has been mother or stepmother to a host of social agencies, organizations and movements that have become integral parts of urban life. Many agencies for child welfare, immigrant protection and education, adult education, labor legislation, food inspection, factory inspection, legal aid, music, art, recreation, etc., found shelter during their experimental stage in the settlement. (3) As a point of observation and contact center for budding scholars and social philosophers of the past generation, the social settlement rendered social science a great service. It was a forum and discussion circle, until social science passed from its empirical stage to a more mature stature and began to range abroad for more substantial diet than the inspiration of the round table. This was a form of warming-up period for social science.

Social science left the dialectic laboratory of the settlement with the rise of research foundations. The point of departure might be put at 1909, which was the date of the publication of the first volume of the Pittsburgh Survey.[16] The transition from discourse and common sense

13. R. A. Woods, *The Neighborhood in Nation-Building* (1923), chap. 2, "University Settlements as Laboratories in Social Science."

14. Jane Addams, Twenty Years at Hull House (1923); Mrs. H. O. Barnett, *Canon Barnett, His Life, Letters and Friends* (1919); W. I. Cole, *Motives and Results of the Social Settlement Movement* (1909); R. A. Woods and A. J. Kennedy, *The Settlement Horizon* (1922). The Welfare Council of New York City has a survey of settlements in preparation.

15. On the relation of the community center and settlement to community organization, see M. P. Follett, *The New State* (1918), p. 205. For a study of an attempt at community organization in a slum see H. W. Zorbaugh, *The Gold Coast and The Slum* (1929).

16. E. B. Butler, *Women in the Trades* (1909). Compare with *Hull House Maps and Papers,* which represents the zenith reached by social science under the tutelage of the settlement.

to research has been gradual but consistent, acquiring momentum apace with the piling up of endowments for research. With increasing access to funded wealth, social science is shifting its emphasis from philosophy to objective study, from seeing "how the other half lives" to the methods of the clinic and the laboratory. The pursuit of truth has become a pursuit of specialties. Obviously this must relieve social science of its former burden as moral appraiser conceiving problems in terms of social evils and, after the thinking of the social reformer, following the social evils to the point of identifying them with persons. Social reform thinking characterized most early attempts to treat the city and its problems. The treatment of such social evils generally involved vindictive attacks on persons who were the symbols of the problems. In the days of housing reform the landlord was the symbol of the housing problem, just as the fat man with a silk hat and dollar signs on his vest is still the symbol of capitalism in the struggles of labor for justice. The saloon-keeper was the *bête noir* of the drink evil; the vice lord was blamed for the social evil, and the ward boss was the villain in all political corruption. We can get an urban sociology no faster than sociology is able to rise above such thinking. We have the beginnings of objectivity here and there, and the purpose of this paper is to take brief cognizance of these tendencies.

The Slum and the City as a Whole

We cannot separate the beginnings of urban sociology from the perennial battle to wipe out the slum. This struggle with the slum, which is still going on, illustrates as well as anything how futile and segmented have been our attempts to understand the city. Boiled down, the slum problem has rarely been anything more than isolated attempts, according to preconceived notions, to improve the housing, to transfer the people from congested tenements to attractive dwellings, to move them out of the district. Most drives on the slum seem to assume single causal factors, and so we have attempts to build up community spirit, to build model houses, to condemn the worst houses, to move out the "good" people, to isolate the "dirty" tenant, and many other schemes.[17] The chief indictment of most of these efforts to relieve the city of the slum is that they have never defined the slum with reference to the spatial and functional patterns into which it fits, nor have they ever attempted to determine the interplay of forces that create the slum and

---

17. "Slums and Slummers," *Municipal Engineering and Sanitary Record* (August–October 1916). Compare with C. E. Morrow and Chas. Herrick, "Blighted Districts, Their Cause and Cure," *City Planning*, October 1925.

make for its continuance.[18] The slum is no isolated phenomenon, and any approach to it must take into account other matters, including labor efficiency, income, population mobility, standards of living, race, nationality, and, by no means least, such apparently remote matters as comparative rents, land values and the future use of immediate and adjacent space. Colbert calls the slum in the American industrial city an investment area. Thrasher describes it as an interstitial area.[19] It is an investment, because it tends to be used for lesser residential purposes pending a change in use for business, industrial or better residential purposes. Like interstitial tissue, it is filler-in. The slum in a changing city is generally a temporary and tolerated occupancy of space, its future being determined by the uses to which adjacent space is put. Thus the problems identified with the slum are problems in relationships. The slum itself is a relationship, most extensive in its ramifications. It is not a problem that will submit to simple local therapeutics.[20]

Urban Areas and the Spatial Pattern

Any problem involving any part or function of the city cannot help involving the city as a whole, though it may involve other parts or functions in varying degrees. Closer examination convinces us that the city is a complex of interdependent occupational units. According to use, areas are devoted to residence, commerce, industry, transportation, recreation, administration, etc. Each of these types may be subdivided into lesser related uses. Residence areas, for example, reflect a distribution of population according to racial and national type, group interests or purse capacity. An area receives its identity through its functional relations to other areas. It gets its status as it participates in the total life of the community, just as the city gets its status by its rôle in the larger situation to which it is coördinated. Thus, the city may be involved in a regional, a national, and also a worldwide economy.

The urban area is not so much the creature of design as of the hit-and-miss operation of expediency, economy, social preference and convenience. It is the natural product of the relatively unguided forces, of

18. "The Slum Endures," *The Survey* (March 15, 1927), and "The Slum: A Project for Study," *Social Forces* (September 1928), both by the writer. Also see B. S. Townroe, *The Slum Problem* (1928), and E. D. Simon, *How to Abolish the Slum* (1929). Simon considers the economic possibilities of model housing.

19. Correspondence with R. J. Colbert, Bureau of Economics and Sociology, University of Washington; F. M. Thrasher, *The Gang* (1926).

20. J. F. Steiner, *Community Organization* (1925); A. E. Wood, *Community Problems* (1928).

tendencies to segregation and mobility.[21] The urban area, artifact of urban life, becomes an object of sociological inquiry as it imprints its character upon its occupants, and as that character is impinged upon the rest of the city. This introduces us to a city which is a spatial pattern, and practically an unexplored field to sociology. Moreover, it has a related functional unity, of which sociology is only beginning to be aware.

The dynamic aspects of the urban entity are equally significant, especially the manner of urban growth—the tendency of areas to spread in zonal array about the center of the city. There evolves from the interrelation of areas a balanced occupancy of space, the organization of which is constantly being disturbed by the dynamics of change.[22] The concentric (*Ringstrasse*) pattern reveals striking correlations between the occupation of space and the distribution of poverty, wealth, crime and vice, homeownership and renting, rent levels, and other social phenomena, such as the distribution of age, sex, racial and other groups.

With reference to land values and rents, the uses of space tend to be dispersed in a manner consistent with other uses, both within the occupational area and adjacent to it. The clothing trade and kindred industries in New York City are packed together at the heart of Manhattan where rents would be prohibitive for textile mills or dye works that figure in the making of the cloth. Adjacent to the banking area where we find the highest-priced land in the world, we have the homeless-man district. Here men are crowded in, one to each four hundred cubic feet of air space. While these lodgings are low priced, also at the heart of the city we find the most expensive hotel lodgings. Tenements are often found near the heart of the city, but in areas of change or isolated areas. Apartment houses tend to be more remote from the center; and still more remote, where space is not so much in demand, are the zones of single homes. The concentrated uses seek the high-priced land toward the center of the city, while the uses requiring more space move toward the periphery.

To know the natural area and trace its bounds is imperative for administration and study. Once we are aware of spatial and functional patterns, and the trends of change affecting them, the problem of con-

21. E. W. Burgess, *The Urban Community* (1926); papers by R. D. McKenzie, N. S. B. Gras, W. C. Reckless, S. M. Harrison, and H. W. Zorbaugh.

22. H. Bonnet, "La carte des pauvres à Paris," *Reveue des deux mondes* 35 (1906): 380–420; E. W. Burgess, "The Determination of Gradients in the Growth of the City," *Publications of the American Sociological Society* 21 (1927); R. E. Park and E. W. Burgess, *The City* (1925); E. F. Young, "The Social Base Map," *Journal of Applied Sociology* (January–February 1925).

trol becomes one of allocating functions and guiding development in some manner consistent with what is practical and possible. We are beginning to recognize how vital to urban life the area is, and how important it is to know the vital facts that relate to it; hence movements are under way in a number of cities to collect census and other statistical data from areas coterminous with the natural divisions of the city. The obvious advantage of such a procedure, which has been adopted in Chicago, Pittsburgh, the cities of New York, St. Louis, and Cleveland, should be that figures on vital social phenomena would be made available for the natural local area rather than the political areas that often ignore natural divisions. This ought to facilitate community planning and administration.[23]

Beyond the City Walls

Rarely has there been a time when the city has not been under indictment for being the great consumer and destroyer, as opposed to the country, the creator and giver of life. On the one hand, the city has ever been the disturber of culture; on the other hand, it has ever been the center of culture creation. For this more than anything else, it has been the object of protest.[24] Always changing, yet the city cannot change without becoming a menace to the countryside, where change is as much the essence of discomfort as it is the requisite of life in the city. These age-old rural-urban antipathies only bear witness to an age-old interdependence of the city and its hinterland. In the give and take of buying and selling they have always been supplementary segments of a single entity. They are markets, one to the other. In this market relationship the city gets its status, and thus the size of the city is determined by the size of its market. Once the market function was purely exchange or commercial, but gradually the city has added the industrial function until a large part of the goods consumed by both city and country have been partly produced and finished by the urban worker. The reach of the city's social and economic influence is the metropolitan market area to which it distributes its services and from which it draws its supplies.[25]

23. *Proceedings of the National Conference of Social Work*, Cleveland (1926), papers on the natural area as a unit for social work by J. K. Hart, E. W. Burgess, H. I. Clark, and B. Renard, pp. 369–74 and 500–515.

24. L. W. Busbey, "Wicked Town, Moral Country," *Unpop. Rev.* (October 1912), pp. 376–92; E. E. Miller, *Town and Country* (1928); J. G. Thompson, *Urbanization: Its Effect on Government and Society* (1928).

25. N. S. B. Gras, "The Development of Metropolitan Economy in Europe and America," *American Historical Review* 27 (1921–22): 695–708; also his *An Introduction to Economic History* (1922).

The hinterland falls into at least two general zones: the suburb and the region of supply. The suburb is the immediate periphery of the city, and beyond that lie the zones of production or supply. Every community in the hinterland, be it near or far, is in the periphery of some city, or a number of cities. Its status and life is conditioned by the manner in which it functions in the periphery of this or that city. Besides its location and accessibility, the community in the hinterland is conditioned in its functions by its resources. Suburban communities differ from others in that they are more intimately related to the city, being often but overflow functions of the city. It is the commuter zone, the heavy factory belt, the region of warehouses, stables, stockyards, terminals and other accessory functions of the city. The life of the suburb is timed with the urban movements, and the occupation of its space tends to correlate with the spatial pattern of the city proper. The urban habit of mind dominates suburbia.[26]

No clear line marks what we have called the hinterland of supply from the suburb given over to nonproductive uses. The two overlap, though as a rule the agricultural land near the city is put to intensive uses, whereas land more remotely situated is more apt to be extensively farmed—field crops, corn, wheat, hay, or used for pasture. An example of an inner zone of intensive agriculture is Long Island, where truck gardens and duck farms are interspersed between the expansive estates of the wealthy.

The interchange of services and goods between city and country is supplemented by human migrations. According to the Bureau of Agricultural Economics of the United States Department of Agriculture, 1,978,000 persons moved from farms to towns and cities during 1927. During the same period, 1,374,000 persons moved from towns and cities to farms, giving the city a marginal advantage of 604,000. Other years the difference in favor of towns and cities has been larger, which has given students of the situation their cue for viewing the city as the consumer of surplus man power as it is the consumer of surplus food. It has often been charged that this man power comprises the best blood from the country. This viewpoint does not seem to be supported by the facts. The truth seems to be that we know very little about the sociological implications of rural-urban migrations; yet such knowledge is imperative to any comprehensive urban sociology as well as rural sociology. It would involve inquiry along the whole line of impact of urbanism upon the hinterland. We would need to study the city as a center of stimulation and its influence upon the periphery through such agencies as the newspaper, the radio, the chain store, the mail-

26. H. Paul Douglass, *The Suburban Trends* (1924).

order house, the automobile, the movie, and other factors.[27] A comprehensive urban sociology would include an inquiry into the rural reactions to urbanization, as, for example, the Ku Klux Klan, prohibition, farm "blocs," and numerous reform movements. On the urban side, the inquiry would have to include the emancipation movements and the various activities specifically urban that menace rural placidity.

Geography, Ecology, and the City

To the geographer the city has meaning because it reveals the extent and manner that man has been able to utilize the earth's surface, especially those parts of the earth that are available for human habitation and exploitation. Cities build where they can—where the food can be grown or procured, where topography, soil, climate and other cosmic factors permit. Thus, in geography the human community gets its meaning with reference to site, location and resources. The geographer sees man using parts of the earth productively for food and mineral resources, and other parts of the earth he uses for unproductive purposes, including houses, roads, parks, etc. This approach is called human geography.[28]

The geographer calls attention to the relation of the human community to roads, and the relation of roads to the facts of geography. This has long been a subject of interest among students of society.[29] Between the city and its hinterland, the road is the life-giving artery for both. In his theory of transportation Cooley points out how the community is essentially a point on the road,[30] that wealth and population gather at the breaks in transportation. We may say, then, that the size of the city is not only determined by the number of roads that lead to it and the quantity of goods moving over the roads, but by the interruption of the flow of such goods, the purpose of the interruption, and the length of the interruption. The community at the break in transportation gets its character and status with reference to the goods thus intercepted, whether to break bulk, to change form or to be consumed.

Economic geography is finding a profitable field of inquiry in its

27. *American Journal of Sociology* 34 (July 1928)—E. W. Burgess, "Communication," J. M. Gillette, "Rural Life," W. S. Thompson, "Population," and other papers on "Social Changes in 1927."

28. J. Brunhes, *Human Geography* (1920); E. Demolins, *How the Route Creates the Social Type* (1923); L. Febvre and L. Batillion, *A Geographical Introduction to History* (1925); P. Vidal de la Blache, *Principles of Human Geography,* (tr.) M. T. Bingham (1926).

29. C. H. Hartman, *The Story of the Roads* (1927).

30. C. H. Cooley, *A Theory of Transportation* (1894). This was given further application by D. Ridgley, "Geographic Principles in the Study of Cities," *Journal of Geography* 25 (1925): 66–78.

study of areas of production. This might be called regional geography. Smith, for instance, conceives North America in terms of about eighteen major production areas.[31] The life and economic organization of each of these areas radiate about one or more key cities. Between the production hinterlands and the key cities a consistency in size, location, and function is maintained. Though mechanized standardization tends to make them all alike, the diverse regional situations in which the key cities are found tend to make them different.

Students of the city sometimes run the risk of being caught in the toils of extreme geographical explanations of social phenomena. In their scrambles over what proves to be an interesting line of investigation, some geographers have attempted to become sociologists, interpreting human society generally in terms of some single phenomenon, such as climate, altitude, topography, moisture and soil fertility.[32] Within limits, however, the geographical approach is valid for the urban sociologist.

The problem of human geography, the relation of man to his environment, is also the problem of anthropology and biology. In biology the study of the relation of the organism to the environment is called ecology. Human ecology, according to McKenzie, is the "science of the changing spatial relations of human beings and human institutions."[33] With changes of the population, the state of the arts, or in the social organization, human spatial relations are also modified. Conversely, changed spatial relations will modify social habits and organization. The human community, like plant and animal communities, tends to maintain a balance of life, a tendency toward equilibrium which holds unless disturbed either by the removal of an occupant or species or by some invasion. After such removal or invasion another equilibrium must be achieved.[34]

The plant or animal ecologist studies the organism in its relation to the environment, watching it behave and noting what affects its behavior. Finding so many parallels, the student of human communities has

31. J. R. Smith, *North America: Its People and Resources, Development and Prospects of the Continent as an Agricultural, Industrial, and Commercial Area* (1925); M. Aurousseau, "Recent Contributions to Urban Geography," *Geography Review* 14 (1924): 444–55; R. Mukerjee, *Regional Sociology* (1926).

32. E. Huntington, *Civilization and Climate* (1915); and *Climatic Changes* (1922); P. Sorokin, *Contemporary Sociological Theories* (1928), chap. "The Geographical School."

33. R. D. McKenzie, "The Scope of Human Ecology," *Journal of Applied Sociology* (March–April 1926); B. Moore, "The Scope of Ecology," *Ecology* 1 (1920): 3.

34. N. Anderson and E. C. Lindeman, *Urban Sociology* (1928), chap. "The City: An Ecological Fact"; F. E. Clements, *Plant Succession* (1916); H. A. Gleason, "Further Views of the Succession-Concept" *Ecology* (July 1927).

ventured to "lift" much of the vocabulary of plant and animal ecology. Some of these appropriated terms describe phenomena that are common to higher as well as lower forms of life. This is especially true of the laws of migration, invasion and succession. In the human community there are also cycles of occupation of space. The problem of adaptation is also present, and the same struggle for domination found in plant and animal communities has its analogue here. In a sense, the processes are somewhat negated by man's cultural heritage and by the control his arts give him over nature, but in no sense are they completely blocked. Such barriers to movement as height and distance, as well as swamps, deserts, forests, and areas of ice and water, tend to diminish in importance. But there are other barriers, some of them created by social differences in the population, or the uses to which space is put. Thus, in the great city the areas of occupation become barriers one to another.

Ecologically explained, the arrangement of urban society, the relation of segments to segments, and the coördination of functions begin to have meaning. It is more than a matter of personal orientation to the natural environment. It includes orientation to the artificial mechanized environment, especially in the city, and also to the social environment.[35] Ecology studies the orientation of individuals within their group relations, and such group relations in so far as they involve environmental spatial adjustments.

The Problem of Space and Population

From the point of view of utility, the surface of the earth plays a twofold rôle in man's life. It is his source of supply and his habitat. The first is a productive and the second an unproductive use of space. The principal value of space is derived from its food-producing capacity and other natural resources, but space also has site value derived from its availability to the market. Most space in the city, used for buildings, streets, parks, etc., is, in the sense used here, unproductively occupied. Its site value takes precedence over its value for food production.[36] While it is true that all land has to have site value even to have value for the production of food, yet with the demand for space the site value ultimately eliminates all other values. Thus we may say that rural values derive chiefly from the producing value of land, while urban land

35. L. L. Bernard, *Introduction to Social Psychology* (1926), chap. 6, "The Environmental Bases of Behavior."

36. J. Brunhes, *Human Geography* (1920), pp. 74–229, on the unproductive occupation of the soil.

values derive wholly from location or site. The fertility of the soil loses its value in the city where the streams of traffic meet. Here space for the city man who trades or sells services gets its value from the number of people who pass. Yet to call such space unproductive is not altogether true, because for the market functions it performs the city does have claim on food-producing land remotely situated.

In its social aspects urban land is basically involved in the evolution of the dynamic city.[37] City land undergoes varied and numerous changes of use, and the uses of space in the city are highly competitive. Because of the changing uses of space, urban land becomes an attractive object of speculation; and land speculation, in turn, becomes one of the most potent factors in urban dynamics, which means that, however he operates, the function of the real estate man in the city is dynamic.

The social values of urban land are confined almost wholly to uses of space for residential purposes. There are social distinctions between residential sections of the city, and these are indicated by rent levels. Social distinctions may also be evidenced by the age of buildings or the up-to-dateness of improvements. Between the slum and the most select street there are many levels of rent and income, many grades of housing, and many degrees of cleanliness. These differences are matched by differences in the attitudes of the people in these sections toward themselves. In relative terms, as public sentiment dictates, areas tend to be more or less desirable for residence. Some areas, as Hobohemia, Bohemia, Chinatown, and others, tend to be unique for certain types of residents. Thus, there tends to be competition between areas for types of residential occupancy as well as between residential and nonresidential uses. City planning and zoning are procedures where types of residential areas, as well as nonresidential areas, are protected by law against undesirable and damaging occupational invasions.

In its earlier stages, city planning concerned itself mostly with garden city projects. In its later stages it is becoming a science of spatial manipulation in the growth of cities. As a method of guiding urban development according to some scientific program, instead of waiting on the old trial and error processes of unguided city building, city planning may be a means not only of achieving urban beauty but economy and social harmony as well. Taking into account the lay of the land, the ecological laws of spatial adjustment, and the possibilities of

37. E. H. Doreau and A. G. Hinman, *Urban Land Economics* (1928); R. M. Hurd, *Principles of City Land Values* (1924).

the urban site, the city planner attempts to inject order into the city's development. In doing this he is beginning to discover certain principles of growth common to all cities.[38]

Just as the city as a functioning whole cannot stop with its political boundaries, so scientific city planning must reach out to the periphery to manipulate the development of areas that may ultimately lie within the city proper. Even though the outlying areas are never incorporated into the city proper, to the degree that they are involved in the life of the city they should be involved in the planning of the city. Recognition of this need has given rise to regional planning movements. An outstanding example is the Regional Plan of New York.[39] The purpose of the regional plan as evidenced in two leading instances, New York and Chicago, is to coördinate the development of the metropolitan area, and it may reach out as much as fifty miles into the hinterland.

The problem of space and food supply is basically a problem of population. Demographically stated, it relates to people in numbers and food in quantities. Assuming that the Malthusian principle works, the population always presses against and tends to outstrip the food supply, but ultimately a final saturation point will be reached. For the usual available quantities of food, congestion in the city is relatively no greater than we generally find on farm land. Yet the sustenance situation in the city has always been more precarious. As a result (and perhaps for other reasons), the city has been more aware of the population problem. It is in the city where the futility of an unrestricted birth rate seems to have been most recognized. In modern times it is the city that manifests uneasiness about overpopulation, so that controversy about the problem is generally identified with the metropolitan centers.

However serious its nature as a problem for science, interest in the population problem has generally been too emotional for candid probing. State policies, church views, and science are usually and uncompromisingly at variance.[40]

---

38. On the theory of city planning, see H. James, *Land Planning in the United States for City, State and Nation* (1927); P. Geddes, *Cities in Evolution* (1915); L. Purdy, "Land Values and Social Values," *City Planning* (October 1927).

39. A point of view growing out of the Regional Plan of New York is found in R. M. Haig, "Toward an Understanding of the Metropolis," *Quarterly Journal of Economics* (May and August 1927); also Publications of the Committee of the Regional Plan of New York and Its Environs.

40. A. M. Carr-Saunders, *The Population Problem* (1922); H. Cox, *The Problem of Population* (1923); E. M. East, *Mankind at the Crossroads* (1923); R. Pearl, *The Biology of Population* (1925).

The Selection and Limitation of Population

There are two approaches to population control: the quantitative and the qualitative. The first relates essentially to numbers and brings up the mooted question of birth control for limiting the population. The qualitative aspect relates also to birth control but with the primary interest in selecting the population. According to either viewpoint, population would or might be limited; but the advocate of qualitative control holds for the increase of certain preferred classes. The selectivist may be against birth control but very strong for a careful selection of population increase through immigration. Behind the idea of selection is the assumption of fit and unfit or superior and inferior classes. Whether they determine fitness by cultural or biological appraisals, the selective protective protagonists are convinced that the unfit breed faster than the fit, and they want to control the sources of supply, be they immigration or the birth rate. In some such circles the fittest Americans are thought to be those from the colonial Nordic stocks, but they are not holding their own against the spawning of the non-Nordics of more recent immigrations.[41]

American cities have become ports of entry for the non-Nordic invasion, hence sore spots to the pro-Nordic eugenists. While there is no denying that certain characteristics, such as feeble-mindedness, do cling to the blood stream, yet it seems that many of these fears are unfounded. As far as immigration is concerned, however, these fears have been so widely accepted as to reverse our "melting pot" policy and to replace it with the present highly selective and pro-Nordic immigration laws.[42] This is essentially a negative legislative approach, being prohibitory to all who would enter the country except the small percentage of so-called desirables.

The selective birth rate through legislation is another matter. It is a problem in eugenics. The eugenist is one who places his faith chiefly in heredity, and he banks on improving the race through proper mating and control of breeding.[43] Pinning his faith on such family histories as those of the Jukes, the Kallikaks or the Edwards, the eugenist is able

41. "A Biological Forecast," *Harper's Magazine*, April 1928; M. Grant, *The Passing of a Great Race* (1916); E. Huntington, *The Pulse of Progress* (1926); T. Simar, *Race Myth* (1925).

42. H. P. Fairchild, *The Melting Pot Mistake* (1926).

43. E. G. Conklin, *Heredity and Environment* (1923); L. Darwin, *The Need of Eugenic Reform* (1926); C. B. Davenport, *Heredity in Relation to Eugenics* (1911); F. Galton, *Hereditary Genius* (1869); H. H. Goddard, *Human Efficiency and Levels of Intelligence* (1920); S. J. Holmes, *The Trend of Race* (1922); P. Jacoby, *Études sur la sélection* (1881); A. Ploetz, *Social-anthropologie* (1923); P. B. Popenoe, *Problems of Human Reproduction* (1927); E. A. Ross, *World Trend* (1928).

to explain most insanity, crime, juvenile delinquency, vice, family disorganization, just as easily as he can account for superior forms of behavior.[44] The city is the great challenge; in fact, the city gives the eugenist much anxiety. There is so much irregularity in the city because of the too rapid increase of Jukes and Kallikaks. The eugenists' answer is as simple as their diagnosis: Jukes and Kallikaks must be limited in their breeding, either by sterilization or institutionalization. This must be done by legislation because such people are not amenable to education.

The superior classes, of which the Edwards family is the shining prototype, must be persuaded to marry and people the earth. This is to be done by education, exhortation, or by making the prospect of family-rearing attractive. According to this point of view, the superior classes are being consumed by the city faster than they are being produced, and the ranks can be recruited only from the surplus from the country. Thus the city continues to attract the "best" blood from the country only to leave the country depleted. At the same time, it draws the "worst" from the foreign countries. Since the best in the city do not keep up their numbers and the worst overbreed, there is only one conclusion: American culture is being destroyed!

The difficulty with such reasoning is that we are not always sure about who is superior and who inferior. Are these qualities that run in the bloodstream, or merely socially acquired behavior traits? Eugenists often mistake one for the other, or make no effort to distinguish the two. In facing social problems in the city, it is important that we begin thinking straight on such matters as this. We can do this and still recognize that there is a place in a scientific social control for something that approaches selective reproduction. We have as yet no grounds for assuming that the differential birth rate between social classes is either eugenic or dysgenic. We need some scientific basis for determining who is fit and who unfit. Certainly there is reason for assuming that by breeding alone we are going to overcome the effects of "bad teaching, bad environment, bad habit formation and evil experiences." We also need to examine the urban population to see what the so-called inferior classes are doing in other ways than in walks of crime.

Mobility and Mechanisms

It has been said that the country is separated from the city less by space than by time; that is, the country, being less stimulated, lags behind the city in its rate of change. The city is active, alert, aggressive;

---

44. As an antidote for this point of view, read C. Darrow, "The Edwardses and the Jukeses," *American Mercury,* October 1925.

the country passive, inert, defensive, doggedly conserving the values of the past. Both city and country submit to change, but at varying rates, making the difference between them principally one of degree. The city is more mobile, mobility being a characteristic of its life, just as stability is characteristic of rural life. In either instance mobility, or the lack of it, has sociological significance.

Mobility has come to be used in a double sense among students of sociology. It may refer to movement through physical or geometric space, or movement through social space. Social space and social mobility are terms that Sorokin has recently put into use.[45] It relates to the movement of people up or down the social scale, and includes movement to and fro across class lines. We might call it the shifting of people from one social status to another. Such mobility is at its minimum in a static society, a society stratified into caste groupings where people stay pretty well put. Social mobility is at its height in the fluxing industrial metropolis, where because of social ladder–climbing no class is immune to invasion, however much they may seek protection through the aid of social registers and "blue books." To avoid confusion, we will refer to movement through physical space as mobility, reserving the term "social mobility" for the kind of movement just described. The two forms of mobility are essentially two aspects of a single phenomenon, social mobility being more subjective and generally a resultant of mobility. Once people shift through space, they have no choice but to form new habits and set up new social relationships.

Urban mobility varies as much with the area as with the types of people. Men seem to be more mobile than women, and adults more than children. The children of the foreign-born are more mobile than their parents, who prefer to cling to language areas. Mobility seems to increase as we approach the urban center. Studies being made by the Institute for Social and Religious Research reveal that downtown churches draw as much attendance from a five-mile radius as a one-mile radius. The suburban churches tend to draw very few people from beyond the one-mile area.

The mobility of the city detaches and undomesticates the city man. It releases him from his primary group associations, the family and the neighborhood, bestowing upon him an independence that serves to weaken local loyalties. The city may give him the provincialism of the specialist, but it does so at the cost of that earlier form of provincialism which we identify with the village or country. The city man gains freedom; but the individualism that he achieves is often at the cost of his locus. He acquires other loyalties and in the flux of life he tends to retain a cultural equilibrium. But the equilibrium that the city

45. P. Sorokin, *Social Mobility* (1927).

man enjoys relates to a poise achieved in the midst of movement. The country man, on the contrary, comes to equilibrium with reference to fixed associations in space.[46] Let it not be supposed that the city man in his gypsy-like orientation does not get in a rut in his spatial relations and stereotyped in his behavior. That tendency is ever present, though in the city, where stimuli are most varied and numerous as well as least constant, the tendency is weakest. But the tendency to equilibrium is constantly being invaded and disturbed; and this is as true of social institutions as of personal relations, though the institution recovers equilibrium with difficulty, if at all. This is especially noted in the case of the urban family.

The persistence of any culture pattern arises not from mobility but from isolation. Main Street and Broadway are at cultural extremes, differing in their tempo of life; yet each is the natural product of a situation. Main Street repeats itself day after day and resents disturbance. Broadway is bored with repetition. Main Street is hemmed in by the natural environment more intimately than Broadway. The environment of Broadway is cultural, being man-made and mechanized; and being mechanized, the urban environment has a mobility of its own quite distinct from the movement of the people. As compared with the man on Main Street, we may say that the Broadway man is nearer the artificial and farthest removed from the natural environment. His movements must gear in with a myriad of movements all about, and these movements tend to contribute momentum one to another. The mobility of the urban community involves movement of the total situation; movement of the people, movement of the home, of institutions and social organizations, movement of occupants in and out of areas, and finally, the movement even of the urban areas.

Equilibrium in the mobile urban society, such a society that calls itself "progressive," is never reached, though it is ever being approximated. To the degree that it is approached, we have the establishment of behavior patterns or behavior mechanisms. Since so much of the urban environment reflects human nature more than nature, an inquiry into the behavior-patterns and mechanisms found there involves a study both of structures and processes. We need to study the movement of people, but also the structural changes—skyscrapers, transportation systems, water systems, lighting systems, sewers, etc.—for these also involve motion. These external non-social mechanisms which constitute the dynamic structural phase of the urban situation are sometimes designated by the blanket term, *the machine.*

---

46. R. E. Park, "Human Migrations and the Marginal Man," *American Journal of Sociology* (May 1928).

Urban Types and Groups

With a mobile society and a mechanized environment, what type of person does the city produce? If human nature is acquired out of experience, what kind of human nature is evolved in the urban situation? In his personality the city man incorporates, as does any other person, "physical make-up, intellectual powers, instinctive tendencies, emotions, feelings, and the will," but the composition of these elements in different people varies as their experience. Type distinctions between people really characterize backgrounds.[47] Personality is an end product, and in some respects a by-product, of association; and through it the person reflects the culture patterns of the groups to which he belongs. Literally he is the group or groups that figure in his life, and to the extent that they figure in his life. He takes on the attitudes, the values and all that characterizes his associates; hence the social scientist, to understand the person, must study him in his social setting. This task is relatively easy in the homogeneous setting, but extremely difficult in the heterogeneous setting. In the great city, where the most variables would be encountered, it would be most difficult.

In their occupational and intimate or primary relations the city differentiates, specializes and separates people, but it tends to reduce them all to a standardized mean in their secondary or impersonal relations. Urban life seems to shunt city people about, group and segregate them into types or classes that differ in interest and activities, in race, religion, nationality, etc. Where country people are bound by propinquity, thrown upon one another by spatial distribution, city dwellers tend to draw together in terms of group interests. Their social relationships incline toward a member basis rather than a neighbor basis. The city man's life may be cast into a number and variety of groups among which he divides his time and loyalty, but his affiliations are the result of interest more than residential qualifications. The shift of society in the city from a neighborhood to a metropolitan character is fundamental to any scientific interpretation of urban life.[48]

The interest group arrangement of the city is both more and less confining than the neighborhood or propinquity group. While it contributes to cosmopolitanism, it also develops forms of provincialism that are as confining as the isolation of the village. If he hopes to under-

47. H. B. Woolston, "The Urban Habit of Mind," *American Journal of Sociology* (March 1912); K. Young, *Source Book for Social Psychology* (1927), pp. 299 et seq.

48. F. H. Allport, *Social Psychology* (1924); E. W. Burgess, ed., *The Urban Community* (1926), see paper by W. I. Thomas, "The Problem of Personality in the Urban Environment," and paper by L. Wirth, "Some Jewish Types of Personality"; C. G. Jung, *Psychological Types* (1923); K. Young, "Integration of Personality," *Pedag. Seminary* 30 (1923): 264–85.

stand and eventually control metropolitan society, the student of urban life needs to acquaint himself with these vital interest aggregates in which urban life is lived. In a common-sense way the urban politician has long known the value of cultivating clubs, fraternities, gangs and other homogeneous groupings through which he keeps his finger on the pulse of the city and manipulates its activities. There is no reason for believing that the social scientist would be less successful, though his objectives might differ vastly. He wants the facts so that those who would manipulate urban life might keep their ideals within the range of the possible.[49]

The Social Pathologies of the City

Social maladjustments in the changing urban situation are inevitable. Old behavior patterns are invaded and broken down and new ones are developed. Pathology begins when the demands for adjustment outstrip the capacity of the organism to make the adjustment. Pathology may involve the individual or person; it may relate to the primary group, or it may concern the community.[50] The person is deemed in a pathological state whenever, because of some physical, mental, or personality maladjustment, he is not able to function normally in his social relations. Whether his problem is one of social friction or dependency, if the condition disorganizes him or inconveniences his associates, or society in general, he is to that extent pathological. The social maladjustments of persons or groups are often traceable to change differentials between stimuli systems and habit response systems. Whether he changes faster or slower than his group, in either case the person may be a behavior problem. He may be more responsive or less to new situations; it's a matter of rate of adjustment, in which he may be lagging behind his group or far in advance. Or it may be that his experience has been different so that his values and attitudes would not be in harmony with his group.[51]

In the final analysis, the pathology of the group becomes pathology of persons in their associational relationships. This is especially true of the family most frequently involved in group maladjustment. It has

49. N. Anderson and E. C. Lindeman, *Urban Sociology* (1928), chaps. on urban types and urban groups; N. Spykman, *Social Theory of Georg Simmel* (1925), chap. 1, "The Concept of Society."

50. J. H. S. Bossard, *Problems of Social Well-Being* (1927); R. C. Dexter, *Social Adjustment* (1927); J. L. Gillin, *Poverty and Dependency* (1921); S. A. Queen and D. M. Mann, *Social Pathology* (1925).

51. J. Colcord, *Broken Homes* (1919); W. Healy, *The Individual Delinquent* (1915); E. R. Mowrer, *Family Disorganization* (1927); W. I. Thomas and F. Znaniecki, *The Polish Peasant in Europe and America* (1927); W. I. Thomas and D. S. Thomas, *The Child in America* (1928).

had so much trouble surviving the impact of urban life that, with its diminishing size, the mechanized apartment life, the passing of domestic social life, the waning of the old domestic economy, and the changing status of women, there is some question as to whether it can survive. The industrial economy of the city, as well as the problem of distribution and habits of consumption, is involved in most pathology of the urban family. The setup of industrial society puts its major emphasis on the employable individual as the unit of production; whereas the unit of production in all previous economies, especially that of the early homestead home, was the family. This contributes to the detachment and mobility of the individual. Group pathology takes other forms. One of the most perplexing of these is the gang, a phenomenon of the city, and particularly of the regions of social disorganization.[52]

Pathology of the community often relates to the distribution, density or the movements of the population, as well as to numerical maladjustments in sex groupings, age groupings, or in death rates, birth rates, divorce rates, etc. These disproportions are important socially only as they lead to social friction or contribute in some way to the social disorganization of the community. Problems of change usually hold the center of attention in community pathology. Such problems are generally characterized by clash between traditional and invading interests or points of view, or between old and new behavior patterns. The challenge presented by the pathologies of urban life is essentially problems in social control, in social case work and community organization.

Social Science and Social Control

The initial purpose of science in its approach to the problems of the city is to describe and interpret them. Where maladjustment is a matter of social change, science measures the rates of change and seeks for generalizations about the trends of change that will be useful in developing techniques for control. But science, as such, ceases to figure in control at the point where fact-finding turns to fact-using. Science does not manipulate phenomena, it studies them. The ultimate objective of social science is social control, to reduce friction in change and to remove the devitalizing forces that prey upon the person or the group, yet the social scientist who assists in creating the tools and techniques for readjustment does not use these tools and techniques. If he did, his role would change from that of a social scientist to that of a technician. This has been a salient difficulty in the development of urban sociology; it has been too often intrigued into the manipulation of urban life. Much of this lies outside the field of measuring, examining, describing and interpreting the phenomena of the city. The manipula-

52. F. M. Thrasher, *The Gang* (1927).

tion belongs in other hands. In so far as it concerns the maladjustment of persons or groups, it is the responsibility of social work.

Social work has been described as the "art of adjusting human relationships." In the turmoil of urban life the social worker functions as a salvaging, reconciling, reorganizing agent. In the great city the social worker has become a substitute for the folk guidance and gossip of the village. It is her function to take charge of the defunct family organization, to rehabilitate the person when his own resources fail, to reconstitute disorganized group life, and to reinforce the community organization. There is some difference of opinion about the possibility of social work becoming a science—that is, the social worker becoming objective—which seems quite beside the point. Social work must remain an art and it can be an art without sacrificing its objectivity. It can be an art in human relations and still be equipped with techniques that grow out of scientific research as well as its own accumulated experience. The social worker at the point of change must rely primarily upon native intelligence and the methods of trial and error to make adjustments, and these adjustments often have less to do with rules than compromise.[53]

In some of the larger cities where social work organization embraces most phases of social maladjustment, at least three tendencies are in evidence: (1) Social work is turning more to research to establish factual bases for action; (2) There is a decided swing toward social planning in the specialization of agencies, the elimination of duplication and the concentration of effort through central guidance; and (3) More emphasis is being put on the coördination of agencies and their programs, also through central guidance. At least these trends indicate that panacea reform as a motive in social work is on the wane.[54]

Other factors than conscious reconstructive controls figure in the life of the city, conditioning its behavior. An example would be the tendency toward the mechanization of movement, including such mechanisms as we have already referred to—those that figure in transportation, communication, supply and waste removal. We have never determined the extent to which such factors as the press agent, the advertiser, the real estate man and others contribute to the social organization or disorganization of the city. Precisely what influence on urban society are such factors as the political machine, the men of influence in civil life, men of wealth, funded wealth guided by the hands

53. For a full discussion of the role of social work, see the chapter by Phelps on "Sociology and Social Work." Also see M. E. Richmond, *What Is Social Case Work?* (1922); and K. de Schweinitz, *The Art of Helping People out of Trouble* (1924).

54. Typical of this tendency is the Welfare Council of New York City; see booklet of this title by W. F. Persons (1925).

of dead men and, not the least, such established institutions as the church?

In the secondary urban society, the pressures of social control are largely indirect, compared with the direct compulsion of the face-to-face groups. Village gossip may not be here, but in its stead we find inner primary groups equally potent. The gang and the institution are typically representative. Both flourish in the complex urban situation, and in a sense both are products of the social disorganization of the city. Thrown on the defensive, social values often retreat to institutions for safety. Once inside, they become aggressive and conservative disciplines, resorting to law for the control that the mores no longer insure. The gang on mischief bent and the institution bent on doing good—both may be powers in dominating public policy, and either may be a problem in social control. In these we have named only a few of the factors that sway the life of the city. How significant they are, how related to one another in making the city the kind of a place it is, and often in spite of conscious efforts to make it different, constitute for the urban sociologist a fertile field of study.[55]

Present Trends of Urban Sociology

The position taken in this chapter is that urban sociology is but a phase of sociology in the process of being formed. As a scientific method in fact-finding it has scarcely found itself, and any attempt to define its scope and aims would be hazardous. Accordingly, we have attempted to go no further than to call attention to some of the subject matter that might properly be included in the field, recognizing that the materials are scattered and fragmentary. The process of gathering these data into a related whole worthy to be called urban sociology can proceed no faster than social science is able to relinquish the well-wishing and often unsystematic reform motives for objective research.

During the formative period of the social sciences in this country, they were involved in numerous welfare moves, aiming at specific problems of the city but particularly those identified with slum areas. They were more concerned with finding solutions than in studying causes and relationships. The trend at present is in the direction of studying the city in larger perspective—in its entirety, rather than in terms of isolated problems. The urban sociology growing out of the more objective viewpoint is essentially a science of interrelationships of segments of the population, of the social processes involved in the creation of attitudes and values. It must eventually become a study of the total situation, of the total physical environment of the city and

---

55. S. Bent, *Ballyhoo: The Voice of the Press* (1927); F. E. Lumley, *Means of Social Control* (1925); P. Odegard, *Pressure Politics* (1928); M. R. Werner, *Tammany Hall* (1928).

of human behavior in response to it. It thus becomes a study of the interdependence of function in the city and the coördinated occupancy of urban space. A very significant approach to this ideal is the recent survey of Middletown conducted by the Institute for Social and Religious Research. It is a study of an average American city with reference to the six "main-trunk activities" of a community: "getting a living, making a home, training the young, using leisure, engaging in religious practices and engaging in community activities."[56]

As a venture in research, urban sociology can only share the progress of social science in general. The research prospects of social science in the city are indicated by a number of trends which include (1) the rapid accumulation of wealth in social science research funds and foundations; (2) the establishment of special projects in urban research (an example would be the institute for the study of land economics at Northwestern University); (3) the increasing number of bureaus for municipal research specializing on problems of administration and taxation; (4) the establishment of schools for city managers, secretaries of Chambers of Commerce, and other municipal workers; (5) the increase in the number of city- and regional-planning commissions, and the tendency among these to base their programs on the findings of research; (6) the trend toward the coördination of social work agencies definitely committed to research and centralized administration; (7) an increasing use of research in business and industry. Examples would be the studies of such organizations as telephone companies, railroad companies, and advertising firms. This includes income and population surveys and such market surveys as the newspapers have been making in the larger cities.

Urban sociology must look to other sources than the findings of social research for its data. It is equally dependent upon progress in the physical sciences as well as in the mechanical arts. Moreover, there is developing another fertile source of data; namely, the field of journalism. The realist in journalism is a potent factor in clearing our vision with reference to phenomena of the city. This, in spite of the fact that in his observations he often alternates between art and science. For an adequate urban sociology these and other sources must be tapped; thus the sociologist's approach to the city becomes a many-sided one. It must be so if he is to have any comprehensive view of the city in its entirety, not only within its limits, but beyond its limits to the most remote reaches of the hinterland.

56. R. S. and H. M. Lynd, *Middletown: A Study of Contemporary American Culture* (1928). Also J. F. Steiner, *The American Community in Action* (1928); and the University of Chicago Community Studies as *The Ghetto* by L. Wirth (1928); *The Gold Coast and The Slum,* by H. W. Zorbaugh (1929); *Domestic Discord,* by E. R. Mowrer (1928); *Suicide,* by R. S. Cavan (1928); *The Gang,* by F. M. Thrasher (1927); *The Hobo,* by N. Anderson (1923).

18

Urbanism as a Way of Life

Our task is to study and understand the modern community and its way of life. In this chapter our attention is directed to a brief examination of modern community life.[1] It is centered in the great cities and it is oriented to industry. It is often referred to as Western, and as a way of life is called urbanism. It is found in its most characteristic form in the United States, but tends to be present wherever a good share of a people live by industry and commerce and, concomitantly, at a tempo which is peculiar to urbanism.

Urbanism as a way of life is not confined to cities and towns, although it emerges from the great metropolitan centers. It is a way of behaving, and that means one can be very urban in his thinking and conduct although he may live in a village. On the other hand, a very nonurbanized person may live in a most urbanized section of a city.

Characteristics of Urbanism

Urbanism as a way of life was once fairly restricted within the walls of the city and, within the city, it was limited to certain sections. The urbanized man remains oriented in the crowd. He is not disturbed by the coming and going of people, hence he is always making new acquaintances and forgetting the old ones; *transiency* is one of his characteristics. He cannot know all persons about him well and he may not wish to. Thus, again to use a term from Wirth, interpersonal relations are marked by *superficiality*. Since the urbanized man cannot know all people, and may not wish to, he acquires the ability to move in the crowd without caring who the people are about him, and he does not invite their approaches; *anonymity* is still a third characteristic.

From *The Urban Community: A World Perspective* (New York: Holt, Rinehart and Winston, 1959), pp. 1–23. © 1959 by Holt, Rinehart and Winston and renewed 1987 by Martin Anderson; reprinted by permission of the publisher.

1. The title of this chapter is borrowed from an early but still widely read article by Louis Wirth, "Urbanism as a Way of Life," *American Journal of Sociology* 41, no. 1 (July 1938): 1–23. This author was a student with Wirth and is very much indebted to him and his pioneering in the urban sociology field.

Certain writers have questioned the transiency-superficiality-anonymity description of urbanism offered by Wirth. For example, Bascom studied the cities of the Yoruba in Africa. He found these cities were not well urbanized, and anonymity was less evident.[2] Sedky found that Alexandria, Egypt, also lacked these marks of urbanism. The people in Alexandria are still joined in extended family networks and they still live by the old tradition. She found little evidence of the emergence of individualism.[3] This writer does not know the cities of the Yoruba, but he does know Alexandria and other Middle East cities. Alexandria, much more isolated than Cairo, is much less urbanized. There is lacking in Alexandria the moving in and out of many strange people of varied races, religions, and nationalities. This may be said of all the cities of Iraq except Baghdad and it applies to all the cities in Iran except Teheran. But neither Baghdad nor Teheran is very industrial and neither could be described as being as urbanized as Cairo.

But urbanism is not merely a way of thinking and behaving. The urbanized man, wherever he may be, is ever adjusting to the new and changing. As he is congenial to initiative, he may also be intolerant of tradition if tradition stands in the way of getting things done. He is not only mobile himself, but he accepts the mobility of others. He may be loyal to his immediate family but he tends to lose contact with other relatives. As he tends to be more urbanized he is also more the individual than is possible in nonurban society.

A third characteristic of urbanism as a way of life concerns the standardizing influences which radiate from the cities. The farmer and the woodsman hear the same radio programs, view the same television programs, and visit the same movies as the most urbanized man. The American farmer, especially, uses machines made in the city and he has a city-made automobile. His children can receive the same education as do city children. He is connected with the world by his telephone and he is a newspaper reader. Not only does the newspaper come from the city, but his farm journals are edited and printed in cities. The farmer's wife buys the same packaged goods for her kitchen as the urban wife, and his children tell the same jokes and sing the same songs that happen to be in vogue among urban youth. A sort of network seems to exist by which all people tend to be mutually oriented.

This network is not merely one which extends urban influence outward. It has many other aspects. By it the thinking and creations of

2. William Bascom, "Urbanization among the Yoruba," *American Journal of Sociology* 60, no. 5 (March 1955): 446–54.

3. Mona Sedky, "Groups in Alexandria, Egypt," *Social Research* 22, no. 4 (Winter 1955): 441–50.

one country are transferred to other countries. Market news travels from one world city to another causing rapid responses in labor markets and industries.

Thus urbanism may be seen from a variety of viewpoints, three of which have been named above. It concerns the ability of people to behave in the urban setting, and it involves a sort of sophistication of the individual. It is also a kind of communication network by which people everywhere are knitted into a vast social system. Urbanism as a way of life is both complex and fluid, and tends to become more so.

Degrees of Urbanism

Urbanism as a way of life in the United States tends to find its extreme form in cities like New York, Chicago, and Los Angeles. In Europe they would be London, Paris, Rome, and formerly Berlin and Vienna. But what of smaller cities and towns, hundreds of which are suburban to the most urban centers? Sometimes the outlying suburban village may be occupied almost entirely by people who work in the city. It may be a very urban population with respect to sophistication, but these people may foster a type of neighborhood community life which may resemble in many respects the neighborhood relations in a remote farm village.

To what extent is the nonurban place oriented in its daily life to the great urban centers, in its buying and selling, in its play and its work, in its family relations? To what extent do nonurban people join secondary organizations which have branches in different cities, towns, and villages? If such tests were applied to American towns and villages it would be difficult to find any place that is not urbanized to some degree. The rural person, often depicted in the mass media as a comic stereotype, hardly exists today, but he did exist in many parts of the United States a few decades ago, although never as a comic character.

The same observation holds for some European countries. The United Kingdom is quite urban, the influence extending from the great cities to all of its shores. Efforts are being made to revive and restore some of its rural way of life. In Holland the peasant with his wooden shoes and wide pantaloons has disappeared, except in areas most visited by tourists and here the old garb is used as a trade uniform. At Arnhem, Holland, is a well-known outdoor museum in which the various farm houses and farm villages have been recreated, and even the modern Dutch farmer visits this place to see what farm life was like a generation or more ago. While the peasant is still found in France, he hardly exists any more in Germany or in tightly inhabited Belgium.

This does not mean that the farmer as a worker in agriculture is disappearing, although his numbers tend relatively to diminish in the industrial countries. It means only that ruralism as a way of life tends to disappear, and is replaced by urbanism as a way of life. As will be seen in other chapters, certain characteristics of that older way of life tend to linger and may be found even in urban communities.

The Process of Urbanization

More and more people in most countries are becoming city or town dwellers. This flow of population from land-bound occupations to other types of work is something new in human history. Such an urban trend could not have happened prior to the industrial revolution, and since the industrial revolution the trend has gone forward even though there have been efforts here and there to curb or guide it.

In a document on the causes and implications of urbanization prepared by the Economic Commission for Asia and the Far East (ECAFE), the term was defined in these words: "In its most simple and demographic sense, urbanization can be defined as the process whereby population tends to agglomerate in clusters of more than a designated size."[4] This definition reflects the definition of the demographer Warren S. Thompson writing in the *Encyclopaedia of the Social Sciences* who called urbanization the "movement of people from communities concerned chiefly or solely with agriculture to other communities, generally larger, whose activities are primarily centered in government, trade, manufacture or allied interests."[5]

This definition cannot be accepted without reservations. Assuming for the moment that urbanization is simply a one-way process, it need only be added that the rate of the process varies from time to time as well as from place to place. During the pioneering settlement period in the United States, for example, it was necessary for governments to encourage the location and building of towns. Before a half-century had passed, town building was moving at a rapid rate, and by 1900 many Americans feared their country was becoming too urban too fast. Yet with each decade since 1900 the United States has become increasingly urban. This trend has been frequently described in terms of the relative percentages of rural and urban population. Moreover, the rate of urbanization, as a one-way process, has been more rapid in

---

4. United Nations Economic Commission for Asia and the Far East, Document E/CW.11/URB.2, 28 June 1956, p. 4. Seminar on urbanization at Bangkok, 8–18 August 1956. The definition was adapted from an article by Kingsley Davis and Hilda Hertz, "Urbanization and the Development of Pre-industrial Areas," *Economic Development and Cultural Change* 3 no. 1 (October 1954): 8.

5. "Urbanization," *Encyclopaedia of the Social Sciences*, 15: 189.

all countries since the industrial revolution. It would, in fact, be difficult for some countries to survive were most of the people not living
in urban agglomerations.

Such a definition of urbanization, however, tends to exclude too
much. It is more than a shifting of people from country to city and
from land-bound work to urban types of work. Merely moving a man
to the city does not necessarily urbanize him (although it helps), while
another rural man may be very much urbanized and never leave his
rural work or habitat. Urbanization involves basic changes in the thinking and behavior of people and changes in their social values. It is not
merely a matter of an individual or group changing from one kind of
work to another, but involves changes in attitudes toward work, and it
means entering a new and ever-changing division of labor. Thus Karl
Mannheim used the term, "urbanization and its ramifications."[6]

Urbanization may assume the form of "idea migration" from the
most urban to the less urban places. In the case of the American dairy
industry we find an example of a rural occupation which has become
quite urbanized. Most of the dairy farms are located in the most urban
parts of the United States. The fact that this type of rural work is often
called an industry is seen in the timing of the dairyman's work with
the tempo of the city. Raper notes that as cities have grown, farm
people have been "brought into closer and closer contact with urban
centers." He then names some characteristic influences of urbanism
on dairy farming and mentions as a second form of urbanization, the
"continued growth of part-time farming and rural residences within
commuting distance of urban or other non-farm employment."[7]

Thus it would be a mistake in our study of modern community life
to think of urbanization as merely a one-way process; the urban way
of life also moves into the nonurban and less urban areas. Urbanization
also means a changeover from one way of life to another. It corre-
sponds in the variety of its application to "detribalization," a term used
by students of social change in Africa. Some Africans move from the
tribal villages to industrial places and there enter the struggle of becoming adjusted to the urban way of life. But the ways of doing and
thinking and the things characteristic of the urban way of life also invade the tribal villages, and there the struggle for adjustment may take

6. Karl Mannheim, *Freedom, Power and Democratic Planning* (New York: Oxford University Press, 1950), p. 62.

7. Arthur F. Raper, "The Dairy Areas." See Carl C. Taylor and associates, *Rural Life in
the United States* (New York: Alfred A. Knopf, 1950), p. 431. On p. 491 Raper observes
that the degree of urbanization varies from one rural region to another, but as urbanization increases "living and thinking of rural and urban populations become more and
more alike."

another form. However the term is used, the end product of urbanization is urbanism as a way of life.

Ruralism

In most countries urban areas of habitation are distinguished from rural areas of habitation in terms of the number of people living there. In the United States if the number is under 2,500 the aggregate is designated as rural. Larger places are divided into classes: 2,500 to 5,000 population, 5,000 to 10,000 population, and so on to cities of 1,000,000 people or more. These are arbitrary distinctions which must be accepted in order to have comparable population statistics for comparison through time, and each country establishes its own arbitrary classifications.

The ambiguities inherent in this system of distinguishing rural from urban are too well known for discussion here. Nor do we need here to go into the various efforts of population statisticians to meet the problem. This much must be said: It is generally recognized that rural population and rural occupations are found in the United States in agglomerations far in excess of 2,500 population, while urban population and urban occupations are found in places of less than 2,500 inhabitants. Thus the size-of-population yardstick, however useful for many purposes, is not very helpful in measuring the presence or absence of a rural or an urban way of life.

Allan Nevins, in a preface to a book on great cities, having in mind the American situation, noted that "quite different faculties of mind and character, broadly speaking, appertain to the city and to the country. . . . The rural outlook is the more serene and conservative; the urban outlook the more volatile, alert and radical." In his discussion he mentioned differences in wit and humor, and the fact that in some important respects rural and urban characteristics tend to be mutually opposite. He implied, however, that the urban are dominant: "But we must make up our minds now to be a predominantly urban civilization, and try to nurture rural virtues in a citified environment."[8]

Without discounting in the least the statistics on population and occupations, we must also recognize that before referring to a person or an aggregate of people as urban or not urban we must take account of their thinking and behavior, which may be very urban, very rural, or some urban-rural mixture. The tendency in most countries is for rural places to assume a more urban way of life. This process of urbanization

8. Allan Nevins, Preface. See Ernest Barker and 12 associates, *Golden Ages of the Great Cities* (London: Thames & Hudson, 1952), p. xiv.

is easily to be seen, as Nelson has observed it in certain isolated Mormon villages:

> Urbanization, or as some sociologists call it, secularization of life, is proceeding at a rapid place. Communication and transportation devices which characterize contemporary life place the remotest corners in instantaneous contact with the world. The diffusion of urban traits to the countryside is everywhere apparent. Farmers are declining in numbers and farms increasing in size. Life becomes more impersonal, mutual aid declines, and contractual forms of association increase. Formal organizations multiply as new interests arise—economic, social, recreational, educational. New occupations come into being as specialization and division of labor grow more elaborate. Homogeneity of the population gives way to increasing heterogeneity. Attitudes change. The sense of community suffers as cleavages develop around special interests. These developments are clearly evident in the Mormon village today, as they are in the communities of the United States elsewhere.[9]

Nelson's closing observation applies to rural villages in most countries, but in particular in the Western countries. The global trend toward the urban way of life touches every community.

The trend of rural change is away from what we call ruralism. The term is not one of depreciation. Communities dominated by ruralism—and they are not numerous—are likely to be described as backward. Raper, quoted earlier, noted that the degree of urbanization (our term urbanism) differs from one region of the United States to another, and this also means that the degree of ruralism differs. The same could be said of regions in other countries, although country-to-country comparisons are difficult to make for we must take into account each country's historical development and traditions. On this basis the United States, for instance, is a comparatively new country and lacks the firmly rooted traditions and long history of Europe.

While emphasizing the global spread of urbanism, it must not be forgotten that more of the world's population lives in a rural than an urban way of life. Many more people live in villages than in cities, but the rate of urbanization is increasing in momentum. In some parts of

---

9. Lowry Nelson, *The Mormon Village* (Salt Lake City: University of Utah Press, 1952), pp. 276–77. In a more recent book he makes the observation that it "seems inescapable that rural and urban segments of American society are drawing closer together, becoming more alike. This is quite likely due more to the 'urbanization' of the countryside than to the 'ruralization' of the city, although the influence of one upon the other is reciprocal." From the preface to *American Farm Life* (Cambridge: Harvard University Press, 1954). For a report which describes rural change in Holland, see E. W. Hoffstee, *Rural Farm Life and Rural Welfare in The Netherlands* (The Hague: Ministry of Agriculture, Government Printing Office, 1957).

the world so many people are crowding into the cities that the labor markets are glutted. Industry cannot be developed fast enough to meet the demands for employment, and so living standards remain low. On the other hand, urban influence is moving to the rural areas at an equally rapid rate. This is another phase of urbanization—the city goes to the country.

The Rural-Oriented and the Urban-Oriented

While it is true that more of the world's population is in the rural-oriented category than in the urban-oriented, the relative proportions are changing rapidly, and have been, particularly since the beginning of this century. The rate of changeover has been especially fast since World War II, due in large measure to programs of aid to underdeveloped countries instituted and continued by the Western countries, in many cases, because of the growing interest of Communist countries in these same underdeveloped areas. These efforts are various, sometimes short sighted and often ambiguous, but the end results are that more and more of the world's population, on the initiative of others, is becoming culturally uprooted by being lured or forced out of the old tribal ways of life. The urban-oriented segment of the population is increasing rapidly.

This changing over from old forms of life and work to new ones, ruthless as far as traditional values are concerned, gives rise to many complex and baffling social problems. Our interest here, however, is not in the problems as such but in the fact that urbanism is spreading. As a way of life, urbanism is becoming global. This growth has always been painful and problem creating, and it continues to be so, although the problems may not be the same. It is, nevertheless, a trend that must be accepted. By many, it is called progress. In Communist terminology this urbanization process is called liberation, and the Communist countries have their active programs for systematically pushing and guiding the process.

At this juncture we must point out that urbanism in its "pure" form would be as difficult to find in most of the Western countries as the "pure" form of ruralism. Any country has, of course, population agglomerations that are the most rural and those that are the most urban, but between these extremes are found various mixtures of urbanism and ruralism; the one diminishing in the urbanward direction and the other diminishing in the ruralward direction. There are no sharp dividing lines.

While the most urban area or the most rural area may be recognizable within the United States, we are likely to find that the characteristics of "most rural" and "most urban" are not the same from country to country. These differences notwithstanding, the relationships between the rural and the urban in all of these countries, particularly the industrial countries of the West, are in a continuous process of change. Change in every country is in the direction of the less urbanized places becoming more urbanized.

The change tends to be a steadier process in the more industrialized and more urbanized countries such as the United States, the United Kingdom, Belgium, Germany, and others than it is in the least industrialized countries. India is an outstanding example of a country where the strains of urbanization seem to be ever at the breaking point. The urban labor market is continuously glutted with hordes of untrained rural job seekers. To quote Deshmukh, "A vast majority of the rural exodus is forced to keep on floating from town to town and from town to village in search of employment, and to earn a precarious living during this migration process."[10]

Urbanism and Industrialization

The urban segment of any population lives indirectly from the land. It must provide goods and services which can be marketed in rural areas in return for the products of the land. Towns and cities have grown, some more than others, as urbanites have found more ways of producing more goods and services. Many cities, besides making things for sale, rendered services by bringing goods, such as raw materials and food, from far places in ships and then redistributing them to other places by other means of transport. However, before the emergence of power industry there tended to be growth limits which were attained by certain urban places and not exceeded for centuries. As we shall see later, growth-limiting factors are ever present, but they are subject to change.

For generations it seems to have been the accepted order in cities that they produced goods and services under conditions of continuous depression. Hand work was the rule, and is so much the rule still in some towns of the Far East that modern textile mills have difficulty in getting started because of resistance from the handloom tradition. In these towns the situation is further complicated by the fact that there is not sufficient other industry to relieve labor market pressure. Most European industrial cities have also lived through this struggle between hand work and machine work. Fortunately, the United States did not have to face such a problem because the westward-moving

10. M. B. Deshmukh, "A Study of Floating Population, Delhi," in *The Social Implications of Industrialization and Urbanization* (Calcutta: Unesco Research Center, 1956), p. 150.

frontier drained off the labor surplus while industry was getting started.

Industry in the Western countries has not relieved cities of growth problems or of occasional deep unemployment, but the population no longer lives in a condition of continuous depression and drudgery. Industry enables more people to find work than was possible before, and while work has become increasingly productive, it has also been lightened and working hours shortened. It was rare that a pre-industrial city in the West exceeded half a million inhabitants living by hand production and commerce, for that system of production and exchange had its limits. Industry has enabled many of the same cities to approach or exceed a million inhabitants, and the people in the new industrial cities enjoy living standards which could not be imagined previously.

An industrialized type of urbanism is much more than a condition involving the industrial cities, for the industrial city has been forced to develop a new kind of relationship with the outside. The old city was a seat of wealth, power, and influence to which people came to sell and to buy. The new city does not wait; it goes out to sell and to buy. The new city had to take the initiative in making roads where they hardly existed before, for the outside had little interest in roads, and often resisted their construction. This is one of the basic differences between ruralism and urbanism: Ruralism conserves its isolation, while urbanism, especially industrial urbanism, encroaches upon isolation.

In order to grow, the industrial city had to extend its networks to improve transportation and communication and to extend its contacts over wider areas. Thus industrial urbanism attains markets and access, but in this process it also becomes more easily accessible to more people, and so circulation and the movement of people parallels the movement of goods.

Industrialization has not only introduced new work ways in the urban centers, new and ever-changing divisions of labor and new work standards, but these innovations tend to be exported into the outside areas, often with disturbing results. Here, again, urbanism and ruralism differ fundamentally. This is another outward-extending urban influence that gathers momentum.

It is true that the factory first made its home in towns and cities, and is still most at home there. However, for reasons of competition and economic advantages, industries may be established in areas from whence the raw materials come—factories near the beet fields, canneries in regions of special farming, sawmills in the forests, and metal-reduction plants near the mines. To a large extent the current programs of aid to underdeveloped countries are concerned with establishing industries in these remote places. Several Western countries, for example, are now engaged in various efforts to industrialize Africa, thereby bringing urbanism to the Dark Continent.

To introduce urbanism to a new region through the development of industry, however, calls for much more than the building of factories. Say Thompson and Woodruff:

> The economic development of an area means the use of more capital, or more labour, or more natural resources, either more of all or more of any of them, to raise the real incomes per head of the inhabitants. In the underdeveloped countries of Africa the emphasis is heavily on the use of more capital; whether social or economic, development involves the direction of resources in the present to uses which will only yield benefits in the future. But in backward countries the people have a low standard of living; the level of national income per head provides little scope for large savings. Left to themselves, therefore, the progress of backward countries would be slow and the attainment of a rapid rate of development is dependent on an inflow of funds.[11]

Bringing industry into a nonurban area in the United States may create some problems, but even the most rural American communities have had some experience with new developments. They have their civil organizations for coping with new and unexpected difficulties; ways are found within the local aggregates for achieving adjustment. But the African natives know nothing of this type of collective living; nor have they been trained in the skills of industry, for the facilities for such training are absent. Community facilities are also lacking, and, moreover, the people know little about the public services a community normally should have, such services as water supply to schools. Civil organization in many areas is still in the hands of outsiders (Europeans) and years may pass before these people acquire the civic consciousness needed for urban living.

Nevertheless, through industry urbanism is being taken to nonurban places, even to peoples emerging from tribalism. The processes of adaption will be long and painful. But it has been long and painful in the developed countries.

Urbanization and Responsibility

President Truman in his inaugural address of January 20, 1949, proposed the so-called Point IV doctrine of extending aid to underdeveloped countries. This was in fact an extension of the earlier Marshall

11. C. H. Thompson and H. W. Woodruff, *Economic Development in Rhodesia and Nyasaland* (London: Dobson, 1953), p. 23.

Plan for the postwar recovery of European countries. The adoption of this doctrine was the basis of a national policy of aid and guidance. It was an expression of interest in the peoples of the underdeveloped countries, not merely in the exploiting of the natural resources of these lands. This idea of national responsibility came to be adopted later by the Organization for European Economic Cooperation (OEEC). A study of the situation south of the Sahara was made and a report appeared in 1951. The following quotation reflects the viewpoint of this interest:

> The countries responsible for the territories have already made a great contribution toward helping the inhabitants in their efforts to achieve better living conditions and enabling the territories to occupy a significant place in the world economy. These joint efforts must be continued and widened in scope, for it is a matter of general concern that the most should be made of the world's resources. It is clear that any expansion of the economy of the area and any rise in the standard of living of its inhabitants will be to the mutual benefit of both the peoples of the African continent and of other continents as well, and that any growth in the trade of the territories is bound to lead to a further expansion of world trade.[12]

The principal OEEC countries with African territories are Belgium, France, and the United Kingdom. It should be mentioned that each of these countries has now established its social science institutes in Africa. The support of these efforts seems to indicate an attitude of public responsibility for the underdeveloped areas. Whatever else may be said of these efforts, this is pertinent to the present chapter: Industrial urbanism is being systematically introduced into Africa, and Western governments are accepting the responsibility for coping with the social problems involved. The expansion of urbanism to global dimensions is being supported by national policies.

Specialization of Work and Place

The city has always been the haven of specialists, but never to such a high degree as today. This springs in part from the complex division of labor in the urban center and partly from the complexity of its social life. Although there is much in the urban situation to stimulate specialization, it tends also to level people in their occupations. Yet this same "level-down" worker is able to range forth and back between a variety of related jobs. Individual specialization, however, is less pertinent to the theme of this chapter than is the specialization of aggregates of

12. OEEC, *Investments in Overseas Territories: In Africa South of the Sahara* (Paris: OEEC, 1951), p. 8.

population. Cities, towns, and smaller places, because they are so interrelated in their market relations, tend to influence each other and to specialize.

For reasons of cost and market advantages, cities tend to specialize in products for which the raw materials are most conveniently available. Thus it was natural at one time that Minneapolis, located in the wheat belt, should become a flour-milling city. It was just as natural that Milwaukee and St. Louis, near the same wheat belt, should become leading brewery cities. However, it was also natural for other cities in the Middlewest to embrace both industries, as they have done. Gary, Indiana, has a natural location for the kind of city it is, a steel center. Other factors may also be influential in determining the work of a place—the type of labor available, the distance to markets, costs of transportation, and so on.

Specialization in some cities may be due to a chain of coincidences or to some type of human initiative. Thus, Los Angeles is the film capital of the world; Detroit is the automobile capital; New York is coming to be, if it is not already, the publishing capital of the world; and Paris holds the title of the world's fashion capital.

Older cities also specialized, but for very limited markets. The modern city cannot operate this way, and precisely because the markets are not limited, the principal work of an urban center may suddenly change. Here we have still another difference between modern urbanism and ruralism: The economic base of a rural aggregate is usually fairly constant. For example, Iowa and corn are about as permanently associated as are Kansas and wheat, or as California and citrus fruits. Thus the rural way of life tends to be more secure with reference to work than is possible with the urban way of life; urbanism is much more beset with hazards.[13]

Unfortunately, the industrial-urban way of doing things has operated in many ways to introduce this kind of insecurity into large sections of agriculture. Farmers may be induced to neglect general farming in favor of single crops—sugar beets, for instance, in one area to

13. Of the Yoruba cities in Africa, Bascom reports that many inhabitants are farmers. Others perform other work, "weaving, dyeing, ironworking, brass-casting, wood-carving, ivory-carving, calabash-carving, beadmaking, and leather-working, as well as drumming, divining, the compounding of charms and medicines, and certain other activities or crafts whose techniques are known only to a small group of specialists. These specialists, who are organized into guilds, supply all other members of the community with their particular goods or services. Formerly these occupations tended to be more hereditary within the clan or lineage, but the apprenticeship system provided a method by which individuals from outside the kinship unit could be taught a craft." This is the ancient type of handwork specialism, quite remote from that of industrial urbanism. Ibid., p. 449.

keep the sugar factory going, and other crops in other sections. Compared with other parts of the world, however, industrialized farming in the United States is hardly a source of rural insecurity. The OEEC report, already quoted, makes this observation about Africa:

> The vulnerability of the territories is all the greater for the fact that the economy of most of them is based on a limited number of commodities. For example, groundnuts represent 99% by value of the exports of Gambia; metals and ores 95% of those of Northern Rhodesia; tobacco and tea 78% of those of Nyasaland; cocoa 69% of those of the Gold Coast and 45% of those of the French Cameroons; and sisal 55% of those of Tanganyika.[14]

The Money Economy

It would be difficult to find areas in the United States today that are not operating wholly on the money economy, although this was not true a century ago when large sections of the frontier population were getting on quite well with various exchange economies. The changeover into the money economy, however, involved no adjustment problems. This is not the case when industrial urbanism enters certain underdeveloped countries where the introduction of money into the native groups may be the source of breakdown in the social order. The native wife, for example, who is able to sell produce for cash is likely to be less obedient to her husband. But usually it is the young male who is soonest influenced by having money in his pockets. He is encouraged to be mobile to a degree never possible under the subsistence economies. Although he may have much bitter experience learning to use money, at least in the learning he has the adventure of feeling emancipated. He may return home later, if only to visit.

Textor made a study of samlor drivers in Bangkok, mostly young men from the remote villages of Thailand. They leave home to earn money and they enjoy a kind of freedom while doing so, but their primary interest is to return home one day with their pockets full. For this they work long hours, make sacrifices, and save, and become somewhat urbanized in the process. Finally the young man is ready for the home journey:

> Very commonly the returner will devote much of his savings to building a new house or house addition. Besides treating friends and relatives to refreshments, he is likely to devote some of his money to merit-making at the temple. A particularly devout returner might spend many hundreds of *baht* to purchase a Buddha or some other improvements for the local temple. Another common type of expen-

14. Ibid., p. 24.

diture, difficult to classify as exclusively a consumer or capital item, is the bride price. Local maidens and their parents are far from completely unimpressed by the new opulence of the young bachelor returner, and the youths in turn regard the stint at samlor-pedaling in Bangkok as a promising route to finding a bride possessed of beauty, wealth or both.[15]

Such young returners bring back to the village some flavor of urbanism and hence, indirectly, the isolation-invading medium of money facilitates the accumulation process of urbanization.

Urbanism and Individualism

We are told in many ways that the individual enjoys greater freedom under the urban way of life than is possible under ruralism. There are more choices to make under urbanism, and they are choices which the individual himself must make. In addition, one is less obligated to the demands of a wide kinship group.

Americans are regarded by other peoples as being individualists, and they often describe themselves as such; in fact, individualism is sometimes regarded as a type of American cult. It was perhaps necessary during the frontier period which is only now coming to a close and during which rule by tradition was not very useful for getting things done. People had to learn to stand alone if necessary and to make their own decisions, but they took the consequences of their decisions. If the individual's adopted course led to failure, according to the rules of the game, he would try again, or try something else. Each of the new countries where European civilization was planted developed some brand of individualism, but it took a different course in the United States because the opportunities here were more ample, and perhaps because there was a greater mixture of peoples among the pioneers. Because the frontier situation did not encourage much carry-over of their Old World traits and traditions, the pioneers were forced to operate as individuals.[16]

This peculiar background may explain the extreme individualism of

15. Robert B. Textor, "The Northeastern Samlor Driver in Bangkok," in *Social Implications of Industrialization and Urbanization* (Calcutta: Unesco Research Center, 1956), p. 33. The samlor is a three-wheeled vehicle pedaled as a bicycle, with a seat for two passengers behind the driver. It is an invention which began in Bangkok, but is spreading. Sometimes the samlor is equipped with a motor. It is more suitable than taxis in cities having great street congestion.

16. For a presentation of the American idea of individualism, see Abbott P. Herman, *An Approach to Social Problems* (Boston: Ginn, 1949), Chap. 8, "Our Values of Individualism."

the American brand of industrial urbanism, but another cause is found in the fact that urbanism generally is conducive to encouraging in the person the development of unique qualities and capacities, usually designated as "individuation." Urban individualism, to quote Hayek, "does not deny the necessity of coercive power but wishes to limit it— to limit to those fields where it is indispensable to prevent coercion by others and in order to reduce the total of coercion to a minimum."[17] It favors rational and immediately realistic control rather than merely traditional control, and these rules must be subject to change.

The individual under urbanism participates in a changing manner to the life about him, but he is an individual and so regarded in the labor market. This does not mean that he operates without social obligation to family and friends; rather, it means that he is not represented by his family. He votes as an individual and,[18] after reaching adulthood, he is responsible as an individual to the law. He usually enjoys the right to choose his own occupation and his place of work, although for some social groups family control may be very strong still even in great cities, especially for families of wealth. With the same reservations the urban individual is free to choose his marriage partner, and they are free to live separate from their extended families. The fact that these characteristics of urban individualism are today not peculiarly urban in the United States tends to indicate how much the values of urbanism have extended outward to the hinterland.

By the rural as well as the urban American it is generally accepted that the individual who works is entitled to keep and to expend his earnings. This was not always the case even among Americans two generations ago, and is certainly not true today in the less urbanized countries. Hoselitz speaks of the industrial worker in underdeveloped countries:

> Similarly, any compensation he may get for his effort is regarded by him not merely as a reward to be employed for his individual purposes, but to be shared with other members of the collectivity of which he forms a part. In many societies there are still recognized traditional arrangements for the control of money income which secure to the older members of the community the major handling of what money income is secured. Laborers must share their income

17. F. A. Hayek, *Individualism and Economic Order* (London: Routledge & Kegan Paul, 1949), p. 27.

18. Despite the clearly important influences on how people vote. See, e.g., Bernard R. Berelson, Paul F. Lazarsfeld, and William H. McPhee, *Voting* (Chicago: University of Chicago Press, 1954).

with chief, parents, fathers-in-law or other relatives and persons of re-spect.[19]

When such a native goes to a town for work he finds himself in an agglomeration of people in the process of being urbanized. He settles with a group from his own village and area, usually with members of his own family group present. He retains his old loyalties, although they may weaken a little. His children born in the town may become less attached to the village. He and they gradually become "detribal-ized." They find about them increasing numbers of former villagers who have broken completely with the village. They begin to assume the roles of urbanized individuals which the situation demands, for even these places become increasingly urban in thought and conduct.

Individualism and Uniformity

The idea of individualism as a characteristic of urbanism can be over-emphasized. It is generally true both that the urbanite has more oppor-tunities for choice and for expression than has the person under rural-ism, and that it is therefore necessary for him to make individual and often unusual choices. While he is expected to behave as an individual, however, more so than would be expected under ruralism or tribalism, his freedom to behave as one is not entirely complete. He still must conduct himself according to rules, and many of the rules are second-ary and impersonal.

The urban man must learn to live with groups of people and to associate with others on levels of intimacy ranging from friendship to anonymity. He must be able, as Wilson observed, to "convert people into things," but there is method and control even in this.

> Clearly we cannot treat the thousands of people whom we meet daily with the intimacy and emotional tone characteristic of human rela-tionships. People come to have no particular significance in and of themselves, in their own rights. They become pre-eminently means to our ends (and, of course, vice versa). We relate ourselves to others insofar as they are of service to us, and shrink from contact beyond a kind of contractual relationship. . . . Thus we are likely to deal with people in terms of those symbols which define the utility of the rela-tionship. Uniforms, badges, headgear, labels—these all tell us that we are dealing with the laundryman, the milkman, or mechanic. We deal with patients, clients, customers. Beyond whatever these labels

19. Bert F. Hoselitz, "The City, the Factory and Economic Growth," *American Economic Review* 45, no. 2 (May 1955): 182.

imply we need not know—nor do we want to know. The relationship is purely instrumental.[20]

The same urban situation that stimulates individuation also tends to create uniformities and conformities. The individual must see large groups in stereotype terms; he finds stereotyped patterns of behaving, which he accepts and helps to maintain. By accepting these uniformities and conforming to them, he becomes at once a person under mass control and a factor for maintaining that control. Without such adjustments, varied and global, the individual would be in a state of confusion. These ways of adapting are productive of order, and although it is a changing order, the individual is able to maintain equilibrium within it.

The uniformities peculiar to urbanism as a way of life in thinking, behaving, and conducting social relationships tend to acquire mass dimensions. Thus people by the millions eat certain foods, wear certain types of clothes, live in houses of a strikingly uniform kind furnished in much the same way (although varying with social class), and enjoy their leisure in fairly similar activities. Although these uniformities may vary from country to country and everywhere they may be in process of change, urbanites acquire a generally uniform capability for adjusting to change. The urbanite, then, lives within a framework of uniformities but is at the same time afforded a multitude of choices in which he may act as an individual.

The Problems of Social Change

These mass uniformities are ever-changing and, for competitive commercial reasons, they must change. Detroit changes car models each year and Paris brings out new fashions. Interior decorators, competitive and creative, are constantly working on new designs for house furnishings. These continuous change-working efforts regarding what consumers will by reflect the spirit of urbanism. All the media of mass communication are used to spread ideas and to induce the desired conduct. These manifestations of the urban way of life are wide-reaching. All people are reached but different groups of people respond differently.

Changes in the things with which man works or uses in his free time lead to changes in his thinking and behavior. Changes in man's means of transport which facilitate his movement, or changes in his means of communication, affect his relationships with others, for such changes permit a man to move about more freely and communicate with

20. Everett K. Wilson, "Some Notes on the Pains and Prospects of American Cities," *Confluence* 7, no. 1 (Spring 1958): p. 9.

greater facility. Changes in the house or in house furnishings as well as changes in the individual's place of residence have their effect on his social values, and his conduct may be in some way modified. This is the essence of social change.

All people are affected by these changes in the material environment, whether they live in the densely urbanized eastern states or in the more open regions of the West or Middlewest, but their reaction patterns may be very different. Some people are not able to maintain social and psychological balance in making their adjustments. At the other extreme are those who never seem to lose balance, however varied the adaptations required. Many who seemed unable to adjust during their youth may be wholly adjusted, urbanized, in their later years. Still others who were very much oriented to urbanism during their early years may become very much out of balance in their later years. Years may pass before some persons of rural origin are able to feel adjusted to the urban situation, much as some urbanized people are unable to feel at home if it is necessary to change from a more urban to a less urban place of residence.

While adaptation is largely individual, it is not entirely so. Reactions vary among different groups or categories of people. Country or place of origin, age, education, economic class, and religion are factors which influence the group-adaptation process.

Because change in the urban community is continuous, the necessity for adjustment is continuous. The rate of social change may vary with times and conditions, and tends to move more rapidly under certain circumstances than under others. And just as there are different rates of change, so there are different rates at which people and groups adapt to change. The community of more rapid change is likely to be more the scene of social conflict than a community of less rapid change. Such an area is also likely to be one with some degree of social discord and various acute social problems.

The urban milieu is of its nature an ever-changing center of work and living, and technological creativity. Social change in the less urban places cannot help but be stimulated by the dynamic influences which radiate from such centers. Here more than elsewhere people work and create and compete sharply, and while at it seek new ways of working and competing to greater advantage. Here the people of many origins meet and mix and, whether willingly or not, change old ways of living for new ones.

Urbanism and Mobility

We have noted that industrial urbanism abhors isolation. Its nature is to expand. In many respects it is a market-finding process, which means that it is naturally occupied with finding or making transportation routes, and with gaining access to those markets. Urbanism's effort to expand stimulates people to move from one place to another, generally from smaller to larger places. This stimulation to move is of a kind that does not permit rest, and the individual, once having moved, may be stimulated to move again. That is one type of mobility which must be associated with urbanism. There are others.

Work must necessarily also change in response to the creation of new tools and machines and the making of new products. Hoselitz called attention to work changes that follow the migration of natives from the tribal villages to industry where they must use tools and perform tasks previously strange to them. Each of these migrants had his fixed place in the village, which was usually determined by some combination of family status and seniority. These criteria for status have no place in the factory where villagers meet under disturbing conditions.

> Older men or chiefs or other persons with high traditional status may be subordinate in the factory to younger men, and this subordination may express itself not merely in a lower wage but in actual positions of inferiority in the factory hierarchy of a work crew. The disruptive effects not only on traditional structures but also on the psychological security of the persons involved, are obvious if a man with high traditional status must obey orders of someone who in the traditional ranking is far below him simply because the new distribution and valuation of skills makes the new relation mandatory.[21]

When people move physically from one situation to another and change from one work to another, professional or occupational mobility may result, or one may remain in the same locality and still move from one occupational or professional level to another. Or, this professional mobility may take place between generations—the father may be a laborer, while his son may become a skilled worker and his daughter a private secretary. Not only is the urban way of life conducive to physical and professional mobility, it is also tolerant of mobility from one social class to another.

Such changes often take place under urbanism, and the urban man does not regard them with wonder. These types of mobility may be found in American rural society, but to a lesser degree. They are even less evident in Old World rural society, which is more tradition bound than rural society in the United States and less under the influence of urbanism. Such changes, however, would hardly be found in the tribal society, even within walking distance of a factory.

21. Hoselitz, p. 182.

The Two Sociologies

There are two community sociologies, rural and urban, and each is prominently recognized by that discipline in the United States. The field of rural sociology is rural society and rural living while that of urban sociology concerns society and living in towns and cities. The pages of this chapter could be interpreted as a challenge to the existence of two separate sociologies, or as the basis for a single community sociology which is at once both rural and urban.

Much that has been called rural sociology in the past was either a plea for the old basic values of rural life or was on guard against the "evils" of urbanism. As Caplow writes, "Much of what passes for sociological literature consists of sermons of protest against the uprooting of old beliefs and the emancipation of the secularized urban dweller from the tight control of the primordial village community in which most of the men who ever lived have passed their lives."[22] Observations of this type do not apply to either the literature of rural or urban sociology today, but these sociologies have other limitations.

One of these limitations is the fact that many rural sociologists stand with their backs to the city. The reverse is also true—many urban sociologists feel somewhat less self-conscious if their work keeps them out of the hinterland. Each avoids the possible embarrassment of being caught in the territory of the other. The fact is that neither knows exactly where his territory ends and that of the other begins. The time has come, it seems, when we must recognize that it really makes no great difference where the line between rural and urban is drawn. In fact, it might be just as well if we stopped thinking about the dividing line. Rural and urban tend to take on more meaning if seen in terms of social organization and interpenetrating social processes, even in relation to a division of labor pattern.

The approach in this book is essentially that of urban sociology, but it is urban sociology that draws heavily on rural as well as urban data. It must be recognized that the urban is not only dominant but is becoming increasingly so as this way of life becomes global in its reach.

Such trends do not render obsolete the need for rural sociology. On the contrary, rural work and rural living are vital to society. The people who do this work in the United States are no less rural even though they become more urban in their way of life, nor are they less a special segment of society even though they come increasingly to be regarded as a specialized occupational group. While this segment of the Ameri-

---

22. Theodore Caplow, *The Sociology of Work* (Minneapolis: University of Minnesota Press, 1954), p. 284.

can population is percentagewise small, it has its social needs and its social problems just as the nonrural people have theirs. The difference is in the spheres, one of which is primarily the field of rural sociology and the other field of urban sociology. Each penetrates the area of the other but does not obviate the work of the other.

Summary

Urbanism as a way of life is primarily, although not entirely, associated with living in towns and cities. It differs from ruralism mainly in ways of work, habits of thought, and with respect to traditional controls. The tempo of life and work is faster under urbanism. Urbanism is the more dynamic of the two, while ruralism is the more self-isolating. Urbanism is more given to creativeness and to extending its influence outward. Ruralism is the more passive and negative, although the use of such terms does not involve negative implications.

We have distinguished between those characteristics of urbanism which concern living in large cities and those which relate to urbanism as an outward-extending, change-stimulating influence emanating from urban centers. In the city, urbanism has been described as superficial, anonymous, and transient. But this way of life as it extends outward may not be anonymous, although it tends to be contractual and secondary. The superficiality, so much a part of urbanism in the city and outside, is not always superficial, for urbanism is also profoundly creative. Transiency is a mark of urbanism wherever its influence extends, and transiency tends to increase with nearness to urban centers.

We noted that different elements of urbanism may be present in different degree, depending on the relative mixture of ruralism and urbanism in particular areas. We took notice of the term "urbanization," commonly used to describe the moving of people from less urban to more urban places and from nonurban to urban types of work. We recognized that urbanization must also mean the changeover from rural to urban ways of living, and that this may take place without migration to the city. The influences that affect people and promote urbanization may be exported by the city. Wherever people live in the hinterland, they may be described as more "rural-oriented" or more "urban-oriented"—that is, urbanized to a lesser or greater degree.

We have noted that, within limits, cities can grow and be important without being industrial. Yet, urbanism as we know it has been made possible by the expansion of industry and commerce, the second being largely an auxiliary activity of the first. Just as industry must be urban-centered, so it must extend outward for markets and raw materials. It disturbs old work ways, old consuming habits, and established social relationships. It requires new and ever-changing divisions of labor. It encourages specialization, but it also reduces mass work to common levels. It raises levels of living.

Urbanism tends to "individuate" people, liberating them, putting them in a position favorable to making choices and being creative according to their ability. The individual and not the family is the unit in the labor market and before the law. But urbanism also imposes uniformities on great masses of people over wider areas. Uniformity applies to machines, tools, clothing, houses, means of transport and communication, commercialized leisure activities, and so on. These mass uniformities are continually changing. As they change they effect changes in ways of thinking, behavior, and relationships, giving rise to problems of social change.

Urbanism as a way of life encourages mobility, and could not be possible without increasing mobility. This is not limited to the moving of people from place to place; it also means mobility from one kind of work to another and the movement of people from one social class to another. Mobility-connected social changes may also give rise to social problems, yet mobility is essential to urbanism.

The approach to the understanding of the urbanized community which this book undertakes may be described as urban sociology. It is not an encroachment on rural sociology. Even though the rural way of life changes to become more urban-oriented, *rural* as a way of work and life remains and that means a continuing need for rural sociology.

Selected Bibliography

Anderson, Nels. 1923. *The Hobo: The Sociology of the Homeless Man*. Chicago: University of Chicago Press.

———. 1923. "The Juvenile and the Tramp." *Journal of Criminal Law, Criminology and Police Science* 14:289–312.

———. 1926. "The Mission Mill." *American Mercury* 8:489–95.

———. 1926. "Pontifex Babbit." *American Mercury* 9:177–82.

———. 1927. "Old Whitey." *American Mercury* 9:101–5.

———. 1927. "The Slum Endures." *The Survey*, 15 March.

———. 1928. "The Slum: Project for a Study." *Social Forces* 7:87–90.

———. 1930. *The Milk and Honey Route: A Handbook for Hobos* by Dean Stiff [N. Anderson]. New York: Vanguard Press.

———. 1934. *The Homeless in New York City*. Manuscript. Welfare Council of New York City Research Bureau.

———. 1938. *The Right to Work*. New York: Modern Age Books.

———. 1940. *Men on the Move*. Chicago: University of Chicago Press.

———. 1942. *Desert Saints: The Mormon Frontier in Utah*. Chicago: University of Chicago Press.

———. 1952. *Unsere Lieder: Liederbuch der Gewerkschaftsjugend*. Köln: Bund-Verlag.

———, ed. 1956. *Studies of the Family*, vol. 1. Tubingen: J. C. B. Mohr.

———, ed. 1957. *Studies of the Family*, vol. 2. Gottingen: Vandenhoeck & Ruprecht.

———, ed. 1958. *Studies of the Family*, vol. 3. Gottingen: Vandenhoeck & Ruprecht.

———. 1959. *The Urban Community: A World Perspective*. New York: Holt, Rinehart & Winston.

———. 1960. "Western Urban Man Faces Leisure." *International Journal of Comparative Sociology* 1:3–16.

———. 1961. "Diverse Perspectives of Community." *International Review of Community Development*.

———. 1961. *Work and Leisure*. London: Routledge & Kegan Paul.

———. 1962. "Rethinking Our Ideas about Community." *International Review of Community Development* 10:143–52.

———. 1964. *Dimensions of Work: The Sociology of a Work Culture*. New York: D. McKay.

———, ed. 1964. *Urbanism and Urbanization*. Leiden: E. J. Brill.

———. 1964. *Our Industrial Urban Civilization*. New York: Asia Publishing House.

———, ed. 1969. *Studies in Multilingualism*. Leiden: E. J. Brill.

———. 1969. "The Private and Last Frontier." *Sewanee Review* 77:25–90.

———. 1971. *The Industrial Urban Community: Historical and Comparative Perspectives*. New York: Appleton-Century-Crofts.

———. 1972. "Early Years of the Chicago School of Sociology." University of Chicago, Regenstein Library, Department of Special Collections, Robert E. Park Papers and addenda, box 6, folder 6.

———. 1974. *Man's Work and Leisure*. Leiden: E. J. Brill.

———. 1975. *The American Hobo: An Autobiography*. Leiden: E. J. Brill.

———. 1980–1981. "Sociology Has Many Faces." *Journal of the History of Sociology* 3(1):1–26, 3(2):1–19.

———. 1983. "A Stranger at the Gate: Reflections on the Chicago School of Sociology." *Urban Life* 11:396–406.

Anderson, Nels, Read Bain, and George A. Lundberg, eds. 1929. *Trends in American Sociology*. New York: Harper.

Anderson, Nels, and K. Ishwaran. 1965. *Urban Sociology*. New York: Asia Publishing House.

Anderson, Nels, and Edward C. Linden, eds. 1928. *Urban Sociology: An Introduction to the Study of Urban Communities*. New York: Knopf.

Beveridge, William Henry. 1934. "Some Aspects of the American Recovery Programme." *Economica*, February.

Brown, Malcolm J., and O. C. Cassmore. 1939. *Migratory Cotton Pickers in Arizona*. Washington, D.C.: Government Printing Office.

Coyle, David Cushman. 1939. *Depression Pioneers*. Social Problems Pamphlets no. 1. Washington, D.C.: Work Projects Administration.

Lewis, M. H. 1936. *Migratory Labor in California*. Report by the State Relief Administration of California. San Francisco: N.p.

McMurry, Donald Le Crone. 1929. *Coxey's Army: A Study of the Industrial Army Movement of 1894*. Boston: Little, Brown.

McWilliams, Carey. 1939. *Factories in the Field: The Story of Migratory Farm Labor in California*. Boston: Little, Brown.

Melvin, Bruce L., and Elna N. Smith. 1938. *Rural Youth: Their Situation and Prospects*. WPA Research Monograph no. 11. Washington, D.C.: Works Progress Administration.

Queen, Stuart Alfred. 1920. *The Passing of the County Jail*. Menasha, Wis.: George Banta Publishing.

Ravenstein, Ernest George. 1889. "The Laws of Migration." *Journal of the Statistical Society* 52 (June). Reprint, Indianapolis: Bobbs Merrill, 1960.

Ribton-Turner, C. J. 1887. *A History of Vagrants and Vagrancy, and Beggars and Begging*. London: Chapman & Hall.

Schubert, Herman Jacob Paul. 1935. *Twenty Thousand Transients: A One Year's Sample of Those Who Apply for Aid in a Northern City*. Buffalo, N.Y.: Emergency Relief Bureau.

Schneider, David Moses. 1941. *The History of Public Welfare in New York State, 1867–1940*. Chicago: University of Chicago Press.

Solenberger, Alice Willard. 1914. *One Thousand Homeless Men: A Study of Original Records*. New York: Charities Publication Committee.

Sutherland, E. H., and H. J. Locke. 1936. *Twenty Thousand Homeless Men: A Study of Unemployed Men in the Chicago Shelters*. Chicago: J. B. Lippencott.

Taylor, Paul S. 1939. "The Place of Agricultural Labor in Society." Paper read before the twelfth annual meeting of the Western Farm Economics Association, June 15.

U.S. Commission on Industrial Relations. 1915. *Final Report of the Commission on Industrial Relations*. Washington, D.C.: USCIR.

Vreeland, Francis M., and Edward J. Fitzgerald. 1939. *Farm-City Migration and Industry's Labor Reserve*. National Research Project on Reemployment Opportunities and Recent Changes in Industrial Techniques, Report no. L-7 (gov. doc. FW 4.7). Philadelphia.

Webb, John Nye. 1935. *The Transient Unemployed: A Description and Analysis of the Transient Relief Population*. Washington, D.C.: Works Progress Administration.

———. 1937. *The Migratory-Casual Worker*. WPA Research Monograph no. 7. Washington, D.C.: Government Printing Office.

Webb. J. N., and Malcolm J. Brown. 1938. *Migrant Families*. WPA Research Monograph no. 18. Washington, D.C.: Government Printing Office.

Woofter, Thomas Jackson, and E. Winston. 1939. *Seven Lean Years*. Chapel Hill: University of North Carolina Press.

Yarbrough, W. H. 1932. *Economic Aspects of Slavery in Relation to Southern and Southwestern Migration*. Contribution to Education, no. 101. Nashville.: George Peabody College for Teachers.

Index